Strategy
Pure and
Simple II

Also by Michel Robert

STRATEGY PURE AND SIMPLE

Strategy Pure and Simple II

How Winning Companies Dominate Their Competitors

Michel Robert
Founder-Partner
Decision Processes International

Revised Edition

McGraw-Hill

New York   San Francisco   Washington, D.C.   Auckland   Bogotá
Caracas   Lisbon   London   Madrid   Mexico City   Milan
Montreal   New Delhi   San Juan   Singapore
Sydney   Tokyo   Toronto

Library of Congress Cataloging-in-Publication Data

Robert, Michel.
   Strategy pure & simple II : how winning companies dominate
their competitors / Michel Robert.
       p.   cm.
   Includes bibliographical references.
   ISBN 0-07-053133-1
   1. Strategic planning—United States.   2. Competition.
3. Success in business—United States.   I. Title.
HD30.28.R635   1997
658.4'012—dc21   97-39581
                                                                CIP

McGraw-Hill

*A Division of The **McGraw·Hill** Companies*

1 2 3 4 5 6 7 8 9 0   DOC/DOC   9 0 2 1 0 9 8 7

ISBN 0-07-053133-1

*The sponsoring editor for this book was Betsy N. Brown, the editing supervisor
was Caroline R. Levine, and the production supervisor was Tina Cameron. It
was set in Baskerville by Don Feldman of McGraw-Hill's Professional Book
Group composition unit.*

Printed and bound by R. R. Donnelley & Sons Company.

McGraw-Hill books are available at special quantity discounts to use as
premiums and sales promotions, or for use in corporate training programs. For more information, please write to the Director of Special
Sales, McGraw-Hill, 11 West 19th Street, New York, NY 10011. Or contact your local bookstore.

 This book is printed on recycled, acid-free paper containing a
minimum of 50% recycled, de-inked fiber.

To my wife Ellie, my best critic, for enduring my writing books on our honeymoon and our vacations. And to my daughters, Emma and Samantha, who I hope will be inspired to realize that achievement in life is totally unrelated to one's origin.

Contents

Preface

Since 1970, American companies have lost enormous chunks of markets that they had dominated since the turn of the century. The following is a partial list from Dean Witter Reynolds, Inc., of industries once dominated by American companies but are no longer:

Loss of U.S. Dominance

- 8 of the 10 largest automobile companies
- 8 of the 10 largest electrical/electronics companies
- 8 of the 10 largest chemical companies
- 8 of the 10 largest machinery companies
- 8 of the 10 largest financial services companies
- 8 of the 10 largest household durable goods companies

Here's another perspective about the same issue. Joseph Pattison, an expert on international trade, makes the following observations in his recent book entitled *Breaking Boundaries*:

- In 1976, U.S. firms dominated the list of the world's 50 largest companies; today, the number of U.S. entries is only 17.
- Of the top 10 worldwide producers of electronic goods, only one is based in the United States.

- Since 1950, the U.S. share of world trade has plummeted 50 percent.

- The entire export production of the United States is equivalent to the output of only one midsize state, such as Illinois.

- Of the top 20 banks in the world, none are based in the United States, and in the last 10 years the international market share of U.S. banks has slumped 50 percent.

- In 1960, U.S. firms made one-half of all the cars in the world—today, they make one-fifth; since 1967, the United States has gone from an auto-export surplus to an auto-export deficit of $60 billion.

- In 1965, the United States produced one-fourth of the world's steel; today it produces one-eighth.

This is the phenomenon that has contributed to the "hollowing of America" and the loss of millions of well-paying, highly skilled manufacturing jobs.

All this has occurred during a time period that has engrossed management in an avalanche of new management concepts, each expected to propel the organization to unparalleled prosperity.

What happened?

The answer, in my view, is the lack of strategic thinking ability in most American corporations. The key impediment is their inability to distinguish between *strategy* and *operations*.

Over the last two decades we have watched American companies get involved in a number of management techniques that were entered into to make the company "more competitive"—techniques such as *Total Quality Management (TQM), Kaizen, Kan-Ban, reengineering, computerization, benchmarking,* and the like. These techniques are all *operational* in nature and *not strategic*. They are techniques designed to make the corporation more efficient at *how* it currently does things but they do nothing to help an organization determine *what* it wants to become in the future.

Most of the time these techniques have led to programs to downsize the organization. Any company that has to "downsize" is one which has a *failed* strategy. A successful strategy, on the other hand, is one that creates growth in revenues, profits, and, usually, employment. Instead of bidding up the stock of a company that announces a downsizing program, Wall Street should ask for the CEO's resignation.

Downsizing, by itself, does not address the STRATEGIC problem that may be at the root of the organization's difficulties. Kodak is a typical example. In just 8 years, Kodak reduced its workforce by 34,000, without any improvement in profits. The issues at Kodak were not *operational*, but *strategic*. Kodak, in the '70s and '80s, had diversified into unrelated businesses such as pharmaceuticals, clinical diagnostic machines, and batteries, and had taken its eye off their core business. It was not until George Fisher was brought in as CEO and addressed the strategic issue by refocusing the company on photography and digital imaging that the company's fortunes started to turn around.

In fact, the underlying thesis of this book is that most companies are so operationally focused that they miss major changes and trends that could have brought them huge new strategic opportunities, and the reason for this, in our view, is their inability to *think strategically*.

Kodak should have been the first company to recognize the opportunities that digital imaging represented. Yet, when Sony unveiled its first digital camera in the early 1980s, it sent earthquake-size tremors throughout the Kodak empire. The same has happened in a number of other industries.

When computers were just in their infancy, the two companies in the best position to capitalize on that emerging trend were GE and Siemens. However, both companies missed the boat and the trend was exploited by an upstart called International Business Machines. In the telecommunications industry, AT&T, the giant, completely missed the move to cellular telephones even though it invented the technology. The major drug companies, such as Merck, Hoffman-LaRoche, CIBA-Geigy, Pfizer, and many others, completely missed the advent of biotechnology. In the car industry, General Motors—the industry's Goliath—was never able to capitalize on the market shift to smaller, more fuel-efficient cars, brought on by the 1974 oil crisis. Even mighty IBM initially refused to recognize the advent of personal computers and the accompanying need for software. It took a Harvard dropout by the name of Bill Gates to see the potential of that opportunity and then capitalize on it so effectively that Microsoft today has a higher market value than IBM.

This lack of *strategic thinking* ability is not restricted to the United States only. It afflicts other companies in other countries as well. The entire Swiss watch industry was brought to its knees by the introduction of the first Japanese Seiko digital watch, even though, again, the Swiss had invented the technology.

One U.S. company that bucked the trend towards exporting its manufacturing base to low wage countries, and should be admired for having done so, is Caterpillar. During the 1970s and 1980s, Caterpillar was the target of a major attack by Komatsu and, by the late 1980s, Caterpillar was feeling the pain. To improve their competitive position, Caterpillar could have taken the easy way out and transferred much of its manufacturing to low wage countries which would have had a disastrous economic impact on the state of Illinois, where most of that base is located.

Instead, under the leadership of ex-CEO George Schafer and current CEO Don Fites, Caterpillar decided to address the *strategic issues* facing the business. With the help of our *strategic thinking* process, Caterpillar management set upon a new direction and identified a short list of critical issues that they needed to address in order to survive and prosper in the next century. They then worked these issues diligently, and the proof is in the pudding. In the last 5 years, Caterpillar has reversed its fortunes and has surprised Wall Street with its spectacular results. And Caterpillar is now the industry's low cost producer, all achieved with its manufacturing base still in Illinois!

Over the last 20 years, using the *strategic thinking process* described in this book, we have worked with over 300 companies around the world and have achieved radically different results. We pride ourselves on the fact that *none* of our clients have had to engage in downsizing programs. In almost every case, the use of our process has led to substantial increases in revenues, market share, profits, and shareholder value. These include well established companies—such as 3M, Caterpillar, Noram Energy, GATX, Hartford Insurance, Dow Corning, and Union Pacific Resources—to fast-growing mid-size companies—such as Material Sciences, American Precision Industries, and OMG Group—to privately owned firms such as FLEXcon and Behlen Manufacturing.

Although each CEO would not attribute their success exclusively to the use of our process, he would, however, offer that the use of our process was the *key catalyst* that re-energized and mobilized that company's people and resources to attain results far greater and more quickly than anticipated. The reason is simple. One cannot grow an organization while practicing management concepts that are strictly intended to improve its operational effectiveness.

There are some macrochanges currently occurring that will have significant effects on all companies in the next two decades. These changes include the fall of the Berlin Wall, the collapse of Communism, the democratization of Eastern Europe and Latin America, the spread of free markets all around the world including China, the aging of the population in the United States, Europe, and Japan and the reverse trend happening in Asia, Mexico, and South America. The last time that changes of this magnitude occurred was after World War II.

Change, as we all know, can bring major opportunities or major threats for companies. In my view, the companies that will prosper and outpace their competitors during the next two decades will be those that will be able to *outthink* their competitors *strategically*, not *outmuscle* them *operationally*. The winning CEO in the future will be the one who can craft a singular strategy that gives the company a *distinctive advantage*.

Too many companies attempt to compete by imitating their competitors and then attempting to outperform them operationally. A successful strategy is one that makes competition almost irrelevant.

Good reading!

Mike Robert

1

A Winning Strategy Needs to Be Distinctive

The best competitive position to be in is to have *no* competition. That position can only be achieved by not playing the game the way your competitors play the game, but rather by formulating and deploying a *distinctive strategy that changes the rules in your favor.*

Many theories have emerged over the years as to how a company goes about growing at a competitor's expense. The obvious method is to duplicate the competitor's strategy and then attempt to outmarket, outsell, outmanufacture, and outservice these competitors. This is called *imitation strategy.* In my opinion, imitation may be the finest form of flattery, but it is the *worst* form of strategy.

All the company is doing with this approach is entering a race with no finish line. One competitor surges ahead of the other for a short period, only to be overtaken by another competitor for another period, to then regain the lead for another period, to...I think you see what I mean. A race with no end—and no winner!

A company does not gain at the expense of a competitor by imitating, or cloning, that competitor's strategy, but rather by crafting and deploying a *distinctive* strategy that changes the rules of the game in its favor. What wins in business is not trying to *outmuscle* competitors with brawn, but rather to *outthink* those competitors with some brainpower. There are examples to be found in every industry.

The three major U.S. networks—CBS, NBC, and ABC—have not had a significant shift in market share in 30 years. Each network's share varies between 23 and 26 percent per year while they play musical chairs to determine who will be number one in any one year. The only network that has grown significantly over the last 15 years has been the Turner Broadcasting System, better known as CNN. Why? The reason is simple. The three networks are aping each other with three *identical* strategies. Only Turner has a *distinctive* strategy.

Instead of going standard broadcast, Turner went cable and satellite; instead of going with variety programming, Turner went with news programming; instead of staying domestic, Turner went international. Who's winning? Ted Turner by some $8 billion.

The same is true of the airline industry. For the last several years, we have been told by the CEOs of one major airline after another—American, Delta, USAir, and United—about how difficult it is to make money in the airline business. The result, therefore, is to accept cyclical swings in revenues and profits. Well, there is one airline that has been profitable every day since its first day in business in 1973. That airline is Southwest. Why? It doesn't play the game the way the others do. It, too, has a distinctive strategy. The majors play a hub-and-spoke strategy, Southwest plays a point-to-point strategy; the majors use multiple aircraft, Southwest uses a single aircraft; the majors have invested several billion dollars in sophisticated reservation systems, Southwest doesn't even have one! Who's winning? Southwest. At its current rate of growth, Southwest will be the largest airline in the country by 2000.

Richard Santulli, CEO of Executive Jet Aviation, has turned an entire industry on its heels by crafting a distinctive strategy that has completely changed the rules of the game. Rather than have companies buy corporate jets outright, he devised the concept of "fractional ownership" of corporate jets whereby a company buys a quarter or an eighth of an aircraft in return for a certain amount of flying hours per year. Almost bankrupt in the early 1990s, last year the company's revenues had skyrocketed to over $500 million with record profits to match. The best news is that after six years of operations, Santulli still has no competitors.

In the car rental business, three companies have been slugging it out for over 30 years with no change in market position or market share. Hertz is number one, Avis is still the "try harder" number two, and National trails as number three. However, the real winner and real number one is none of the above. That company is Enterprise. While the so-called Big Three agencies feast on each other by trying to attract business and vacation travelers at airports all over the world, producing meager profits, Enterprise has become the largest and most profitable car rental company in the world by pursuing a different strategy. Enterprise focuses on people who require a car to replace the one they own while it is being repaired or for some other temporary situation. Furthermore, instead of hiring low-paid service employees, it recruits freshly minted college graduates, who are highly rewarded to build profitable locations. It also delivers the car to your home and picks it up at the end of the rental. As a result, Enterprise owns the most cars in the industry (300,000), has more locations than Hertz (2800), and has the largest share of the market—20 percent versus 17 percent for Hertz. A *distinctive* strategy pays off again.

A similar story is unfolding in the car rental business in Germany. Again, the largest company in that country is not Hertz, Avis, or Eurocar. It is a company called Stixt. And the reason is the same. Stixt has yet another, but highly distinctive, strategy. Because it is not owned by a major car manufacturer, as is often the case in European countries, Stixt offers a broader range of cars, including Mercedes-Benz, BMW, Porsches, Jaguars, and even Harley-Davidsons along with the more mundane Volkswagens, Opels, and Renaults. The company also has self-service counters at airports that do not require the customer to have to wait in any line for a rental. The result? Stixt's market share is 20 percent, Eurocar's is 14 percent, Avis's is 10 percent, and Hertz's is 9 percent.

In the insurance industry, it is a well-recognized fact that most companies do not like to insure cars. However, one of the fastest growing and most profitable companies is one that thrives on car insurance. Its name is Progressive Insurance and its success, again, is due to a distinctive strategy. Unlike the other insurers, which try to avoid what is considered a "nonstandard" driver (a person with three speeding tickets in five years), Progressive's strategy *deliberately* focuses on these people. Its CEO, Peter Lewis, figured out long ago that speeding tickets, per se, are not predictors of future accidents, but that *one* accident is the true predictor of future accidents. With this strategy, Progressive has become the tenth largest of the industry's 250 companies.

In the shoe retailing industry, the last few years have seen the disappearance of such chains as Shoetown, Fayva, and, more recently, Thom McAn. Yet there is one chain that is prospering. That company is called Payless Shoesource and, again, its success is due to a distinctive strategy. While traditional shoe stores have a number of attendants to serve their customers, with most of the shoes stocked in a back room, Payless does it differently. Its stores display 10,000 pairs of shoes on 6-foot-high shelves, starting with sneakers at one end of the store and ending with dress shoes at the other. All sizes are available and displayed. Customers simply choose their style of shoe, their size and color, try it for fit, and then head for the cashier. Simple, but extremely effective. With this strategy, Payless now sells one of every five pairs of shoes in the United States.

In the financial data industry, the British company Reuters, which sells analytical information to stock analysts, has seen its market share more than double that of its chief competitor, Dow Jones's Telerate. Reuters' distinctive strategy, formulated by its former CEO, Glen Renfrew, and perpetuated by the current CEO, Peter Job, is to supply proprietary data through the use of proprietary software that is downloaded in customized formats to individual users through ordinary PCs. No other competitor does it that way. The result? In 1996 revenues increased 12 percent to $4.7 billion, and earnings, 24 percent to $705 million. The stock has gone from $4 to $70 in 12 years.

In the banking industry, there is currently a wave of consolidation going on, where big banks are merging with each other to become even bigger while small community banks are being gobbled up by other community banks to form "super regional" banks. The strategy behind all this activity is based on capturing the economies of scale from the use of computer technology.

Two banks, however, are going down a different road. Wells Fargo, in San Francisco, will be using computer technology, but in a very different way. It is closing down its traditional—and very expensive—"Taj Mahal" main street branch network and replacing it with a multitude of smaller, more economical branches located in supermarkets. This "minibranch" has a telephone and computer hookup to an operator in a central office. This strategy has made Wells Fargo more easily accessible to its customers and has allowed the company to increase its customer base while reducing its operating costs by over 20 percent, a result which will give it a substantial edge over its competitors.

Another bank, also based in California, that is pursuing yet a different strategy is the City National Bank of Los Angeles. Russell Goldsmith, its CEO, sees the benefits of Wells Fargo's strategy of improving the bank's interaction with its customers. However, instead of imitating Wells Fargo, and relying on computers and ATMs, Goldsmith has decided to embark on a strategy of increased *personal* service. When you enter one of City National's branches, you would think you were back in the 1950s. Human beings outnumber computers, and customer service people can be seen everywhere. Which of these two strategies will win? Stay tuned.

In the lighter industry, which is closely tied to the fate of the cigarette companies, business has been dismal as the volume of cigarettes being sold has dropped from 29 to 24 billion in just 10 years. Dismal, that is, for every company except one, the Zippo Manufacturing

Company. While Scripto, Cricket, Bic, and Calico Brands are clawing each other out in a winner-loses-all catfight, Zippo Manufacturing Company sticks out like a sore thumb. While the four companies are battling it out in the low-end, 99-cent disposable market, Zippo has decided on a different strategy. Its lighters sell for $13 to $40 each. The company focuses on making lighters that become "collector items." It offers a wide variety of designs, such as the Elvis model and models commemorating special events like the Woodstock 1994 Rock Festival. Zippo also makes lighters with corporate logos. There are even some for the cigar aficionado market that are leather-bound. The result: Sales have jumped from $30 million to $150 million in 10 years and are expected to continue at that pace for the next 10 years.

Still another company that changed its fortunes dramatically by formulating a distinctive strategy is the pharmaceutical company Eli Lily. Historically, Eli Lily had viewed itself as a "pill company." As such, its sales force consisted of people with pharmacy degrees who could have an intelligent dialogue with doctors about the characteristics of the company's pills. Recently, the company redefined itself as a "disease management company." Lily replaced its sales force with people who understood the changing environment of the health-care market and who understood the needs of all the players, including patients and HMOs. The result: In three of its key product areas, Lily went from last to first position, and in a fourth, it went from 46th to second.

In yet another industry, furniture, there is a company that has evolved from nothing into a billion-dollar giant in the space of 25 years by pursuing a distinctive strategy. The company is IKEA, and it was founded in Sweden. Instead of selling finished furniture, as other furniture retailers do, IKEA sells unassembled kits that customers can select and pick up in the company's "superwarehouses." After 25 years, IKEA has yet to attract one single imitator.

Our experience has shown that if you are not the leader, *never play the game according to the rules the leader has set*. Otherwise, you are certain to lose! In other words, do not try to "outexcel" the competitor in its areas of excellence or strategic capabilities. Playing by the rules set by the leader in an industry is certain death over time. The leader understands the rules better—it designed them. The leader can enforce them more effectively; it has more resources to do so. And the leader will crush you!

A better approach, in my view, is to create a *distinctive strategy to change the rules of play*. By changing the rules of play, you *neutralize* and *paralyze* the leader. While the leader is temporarily immobilized and on the sidelines, you can make significant gains against that competitor.

Examples of Companies that Have Changed the Rules

In 1980, Xerox had a 97 percent share of the worldwide copier market. In 1985, it had 13 percent. Why? Canon came in and completely changed the rules of play. Instead of offering xerography technology, it introduced its own. Instead of offering big machines, it introduced small ones. Instead of selling through a direct sales force, like Xerox's, Canon went through distributors. Instead of leasing the machines, it sold them outright. It took Xerox five years to decide to sell through distributors, and it took Xerox seven years to wean itself off its leasing revenue stream. Eighty-four percent market share points later!

Significant shifts in market share only occur by changing the rules of play on the leader, not by imitating the leader! Imitating the leader, or others in the industry, does not result in significant shifts in market share. The game is played between the 40-yard lines—up 10 yards, back 5 yards. Up 5 yards, back 10 yards. No one gets to the end zone! The same is true in business. Up one point, back two points. Up two points, back one point. No company's share changes significantly over time.

A company that has had considerable success in a very mundane business over the last 25 years is Domino's Pizza. And most of that success was achieved by changing the rules of play. Thomas Monaghan, founder of Domino's, invented the concept of "guaranteed home delivery within 30 minutes." This guarantee was made possible because of the development of a special envelope that was placed around the pizza to keep it warm during the delivery. As a result, Domino's has grown to several thousand outlets with almost no reply from its competitors.

In the stock brokerage business, Charles Schwab has grown a very successful business from scratch by also changing the rules to its advantage. The firm's net revenues have risen to over $500 million, and its stock price has gone from $7 to $44—by not doing what other brokers do. Schwab's personnel are on salary, not on commission; they take calls 24 hours a day, on three shifts, versus the single-shift day of its competitors; and 20 percent of its business comes from an automated system rather than through direct phone contact with a broker. As a result, Schwab has challenged and changed the most important rule of the industry: Schwab's commission rates are less than half of the traditional houses!

Schwab changed the rules again in 1995 with its introduction of the "One Source" program for the purchase of mutual funds. Rather than buying mutual funds from individual mutual fund companies, the

Schwab One Source program allows customers to choose from an inventory of over 600 funds without paying any commissions and to transfer from one fund to another without any penalties. This concept has completely revolutionized the marketing of mutual funds and caught the industry leader, Fidelity, totally off guard.

In 1997, Schwab decided to go for the hat trick and change the rules of the game again. Schwab introduced a program that allows investors to trade stocks on-line. The firm already has over 700,000 customers trading in this manner and, again, Schwab is giving its competitors fits.

In Europe, another upstart is making substantial gains at its competitors' expense by changing the rules of play. Martin Carver, CEO of Bandag, Inc.—a tire retreading company—decided that his business could not grow by emulating his competitors. Instead of working through Bandag's own distribution system, as it had done for decades, Carver dismantled the company in favor of a franchise system that costs each franchisee $150,000. Unlike its competitors, which insist that customers come to the retreader's shop, Bandag franchisees come to the customer's premises in specially designed $60,000 trucks filled with tires and equipment. Furthermore, the trucks are sent out after hours so that the customer's business is not interrupted. The result? Bandag's share has grown from 5 to 20 percent in Europe and now accounts for 18 percent of the company's total business, as compared with 5 percent in the 1980s.

In the cosmetics industry, Anita Roddick has seen her company, Body Shop International, grow from nothing to over $250 million in business annually by breaking all the rules that the larger companies play by. Instead of using expensive packaging, as its chief competitors do, Body Shop utilizes plain, nondescript material. In an industry that spends millions on advertising, Body Shop spends nothing. In an industry that sells primarily through drug and department stores, Body Shop sells through exclusive franchisees. Its growth is consistently in the double digits, and its net profit is over 30 percent of sales!

In the staid and somewhat dull gas utility business, things have not changed in 100 years—that is, until Kenneth Lay took over as CEO of Enron. For decades, government regulation required a gas pipeline to run directly from a specific gas field to a specific gas utility in another part of the country. As a result, customers were obligated to buy their gas from a single utility because it had a monopoly over a certain geographic market. Lay looked at this maze and decided to change the rules of play. Lay was the driving force behind the deregulation of the gas-distribution industry in the 1980s. Lay envisioned this maze of single-purpose pipelines as a cohesive national network, where broker companies could buy gas at the best price from whatever field they could, have it piped through the most efficient route available, and then sell it to any customer they could find at the other end. Enron was the first company to capitalize on deregulation and hired traders who developed the first "spot" market for gas. Enron's shares have soared while its competitors are still stagnating as they try hard to catch up.

In yet another industry—steel—a group of upstarts are in the process of changing the rules of play and creating major headaches for the traditional giants U.S. Steel, Inland, and Armco. New entrants, such as Nucor and Chaparral, are using "minimills," which represent a complete rethink of the steel fabricating process. Instead of making steel from ore that requires expensive coke ovens and blast furnaces, the minimill employs less costly electric furnaces that melt down scrap metal. As one executive of Chaparral Steel said, "We're Big Steel's worst nightmare, and we're not going away."

In the trucking industry, Don Schneider, CEO of Schneider National, has equipped his trucks with a computer and a rotating antenna. This allows him to keep track of each truck's precise location at all times and to redirect the trucks to respond to clients' requests more rapidly than any competitor. Confronted with some dramatic changes facing the trucking industry—mainly deregulation—most other companies lowered rates in an attempt to keep customers. Schneider opted to develop a distinctive strategy to respond more quickly to customer needs and to maintain price and margins by providing more value.

Roberts Express, another trucking company and a client of ours, has changed the rules of the game in yet a different manner and has a cre- ated a distinctive strategy for itself. Most trucking companies in the United States have organized themselves to serve the just-in-time inventory needs of their customers. As a result, they have short-haul or long-haul routes and prefer back-to-back loads. Roberts Express does exactly the opposite. Its strategy is to exploit breakdowns in this system. An example might be a car assembly plant located in Detroit that receives its engines from another plant in Cleveland. When an engine does not get there on time, Roberts Express comes into the pic- ture. The company has 2000 trucks stationed around the country, on standby, waiting for such a call. While on the phone with the person from the car assembly plant, Roberts (again through a satellite system that connects every truck) will locate the truck that is closest to the supplier's site and promise the customer to pick up and deliver the engine within a 15-minute window at both ends. Not only does Roberts get paid a premium for this service in an industry where low- est price usually is the name of the game, but its growth rate is sub- stantially higher than any other company in the industry.

Another revolutionary is Marty Wygod, founder of Medco Containment Services. Wygod changed the rules of the retail drug store business by providing companies with prescription drugs through the mail instead of through retail drug stores. The effect is a substantially lower per-unit cost for the customer. The result? Medco had such an impact that Merck decided to acquire it in order to guarantee a channel for its products.

Even Gillette, the inventor of the razor blade, has decided that the only way to grow its business again is to "change the playing field," as Colman Mockler, ex-CEO, stated. After having followed the crowd during most of the 1980s by trying to sell disposable razors and not doing very well at it because of the commodity, low-price, low-margin, low-profit attributes of this approach, Gillette decided it "had to change the playing field. Gillette had to convince consumers to pay more for systems instead of buying cheap disposables." Hence its introduction of the Sensor razor and blade system, which has been a phenomenal success even at $3.30 versus a 40-cent disposable, not to mention the endless need for replacement blades at 70 cents apiece. In one swoop, Gillette went from a low-margin business to a high-margin business with an automatic multiplier to boot! It recently repeated this success with the introduction of a version made especially for female users.

Dell Computer is still another example. Instead of marketing computers through stores, as the rules of the industry would dictate, a brash 19-year-old Texan, Michael Dell, decided to market computers using direct marketing techniques. The result: A $4 billion company after only a few years, one that is still going strong.

Dell changed the marketing rules in Europe as well. After having been told by all the so-called marketing experts in Europe that Europeans would never buy computers through the mail, Dell decided to go ahead anyway. Guess what? Dell's business in Europe is fast approaching the $500 million mark. Dell recently decided to change the rules of play again. At the beginning of 1997, the company extended its direct marketing method to the Internet and started taking orders directly from consumers from around the world. Within three months, it was receiving over $2 million of orders *per day*. The company predicts that its first year's revenues from the Internet will be over $300 million and that 80 percent of these buyers are new customers! In fact, Dell's success is causing all the existing makers of PCs to rethink their approach to the marketing of their own products. The company that changed the rules may soon see its new rules become the industry standard, which demonstrates that sometimes one can be so successful by changing the rules that an entire industry may feel threatened enough to convert to the new way of playing the game.

Eyelab is a good example of a company that has changed the rules of play to make significant gains at its competitors' expense. In order to reduce the waiting time for new eyeglasses, it decentralized the manufacturing process from a single, centrally located laboratory to mini-labs at each of its stores. Every Eyelab store has its own lenses, frames, grinding equipment, and technicians who can provide customers with eyeglasses within one hour.

The late Sam Walton, the founder of Wal-Mart, succeeded in dethroning Sears as the largest retailer in the United States. In just 30 years, his company went from nothing to $100 billion in sales to displace Sears, which had been around much longer and enjoyed sales in the billions before Wal-Mart was even conceived. How did Walton do it? Simply by breaking all the rules that Sears had invented. For example, instead of periodic sales, Walton introduced the concept of every-day discount prices; instead of concentrating in large metropolitan areas, he built his stores in small towns that others scorned. By the time Sears woke up to the threat, Wal-Mart's momentum was unstoppable.

In the publishing business, three entrepreneurs have formulated and deployed unique strategies that have changed the rules of play to their advantage. In the United States, Robert Petersen has created a magazine factory by developing magazine formats that are targeted at "niches of niches." His titles include *Hot Rod, Guns & Ammo*, and *Sport*. Each of these "niche" magazines leads to other niches. For example, *Hot Rod* led to *Motor Trend*, which led to *New Car Buyer's Guide*, which led to *Chevy High Performance*, which led to *Hot Rod Junior* for teens. *Guns & Ammo* led to *Handguns*, which led to *Bowhunting*, which led to *Rod & Custom*. The result? This strategy has made Peter a multimillion-aire worth some $400 million.

In the United Kingdom, another publisher has formulated and deployed a distinctive strategy that is changing the rules of play to his favor. Peter Kindersley, CEO of Dorling Kindersley Holdings, has a two-pronged strategy. First, his books are designed around a technique called "lexigraphics," which consists of pages dominated by a main picture surrounded by words, which makes the message "leap off the page," as Kindersley describes it. The second part of his strategy is even more unusual. Instead of selling his books through regular book-stores, Kindersley has built up a 20,000-person direct-selling force which sells books the old-fashioned way—door to door! In 22 years, the company has gone from nothing to over $300 million with nary a competitor in sight.

Yet another U.K. entrepreneur is in the midst of changing the rules about how books are marketed. Tim Waterstone, the founder of

Waterstone Booksellers, has introduced the concept of bookstores with over 100,000 titles—compared to the W. H. Smith stores, which carry less than half that number. Furthermore, Waterstone's stores are open until 9 P.M. every night including Saturdays and Sundays, a practice unheard of in the United Kingdom. Since 1983, Waterstone Booksellers has grown to 85 stores in the United Kingdom and opened several U.S. stores.

Sometimes, changing the rules of play puts an entire industry in jeopardy. Such is the case currently in the pharmaceutical industry. The giants—Merck, Hoffmann-LaRoche, Bristol-Myers Squibb, Sandoz, CIBA-Geigy, and others—are being challenged by a number of upstarts, such as Genentech, Genzyme, Innumex, and Amgen. What do these upstarts have in common? They have changed the rules of play with regard to the process of drug development. Whereas the traditional companies have their roots in chemistry, the challengers have their roots in biology. As *Fortune* reported:

> The conventional approach which still dominates drug development at the big houses, relies on hit-or-miss screenings of thousands of compounds in hopes of finding one that has medicinal properties. Only 1 out of 10,000 winds up on the market.
>
> By contrast, the biotech approach starts with substances the body already manufactures, either to heal directly or to act as signals that mobilize the response to an intruder. Biotech companies analyze the structure of these compounds, which are large protein molecules. Then they use genetic engineering to copy them. With the biotech approach a remarkable one of every ten possibilities has proved out.

Other advantages in the areas of costs, speed of development, and effectiveness have industry experts worried that the traditional approach will not match these new rules. Thus, they question the ability of the conventional, chemically based companies to survive in the mid-to-long term.

In Japan, a market that many companies claim is closed to foreign firms, one U.S. company is doing spectacularly well by changing the rules of play. That company, Amway, has been growing at a rate of 30 percent per year since 1979 to over $1 billion—one-third of the company's total revenues. How has Amway done this? By bypassing Japan's vaunted, closed, and entrenched multitiered distribution system and going direct through a sales force of one million Japanese who sell products door-to-door. So much for those who claim the market is impenetrable.

IBM has made a comeback with a new, distinctive strategy. In the 1980s, IBM floundered as management lost sight of its original strategy formulated by Thomas Watson. It has only been since Lou Gerstner came aboard as CEO and articulated his new strategy of "concentric computing" that IBM has regained its focus. As Andrew Grove, Intel's CEO, said at the time: "Lou Gerstner has defined his sandbox, and it's a very big sandbox and a very appropriate one for IBM to defend." The results since then speak for themselves. I am proud to say that on that day I bought IBM stock. The price? $28 (January 1994). Twenty-four months later: *$106* (August 8, 1997)!

AT&T is another company that is finally starting to think strategically. After years of trying to compete with MCI, Sprint, and the regional Bell operating companies (RBOCs) on the basis of price and losing market share consistently, it has finally decided to try to change the rules of play. Telephone signals are generally carried over copper wires. Once any competitor has access to that distribution system, the name of the game becomes one in which the low-price provider wins. In the local markets, these wires are controlled by the RBOCs, which puts AT&T at the mercy of their key competitors and, thus, in a losing position.

Starting in the fall of 1997, AT&T began market testing a new system called *Angel.* Instead of wires, the company will install a small box on the side of your building that will connect to the phones inside and then transmit the signal from the building to its ultimate destination not through wires, but through the air to a series of antennae, which will then tap into A&T's worldwide network. With this system, AT&T will be able to bypass the RBOCs' network, offer both local and long-distance service on its own network, and unshackle itself from the RBOCs' stranglehold. If successful, this might lead to AT&T's revival.

The Moral of the Story

The moral of these examples is this: When you create a strategy with the intent to change the rules of play on the leader, you paralyze the leader, sometimes for long periods of time. The reason is simple. The leader's organization is structured to do business according to the rules it has set. Changing that structure is not easy and can sometimes take years. While the leader is immobilized, you can make significant and important gains.

When everyone in an industry plays the game according to the same rules, no one wins! In other words, there are only marginal changes in market position. Those who make significant gains at a competitor's expense are those who have found a way to *tilt* the playing field to their advantage and change the rules of play.

After all, the object of competition is *not* to have an even playing field, but to design a playing field that is tilted to your advantage, a playing field that paralyzes the competition. As General Sun Tzu, the famous Chinese war strategist, would say, "To subdue the enemy without fighting is the acme of skill."

The same concept applies to business. Do not play the game according to your competitors' rules. *Surprise* the enemy by changing the rules of play! If *you* are constantly being surprised by the enemy, this is a clear signal of a defensive, reactive strategy. Change it. A proactive strategy constantly surprises the enemy and keeps the competitor in a defensive position.

Even Michael Porter, the guru of competitive tactics, has come around to our way of thinking, as evidenced in a recent *Harvard Business Review* article:

> In many industries, what some call hypercompetition, is a self-inflicted wound. The root of the problem is failure to distinguish between operational effectiveness and strategy. Operational effectiveness is necessary but not sufficient. A company can outperform rivals only if it can establish a difference that it can preserve.

After 20 years of experience with CEOs and their management teams, and after having been present in the "war rooms" of over 300 corporations, both large and small, I have come to the conclusion that the key difference between winners and losers is the ability to *think strategically*. Unfortunately, strategic thinking is not a highly developed ability in most corporations, ergo this book. The remainder of this book will describe the key concepts of strategic thinking which allow a successful company to formulate and deploy a *distinctive* strategy that makes competition irrelevant.

CATERPILLAR ®

Why the Cat Landed on Its Feet

Don Fites

Chief Executive Officer (with remarks by former CEO George Schaeffer)

The time was the go-go 1980s. Stock market boom and bust and boom again. Trump. Boesky. Apple. Honda. The Japanese quality revolution and the realization of a globalizing economy.

It was a decade in which vast fortunes were being made. But for the first time in its history, Caterpillar was stalled in the very steel-tread tracks it had pioneered in the 1920s. A worldwide building recession in the early part of the decade and the emergence of aggressive new competition had caught the Cat napping. The uninterrupted growth it had enjoyed for six decades was grinding to a halt.

Said then-CEO George Schaeffer, "for 60 years Cat was a rocket. Caterpillar could do no wrong. Now our business has undergone profound change. We had 60 years, all very successful, in which we built what *we said* the customers wanted and needed. The whole ball game has changed."

Aided by the post-World War II infrastructure building boom around the world, Caterpillar had been a seemingly invincible juggernaut. Anchored by a vast network of Caterpillar dealers in all of the growth areas of the world, the mighty Cat had the equipment, distribution, and service to dominate the world market for construction equipment and spare parts. Pursuing a classic product-driven strategy, Cat had all the right components—knowledgeable and dedicated people; extensive global manufacturing, a vast field population of machines and engines; and service facilities within easy reach of customers, literally everywhere. This physical presence in every market—a network its competitors could not duplicate—formed the basis of a *distinctive* strategy which allowed Cat to dominate its competitors for 60 years.

But like the Big Three automakers in Detroit, Caterpillar was caught by surprise when new offshore competitors—in Cat's case Japan's Komatsu and others—came on the scene with new high-quality products and a different marketing and sales approach. These new players attempted to establish *new* and *distinctive* strategies of their own to undermine the strategic strength of Cat's dealer network. The strategies included convincing customers that *their* new equipment needed far less service—and hence that the customer would be less dependent on a local dealer to keep equipment and operations running. Their strategy was to change the rules of play in a market Cat had led for as long as anyone could remember. Cat's strategy, so heavily dependent on the value of its dealers, was temporarily neutralized. Further crippled by a widespread building recession that had taken place in the early 1980s, Cat was in trouble.

"This was in the late eighties," says present CEO Don Fites, who was Cat's president at the time. "We'd experienced a decade without really any shareholder value being created....we were very concerned about our Japanese competitors. When I joined this company, all of our competitors were American companies—and they all were put out of business by the Japanese and Europeans who are fierce competitors. *Survival* was a word that we talked about around here."

As its U.S. competitors, such as International Harvester, succumbed one by one to this new environment, Cat management could find no clear path to regaining its growth of the past. Not that they didn't try. "We were floundering despite help from the top consultants available," said George Schaeffer. "We had too much good advice."

At some point Schaeffer came across *The Strategist CEO*, a precursor to the book you are now reading. In it he saw a new strategy-development methodology, the *strategic thinking process*, that he believed would enable the Cat managers to bypass the traditional strategic planning methods in vogue at the major consulting firms. This new approach, he thought, would give him the tools to mine the hundreds of man-years of experience he had right there in Cat's Peoria offices. In the heads of the company's own managers, he believed, lay the answers to their future survival and growth.

Employing the *strategic thinking process,* which will be described in detail later, Cat's management team developed a new strategy that would drastically restructure the company and within two years put it back on the path of record growth.

In the first three-day session, facilitated by Mike Robert, a few things became clearly apparent. Cat had gradually grown complacent over the years, neglecting to nurture the fundamentals of its product-driven strategy. Product quality lagged, and product development and service had lost touch with the real needs of its customers, opening the door to new and unexpected competition. The good news was that it also became quickly obvious what they needed to do to reestablish the company's former dominance and reinvent the distinctive strategy that enabled the Cat to dominate its competition for decades. More important, the team was able to come to these conclusions as a group, gain agreement, and move ahead with the assurance that comes from understanding and ownership.

Says Schaeffer, "Mike and his process helped us sort everything out. We knew that we were moving in a more orderly and focused fashion. We saw it all...businesses entered without commensurate expertise, misunderstood market share, and so on. It was priceless. Noses got bent out of shape...but when noses get bent out of shape you generally get better decisions."

Fites recalls, "The first sessions were an honest, hard look at who we were, how we were organized, and how we were going about doing business. It's a difficult process. It's easier to have somebody else tell you what you are and what needs to be done. In our case, though, I think this process was exactly the right approach to take because ours is a company in which most of the people spend their lifetime. We're very attached to the business and the equipment. We know the market and the customers. We know the business very well, and it's not a business that is easy to grasp. I mean, there aren't a whole lot of companies, there aren't really *any* companies in the world like Caterpillar. We don't have any models to follow. Forcing us to do that assessment process was exactly the right thing because only we, in the end, could have *made* that assessment, arrived at the conclusions, and taken the path that we eventually did.

"I think that the idea of someone from the outside telling people who have spent their whole life in a company that something will or won't work is not really a good idea. They don't have the insight into what really makes the company tick. I think the thing that this process does very well, and I've seen it done over and over again in different circumstances, is it forces *you* to come up with the good news and the bad news. And *you* find the answers to these issues yourselves."

As an integral part of the process, a dozen or so key "critical issues" were identified as imperatives for a successful turnaround: product quality improvement, new product development, customer focus, redistribution of responsibility, and a structure that would enable Caterpillar to respond quickly to changing customer needs. The list was concise, and ownership of each issue assigned to individuals and teams charged with seeing them through to fruition.

Says Fites, "We completely restructured our company from what was essentially a functionally organized company into profit-center divisions and service divisions. Originally there were 18. Now there are 23. We completely distributed accountability and responsibility down into the organization from what had been a structure where virtually all important decisions were made by a few people at the top. We drove the accountability and responsibility broadly into these divisions, held them accountable for their own plans." At the base would be the extensive dealer network that provided a direct line to the changing conditions and needs of every major market—a critical link that no competitor could duplicate.

At the end of the decade of the eighties, Caterpillar was doing business in more than 200 countries, with nearly 60 plants in 16 countries employing more than 60,000 people. In addition, its dealer network of some 190 dealers had truly global reach. Turning around a company of that massive size and inertia is akin to turning around an ocean liner. It takes time, planning, and the coordinated efforts of a lot of different specialists.

No strategy, of course, is worth much if it doesn't get implemented. To make sure all of these newly created units had a plan it could execute in synch with the corporate strategy, each strategic business unit (SBU) went through the *strategic thinking process.*

"Once we got ourselves organized corporately, a lot of the people who are running these divisions had been involved in the first sessions or were aware of the work that had been done. They immediately began using the *strategic thinking process* to flatten their own organizations and also do a self-assessment on a more micro basis of what they were and what they were trying to do."

The goal was to cascade the strategy concepts down through every level of the organization so the company could eventually move forward as one.

Today, more than five years later, those plans have long since become realities and have restarted the engines of long-term growth.

The days of facing extinction are a distant, though chastening, memory in Peoria. The results since 1992 have been nothing short of phenomenal. In fact, the *Wall Street Journal* (February 27, 1997) ranked Caterpillar number three of all the companies it tracked in five-year average shareholder return—at 29.8 percent!

As Fites describes the results of Caterpillar's strategic refocusing: "As far as the shareholders are concerned, it's the creation of shareholder value that has been rather spectacular. But also from a customer standpoint, the acceptance of our products from around the world is at an all-time high. Our product development process is working better than ever. We're expanding into new and related fields. We've just announced a joint venture that's going to put us more into the agricultural equipment business. Instead of having seven people at the top of the organization trying to come up with all these ideas on how we're going to grow, how we're going to be successful, we've got thousands of people in the organization coming up with all sorts of ideas. Our job now at the top of the company has changed—we're put in the position of choosing and picking the *best* ideas. We've got more growth opportunities identified than we really want to try to implement.

"I think it is one of the truly remarkable success stories of the 1990s. The track record is there in terms of financial results, market shares...percentage of sales...the whole nine yards."

Keeping the Global Strategy Alive and Flexible

For a company as large as Caterpillar the major challenge in achieving results like this consistently is keeping all of its global businesses focused on the strategy—yet flexible enough to change with conditions. The company now has in place a management accountability structure that assures ongoing implementation and progress on critical issues. At the basis of it is the common understanding and consensus on the underlying strategy developed in 1989 and 1990 through the *strategic thinking process.*

"We have a process and we stick to it. It's all been very well documented. Our mission. Our vision," Fite explains. "And where it's really well documented is in what we call our critical issues. We have an ongoing strategy committee whose work it is from time to time to look at all those documents drawn from people at various levels in the organization...take a look at our mission, vision, and particularly the critical issues. Our mission and vision are in place. But critical issues can change as the world changes, as competitors change. We make sure that those are kept up to date.

"Our people are motivated personally; they're motivated financially to stay on strategy and to demonstrate that the strategy is not something that's just been pulled out of the air. It's something they're going to implement...in fact are implementing. And there's a timeline for that implementation."

The role of top management is to monitor progress, set ambitious goals, and manage the strategic processes. A formal management structure was created as part of the process to assure ongoing reevaluation and implementation.

As Don Fites lays it out: "We have, what we would call EORs, which are our Executive Office Reviews, through which each division meets with the executive office, anywhere from a half day to a day. We do these generally in the February–March time period, and this is a detailed explanation by the division of what their strategy and what their plans are, which the executive officer approves. We're essentially looking at a three-year plan, and we measure that against what we were told three years ago, or two years and one year ago, and if we like what we see, and they're meeting the benchmarks that we have jointly established, then the division is further funded or further encouraged or given the green light to proceed. If they're not meeting the long-term benchmarks that we think are required by the enterprise, then we mark off some other plan for that division.

"And then to further enhance that process, so that knowledge just doesn't rest with the five members of the executive office, we then meet once a year with all of the divisions, and for a week each division explains to the rest of the organization, i.e., to their peers, what their strategy is, what their performance has been against their plans, and what it looks like three years out. At that point we also just take a look out as far as six years ahead as to what might happen. That meeting encompasses about 100 people—our top people from around the world. And I think those reviews are even tougher for the divisions because they're a committee of your peers, who are judging your plans and your performance against how it will interface, whether it will have synergy with what they are doing.

"And that's how I think we keep driving the vertical integration throughout the company, which is very important to us. But also I think it's important to how each division strives to maximize performance. And particularly peers tend to be tougher, I think, on each other than perhaps we are."

Because of the remarkable resurrection at Cat, Fites has become a firm believer in the use of the *strategic thinking process* to face the tough issues and find real answers. But with a cautionary note he adds, "It's not a process you dare take lightly. It's not a process where somebody's going to give you the answer. If you're concerned about your survival, it's very worthwhile doing because it *drives* you to make the best decision you can make, *because it uses the best knowledge available* and that's the knowledge within you and the people you're surrounded with—who really are your best and brightest. It uses *their knowledge* to identify and correct those things that can be corrected and also weds the organization to that new plan and that new organization. It makes you very determined to implement and make it work.

"*This is not a process for wimps.* It is not a process where somebody is going to tell you how to save or maybe even improve your organization. But it is a process that if you go into it recognizing that you've got to change, that you've got to do better—if you want to maintain your leadership or even survive—this process, better than any I've seen, will get the job done.

"Nobody likes change. But it helps you reach the *right* conclusion. If you implement with candor and with determination and with honesty in terms of telling the organization where you're going, what your goals are, 90 percent of the people are going to buy in, and they're going to try and make it work. There are always going to be a few people who don't, but that's part of the process. If you reach the right conclusion, your organization is smart enough to understand it. They realize the tremendous upside—a brighter future than they ever thought about."

Could Caterpillar have survived and prospered using the traditional strategic planning methods espoused by the major consulting companies in the seventies and eighties? Fites is quick to emphasize that the combined experience, energy, creativity, and drive of the company's people are what has made Cat's turnaround possible. Yet he credits the *strategic thinking process* with being the catalyst that enabled all those forces to work together toward a common goal. Looking back, CEO Fites concludes: "Had we come up with the same strategy, we would have been just as successful. But I'm not sure that we would have. We worked with several very well known consulting organizations....we never could come to a conclusion. In fact the conclusions that we semi-reached, a lot of us never really bought into. And I think it was because we didn't feel the ownership of those conclusions. So, I'm not sure we ever would have gotten to that point. Or if we had, it would have taken too long. Perhaps we would have gotten there at some point but that would have been too late...too late for the company or certainly too late for some of us charged with running the company."

For the record, the bright future at Caterpillar has already materialized and, by all indications, will continue. The competitors, such as Komatsu and Hitachi, are still there and still battling tenaciously. Yet, in 1996, Cat's sales were a record $16.52 billion versus about $8 billion in 1989, and its record profit reached $1.36 billion. Exports were the highest in company history at $5.5 billion. The stock price has gone from $10 (split adjusted) to $61 (August 1997), for an increase in shareholder value of over $16 billion. All made possible by creating and adhering to a *distinctive strategy* that enables Cat to monitor closely and respond to the changing conditions and product needs in every market around the world. Cat has, after a brush with extinction, landed squarely on its feet.

2

What Is Strategic Thinking?

The word *strategy* has a military origin. It comes from the Greek word *strategia*, which means "office of the general." Over time, it has taken on a variety of different connotations, such as...

> "the science or art of military command as applied to the overall planning and conduct of large scale combat operations."

or...

> "a military maneuver designed to deceive or surprise an enemy."

or it has been extended to other phases of life...

> "the art or skill of using stratagems in politics, business, courtship or the like."

As you can see, the word *strategy* has come to mean different things to different people.

I have been involved in developing business strategy since the mid-1970s. For those of you who were around back then, you will recall that there was an avalanche of books that came out on this subject under a variety of titles, *Strategic Planning, Corporate Strategy, Strategic Management*...strategy this and strategy that. Since my background includes many years in marketing positions for a variety of multinational companies, these books immediately caught my attention. I started browsing through them to get a better understanding of the meaning of the word *strategy*. However, as I began my browsing, I made two very quick discoveries.

First, every author who used the word *strategy* used it with a different meaning. One author would write that "strategy is the *goal* and tactics are the *means*." Another author would say, "No, that's wrong. The *goal* is the *objective* and *strategy* is the *tactic*." This is a 180-degree difference in definition! Still another author would claim that "strategy is *long-term thinking* and that tactical, or operational, was *short-term thinking*." Each author used the word *strategy* with a different meaning.

All this is to say that the more books I read, the more confused I became. But then I noticed that the same thing happened in the real business world. Whenever I attended one of our management committee meetings to discuss "strategy," I noticed that each person around the table had a different meaning for the word *strategy* and very quickly we would start bouncing off the walls.

The second observation I made about all those books back then was that they had all been written by business school professors of one kind of another who had spent "$7\frac{1}{2}$ years in the business school library" asking themselves the question of the decade, which at the time was, and to some extent still is today: What is it that has made GE (General Electric) so successful? And then, without ever talking to anyone at GE, they would concoct the "miracle recipe" that GE supposedly had used for its success. In other words, they had been looking into these companies as "outsiders" trying to re-create a magic formula without any firsthand knowledge of what had really occurred.

It was then that I said to our people at Decision Processes International: "Let's do things a little bit differently. Let's go out and let's talk to *real* people who run *real* organizations, and let's ask them what the word *strategy* means to them and let's sit in on their meetings to see how they go about doing it." And thus we set out on our journey.

We started by interviewing CEOs in companies of various sizes—small, medium, and large; in a variety of different industries; in dozens of countries. Gradually, we started participating in their strategy meetings. Therefore, what you will read in this book is not a miracle recipe pulled out of the blue, but rather concepts and a process extracted out of the heads of *real* people who run *real* organizations. All we have done is to codify these concepts into a process and to build some instruments around them, so that we could bring more structure or discipline to these types of strategy meetings.

The CEO's Vision: The Starting Point for Strategic Thinking

As we began interviewing a number of CEOs about the future of their businesses, we came across an interesting phenomenon. Very early on in such discussions with these individuals, they would begin telling us about a certain "vision" that they had in their heads (Figure 2-1).

Figure 2-1. The strategic thinking process starts with a vision.

Frequently, however, the CEO envisioned the "look" of the company in the future as different than the look the company had at that moment (Figure 2-2).

Figure 2-2. The process of strategic thinking looks into the future of the organization.

We came to define *strategic thinking*, then, as:

The process of thinking that goes on in the head of the CEO and the key people around him or her that helps them determine the look of the organization at some point in the future.

The look of the organization in the future can be different from what it is today. Strategic thinking, in our view, is akin to picture painting. It is this picture or profile that will determine the direction, nature, and composition of the business. *Strategic thinking*, then, is the *type of thinking that goes on within the mind of the CEO, the strategist, to shape, and clarify the organization's future strategic profile* (Figure 2-3). Decisions

Figure 2-3. The organization's strategic profile is clarified by the strategic thinking process.

that "fit" within the parameters of this profile are taken and implemented, and decisions that do not fit the profile are rejected.

Strategy versus Operations

Strategic thinking is different from both *strategic planning* and *operational planning*. In fact, strategic thinking is the *framework* for the strategic and operational plans (Figure 2-4).

Figure 2-4. Strategic thinking framework.

Strategic thinking is the type of thinking that attempts to determine *what* the organization should look like. In other words, the *strategy.* Operational planning, and even what has become known as strategic planning, is the type of thinking that helps us choose *how* to get there. To illustrate the difference between the two types of thinking, we can develop a matrix with the *what* on the horizontal axis and the *how* on the vertical axis as shown in Figure 2-5.

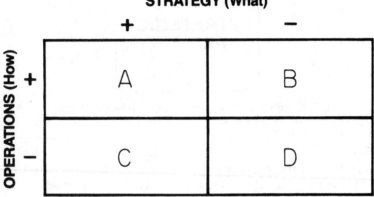

Figure 2-5. Strategic thinking matrix.

We can complete the matrix by further dividing each axis into *good* (+) strategic thinking and *poor* (−) strategic thinking as well as good (+) operational or strategic planning or poor (−) operational or strategic planning. Although both of these activities go on in all organizations, what we have noticed is that they go on with various degrees of proficiency.

In quadrant *A* (Figure 2-6), we find companies that do both very well. They have developed a *clear profile* and explicit strategy, and they

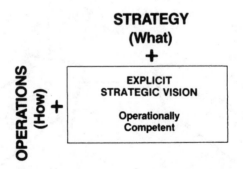

Figure 2-6. Companies in the *A* quadrant of the matrix.

manage their business successfully on an ongoing basis. Companies that fall into this quadrant include Wal-Mart, Sony, 3M, Harrod's, Merck, Johnson & Johnson, Marks & Spencer, Honda, Boeing, Procter & Gamble, and Caterpillar.

In quadrant *B* (Figure 2-7), we find companies that have been successful by managing their ongoing operations effectively, but manage-

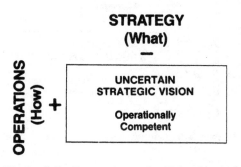

Figure 2-7. Companies in the *B* quadrant of the matrix.

ment cannot articulate *where* they're going. Generally speaking, many of the companies in the United States have been in this quadrant since the early 1970s. In other words, management can keep churning out good operational results quarter after quarter, but they frequently do not have a shared vision of *what* the company will "look like" as a result of all that churning.

In quadrant *C* (Figure 2-8), we find the opposite situation. Here are companies that have a very clear strategy, but management has diffi-

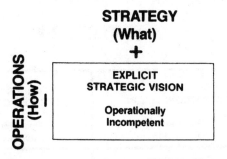

Figure 2-8. Companies in the *C* quadrant of the matrix.

culty implementing it operationally. During the 1980s, one such group of companies were the manufacturers of PCs. Each company probably had a very clear strategy: "Be the best IBM clone we can be." However, many of these companies had great difficulty making this strategy occur; thus, their fortunes went up and down like yo-yos.

The last quadrant (Figure 2-9) is the worst of both worlds. Here we find organizations that do operational and strategic planning poorly.

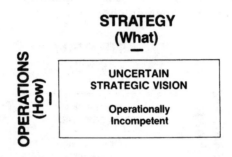

Figure 2-9. Companies in the *D* quadrant of the matrix.

Companies that fall into quadrant *D* usually don't survive very long, so it is difficult to generate a long list. Many companies have wandered in and out of this quadrant over the years—companies such as J.C. Penney, Kmart, Ethyl, American Motors, Friden, Burroughs...and even giant IBM until Lou Gerstner arrived.

In Figure 2-10, which quadrant is your organization in?

Although we would all like to say that we are in the *A* (+/+) quadrant, most of our clients readily agree that they fell into the *B* (−/+). That is, they are effective operationally but aren't always sure what direction they are pursuing. As a matter of fact, our experience has shown that almost 70 to 80 percent of companies are in that position.

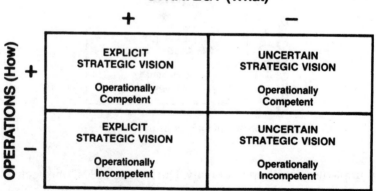

Figure 2-10. The completed strategic thinking matrix.

Surprising? Not really, when we explore some of the reasons for this. Here are three major explanations:.

First, most people who lead and manage organizations got there through the operational ranks. They were promoted from one level to the next because of their operational skills. They were good managers and made good operational decisions. They did not spend much time thinking about, or charting, the direction of the company. As a result, they have not acquired the skill of setting direction and being the organization's strategist. *That* skill takes time to develop.

Second, the need for management to think strategically surfaces only when a company starts going into markets that represent unfamiliar terrain. This occurs when the domestic market peaks and management has to explore expansion into other geographic markets and countries, where the rules of the game are different. This shakes management out of its operational thinking boots.

Working both sides of the Atlantic, we have come to respect the strategic thinking ability of Europeans—particularly the Germans and Swedes. These two countries export the majority of their GDPs and they have a long track record of doing business outside their natural borders. This has forced them to think much more carefully about products, markets, and the allocation of resources. Sweden, with a population of only 14 million, has 20 companies among *Fortune*'s 500.

Third, there is a tendency when a large domestic market is at our disposal to pursue only two elements from an operational point of view—*market growth* and *market share*. As long as the market grows and we can find new ways to increase our share, we will do well—thus there is little reason to think about strategy and direction. Momentum alone will carry us forward. This has been the case in the United States during the 1960s and 1970s. Only in the last decade or so has the company become more complex and the need to allocate resources more carefully given rise to the need to think more strategically.

Peter Drucker makes the same observation:

> Not in a very long time—not, perhaps, since the late 1940s or early 1950s—have there been as many new major management techniques as there are today: downsizing, outsourcing, total quality management, economic value analysis, benchmarking, re-engineering. Each is a powerful tool. But, with the exceptions of outsourcing and re-engineering, these tools are designed primarily to do differently what is already being done. They are "*how to do*" tools.
>
> Yet "*what to do*" is increasingly becoming the challenge facing managements, especially those of big companies that have enjoyed long-term success. The story is a familiar one: a company that was a superstar only yesterday finds itself stagnating and frustrated, in trouble and, often, in a seemingly unmanageable crisis. This phe-

nomenon is by no means confined to the United States. It has become common in Japan and Germany, the Netherlands, and France, Italy, and Sweden.

Companies falling into quadrant *B* can be referred to as being part of the Christopher Columbus School of Management.

- When he left, he didn't know where he was going.
- When he got there, he didn't know where he was.
- When he got back, he couldn't tell where he had been!

But he got there and back three times in seven years! Which means that Columbus was operationally very competent although he never knew where he was.

The *strategic thinking process,* therefore, can be described as the type of thinking that attempts to determine *what* an organization should look like in the future. *Strategic planning* systems, on the other hand, help choose *how* to get there.

Strategic thinking is a fresh approach to the subject of strategy. It identifies the key factors that dictate the direction of an organization, and it is a *process* that the organization's management uses to set direction and articulate their vision. For strategic thinking to be successful, it is necessary to obtain the commitment of the organization's key executives and the commitment of others who will be called upon to implement that vision. Naturally, the vision is greatly shaped by the CEO.

It's a process that extracts from the minds of people who run the business their best thinking about what is happening in the business, what is happening outside in the environment, and what should be the position of the business in view of highly *qualitative* variables (opinions, judgments, and even feelings)—not the quantitative ones. Strategic thinking produces a vision, a profile, of *what* an organization wants to become, which then helps managers make vital choices. It enables management to put the corporation in a position of survival and prosperity within a changing environment.

American Precision Industries

Driving Growth by Thinking Strategically

Kurt Wiedenhaupt
Chief Executive Officer

"Managing companies is like standing with your management team in the valley, and you're surrounded by many beautiful and challenging mountain peaks. Your strategic objective here is to decide which mountain are we going to climb," says Kurt Wiedenhaupt, CEO of American Precision Industries, in discussing his approach to creating and implementing strategy.

"Now, there are various ways of doing it. Number one is you sit in an armchair as boss and you point at one peak and say 'charge.' And then these guys are charging up and they come to the first difficult spot. Then they say, 'Do you think the boss is serious? Why don't we take a rest here. He's still down in the valley.' And then after a while they say, 'we're not crazy'...and then 'forget it.' And they come back to the valley and they say 'it was too difficult, it was too dangerous, and it didn't make any sense.' Then the boss gets upset and everyone wonders what comes next.

"The second way is that the boss says 'charge' and he's in front of these guys. Then the only difference is that when they come to the difficult spot, the boss makes the decision that maybe that wasn't the right mountain to climb, so they go back into the valley and try another one, and another one, and another one. They are very busy and expend a lot of energy and money. And the reason they turn back this time is that they are not sure that that was the right peak to climb in the first place. But with DPI's *strategic thinking process* you get conviction because you very carefully select the mountain you want to climb together, and everyone knows the reason why you want to climb that mountain. Then you start working your way up together, and if you hit a rough spot, a crevasse or overhang, you will find a way around, and you will get to the top. The team will think it out because everyone is convinced and *knows* it is the right peak to climb.

"They know the logic, the logic that says to everyone it's the right thing to do. There's ownership, there's pride, there's determination. And the team is united in it. As alternatives, you only have a strategy that is developed by the boss, or by somebody from the outside. So in the team of 20 you might have two or three who are enthusiastic, then you have three or four or five who are followers, and the rest are leaning back."

When Kurt Wiedenhaupt came to American Precision Industries as the new CEO in 1992, he saw no lack of mountains that were worthwhile climbing. The questions, of course, were which ones and how?

Wiedenhaupt had had such consistent success with the *strategic thinking process* in previous assignments as a CEO that he resolved early on to use it to identify the mountains and the means.

API is a "mini conglomerate," a collection of three technology-driven divisions with no real strategic connection to each other. One is in precision motion control, one in industrial heat transfer, one in electronic components. Each has a unique technology at its core. But no synergy potential exists between the divisions, given widely divergent technologies, applications, and markets.

"These three have nothing to do with each other," Wiedenhaupt explains. "That's the way I inherited the company. There had been others, but these were the ones that were left over when I came here. It was a dormant company which at one time had grown but was not growing anymore. There was no clear strategy for future growth. Sales had moved from $38 to $50 million in the 12 years before—below the inflation rate. The company was profitable. There were good products and good people. But there was no R&D, no vision for the future.

"So, I had to give the company a vision, a future. That was my main job, to define the future, to communicate it, and get the company moving. And I knew only one effective way of doing it—the *strategic think-ing process*. Within the first month that I came here, I took the three technology groups separately offsite, and we developed strategies for each of them."

Kurt Wiedenhaupt is a strong believer in the ability of the process to draw out the knowledge, experience, and honest thinking of the participants, as long as the CEO does not try to dominate the discussion or manipulate the outcome.

"I was a very attentive listener," he says, "and the only thing I told the people before we started each session was that the good news is I cannot interfere in the process. I do not have a preconceived idea of where we will take this company. The only thing I know is we're going to grow the company. But you are the ones who will decide the strategy, not I. The bad news is, whatever you decide, I will make sure you implement, so you better make the process yours, and that's what happened. The three technology groups developed strategies. Then, based on that, I developed my own thoughts, with Mike's help, for the company as a whole."

This is a somewhat unusual application of the *strategic thinking process*, since most companies are looking for a way to coalesce the various and sundry business units together into one synergistic dynamo.

"One thing I recognized immediately was that I was not running one company," Wiedenhaupt states. "I was running three companies. And it would have been wrong to push all three groups through the same filter."

In sorting out the future strategic profile of the units, and ultimately of API as a company, the key question became by what route would profitable, stable growth be achieved? By building on each individual technology? Seeking further unrelated technologies? Looking for synergistic, interrelated technologies? As a technology-driven company, the teams decided to focus API's growth on the diversification of products and markets based on the three core technologies. By combining the R&D strengths of all the business units, the company could begin to generate new, differentiated products based on leveraging of each unit's technological strengths. These products would provide opportunities to strengthen API's position in current markets and offer opportunities to break into selected new markets. This two-pronged expansion would then be bolstered by acquiring companies with a direct relationship to these core technologies, thus opening up new geographic and market opportunities.

On the macrostrategy level, the plan would be that when these core technologies begin to run out of growth at some point down the road, *interrelated* technologies would then be added to create new growth, building on the strengthened foundation of three original business units.

"So we did it," Wiedenhaupt says, "and got the critical issues moving. The board approved the strategy in December when I presented it officially, and we started implementation in late 1992, early 1993. And the rest is really history, because we grew the company in four years from $50 million to $120 million last year. And this year we will have at least $200 million in sales."

Communicating to the Troops

API's *management* has a clear understanding of the critical issues and their role in resolving them. But what about the guy in the plant, the machine operator, salesperson, administrator. How did the CEO ensure that the company's direction and purpose would be understood at *all levels* of the company?

"After the strategy was done, the team members who were part of the strategy group and I presented it to every single employee," Wiedenhaupt recalls. "We went in and had meetings from the shop floor to the corporate office. Everyone was exposed to it. We went in at night, at 11, to get the second shift and the third shift; we went in at 6 in the morning. We must have had over a dozen meetings to communicate the details of the strategy to all people. I used to also have quarterly, now will have semiannually, what I call 'Coffees with Kurt,' where people who are interested are invited, they chew on a donut and have a cup of coffee, and they can ask me questions. And I give them a brief update on the state of the nation. It's not a command performance because I don't want to drag people in to see them sleep. So people who are interested come and ask questions. And we also have our *API In Action,* our newspaper, which is also focused on continuous improvement and what's happening in the company. So we are communicating regularly, which I think is one of the most important things. Otherwise, you lose momentum.

"And, of course, one of these days we are going to hit some hard spots and we will get through it because we are solidly committed to our strategy. We don't change course. I think this is another item which is important with the strategy. People have to see their role. We have to define it. And they must know what is expected of them. You have to define clear targets—set the crossbar at the height you expect to jump. We announced to everyone that in five years we want to be a $250 million company. These people thought I had smoked something on my way here from New Jersey to Buffalo. It was pure lunacy in the eyes of many. We put up big banners hanging in the factories, and posted in the offices, saying, 'We are the company, we can do it.' But then you, the management, have to act consistently and people start to believe it."

As any leader knows, setting ambitious goals is critical to inspiring exceptional performance. API's leader illustrates the point with this analogy:

"Running a business is like going into a track and field meet, and you have to make a decision how high to put the bar for the high jump. If you put the bar at three feet, no problem, you step over it. You put it up to six feet, well, you have to train a little bit and then you jump. Put it at seven feet, then you have to change your style but you can still make it. And now comes an idiot who puts the bar up to 15 feet. What do you do now? There are some people who give up and turn away and say this guy is crazy, and there are others who go around back to a shed and pick up a pole and jump the bloody thing.

"So my role is to manage processes in the company, make sure the processes are being followed, help people to find the pole to jump the bar, and put the bar up as high as realistically possible. And then encourage them, but not tell them. You put the bar up and say, okay, now let's figure out how we get over it, and it can be done."

An Expert's View of the Strategic Process

As the first client of Decision Process International back in the 1980s, Kurt Wiedenhaupt has a unique perspective on the *strategic thinking process*. An acquaintance of the author at the time, he learned of the process during the author's visit to Wiedenhaupt's home in the United Kingdom.

"It was at my rustic dining room table in England, which now happens to be my desk in the office," says Wiedenhaupt, looking back some 15 years. "That's where Mike first revealed to me that he was going out on his own. He was full of enthusiasm for this new process he had developed. So I asked him if he had a client, and he said, 'Not yet.' And I said, `Okay, let's start.' I was the first one. At the time, I was with AEG, which became part of Daimler-Benz."

"Mike had looked at what was available in the market and he was frustrated with what he saw there," Wiedenhaupt remembers. "He believed the standard consultant gave the client only 70 to 80 percent of what he really needed to complete the strategy development *and* put it into action. He said that if this 20 or 30 percent cannot be bridged, then the 70 percent is a useless product which you see standing as a book on the shelves of many famous companies that have spent millions of dollars with outside consultants to develop a strategy. And what intrigued me was Mike's commitment, not so much to going into business—he was interested in delivering a benefit, a result, to the client. And that, combined with the simple wisdom of the process, *this* convinced me to go along with him. Number one, there is no mumbo jumbo. It is straight, may I say, street wisdom. It's not an academic challenge to the participants. It is clearly, simply, an application of sound, basic business knowledge."

So they tried out the process on the management team there and were so successful in creating a cohesive strategy that Wiedenhaupt would opt to use the process several more times to help management teams sort out strategies in subsequent assignments. He had identified something new in the process and its mentor that was a refreshing change from other methods of strategy creation he had encountered.

"I have been exposed to McKinsey, Boston Consulting Group, and to Bain & Company. They are all very capable and I'm sure they have a good product that's extremely impressive," he says, "and I'm sure intellectually they're also very sound. The only problem is it's not of the people, by the people, through the people. It's not owned by the people who later have access to it. It is an alien product no matter how well it relates to the company. That's why it fails. I think, *intellectually,* they might even come up with a better product than the process we are using. But when it comes to executing it, they are miles behind DPI. It's simply ownership. We as human beings do what we *believe* in, and we do that with *enthusiasm.* If somebody else tells us something to do, we might do it, but don't expect any enthusiasm.

"But anyone who is considering using the process should not see it as a one-time exercise; it has to become part of the company, part of the everyday life. Language like *critical issues, driving force, areas of excellence, strategic thinking*—this is part of our daily verbiage, this is part of our language, this is part of our culture now. I just came back from a three-week holiday, my first in five years. And what I did during that period was I just wrote a manual for our company where I describe our systematic approach to business, and where I describe the strategy process so that new people coming into the company, after reading that manual, understand our philosophy, our processes, our systematic approach to business. I describe the strategies, the decision analysis, the problem analysis, the strategic creative product development process, and the annual planning process so that a new person reads it and is immediately an insider. This way people start to adopt it, to live with it, and it gets stronger and stronger."

Strategy and the New CEO

Having been called upon several times in his career to take the reins of businesses he did not know as an insider, Wiedenhaupt has come to recognize that strategic thinking can be an especially valuable tool to the CEO coming into a new situation—either as incoming chief executive or in the integration of a new acquisition.

"This process, I have found through my own experience," he says, "can be beautifully used by *any* new CEO coming into a company or business he is not fully familiar with. You have the opportunity in a very short period of time to immerse yourself into this new business. You get a deep understanding of the issues. You get a very good feeling for the players in your organization who are participating in this process. And I have to say it took at least half a year out of my learning process in my last assignment...and I feel much more secure in the path I am walking because my own people have described the path we have to walk and they are walking with me.

"No matter what industry you come from, what industry you go into, the fact is that when you enter a new company, you enter a different culture and a different and new business environment. The most important thing for you to learn is to listen and not tell people what to do until you really know what you're talking about. And going into the strategy session right away and sitting there and listening affords you getting to know the people, their thinking, their emotions. You get to know the issues, the real issues the company has to address. So by just going through the process you get tuned into the company much faster than any other way I know.

"We have just acquired one company in Germany, and we are going through the process immediately. We acquired the company in February. In April we go through the strategy process," says Wiedenhaupt. "Any company we have acquired over the last four years went through the strategy process because it's so important; not that we don't know what to do with the company, but we want to make sure that the people develop their strategy, and that they see the 'light,' and that it is their product and they take ownership."

Why the Process Has Staying Power

"You have all the facts on the table. You're not going down this path just because somebody feels like it. The process does not allow you great emotion. It leads you through very logical details," Wiedenhaupt states.

"And throughout the year the critical issues keep you on your track. You are not going to be diverted by day-to-day business and thrown in one direction one day, and another direction the next. Well, you have to deal with your daily occurrences, but your track of progress and your possibility to measure the progress are the critical issues. And again, it is so simple and yet so powerful.

"You have not dictated these issues to your people. These are *their* findings, and they have to address these critical issues so they have ownership from day one.

"You have to drive the process as a CEO. You have to be committed as a CEO. You have to put in the instruments of regularly sitting down with your people, with the owners of the critical issues. They must know that this meeting will take place. And because everyone knows what's expected, you can automatically guide the team along the path that you have together set out."

These principles have paid tangible dividends since 1993. API's rapid acceleration of growth is assignable to the addition of key components that, as Wiedenhaupt saw it, were missing from the mix: "Direction, definition of the direction, that the people took ownership of it, or at least a large number of people, and the clear vision of what we wanted to be, and an understanding of the market and the world we are living in, in each of these special technology groups. The definition of their future, I think, was one of the most important things for the people. Everyone was working hard and were dedicated, but didn't know where their journey would take them. And now people have direction and they march. It's very exciting to observe the change in the company.

According to API's 1996 annual report, the company has achieved three straight years of record revenues. "This outcome," it states, "is the direct result of the strategy we began to execute in 1993." Revenues in 1996 grew by 42 percent, net earnings by 38 percent. During the last four years, API has generated a compound annual growth rate of 23 percent in sales and 29 percent in net earnings. API's stock has gone from $6 to $22 (August 1997), for an increase in shareholder value of $112 million.

"The best result is the growth. I mean 14 quarters, with increased earnings, 14 in a row," says Wiedenhaupt, summing up the fruits of the past four years.

3

Key Obstacles to Strategic Thinking

If the objective of any company is to be in quadrant *A* (clear profile and operationally effective), then the next question has to be: Why are they not there? This question led us to probe into the obstacles that get in the way of good *strategic thinking*. Let's explore what these are.

The Strategy Suffers from "Fuzzy Vision"

The first observation we made about the behavior of people in top management positions is that they spend a lot of time together—in various meetings and on various committees. Some estimates show that 80 to 85 percent of their time is spent meeting—together. In the course of those meetings, managers talk to one another. One would expect, after all that talking, that the direction of the company would be clear and that they would all share the same vision, particularly after so many years of working together. Yet, in spite of this, an interesting phenomenon occurs when each member of the management team is asked to describe the company's future and direction. Each person has a different perception!

Each person's vision is slightly different than his colleague's, in spite of the amount of time they spend *together*. These different perceptions of the company's future result from the fact that everyone, to some extent, suffers from tunnel vision. Each person sees the company's future profile from their own perspective and function (Figure 3-1).

Figure 3-1. Each member of the management team perceives the company's future direction from a different perspective.

One member of a management team that we recently worked with expressed it accurately when he said, "The reason I see the company's future profile as a triangle is because I've been up to my neck in nothing but triangles for 15 years."

Operational Thinking Dominates Management's Time

Even when there is an "unspoken" strategy in existence in a company, there are many interpretations of it. Delving into this phenomenon a little further, we find that the reason is simple—most of the time management spends in meetings is spent discussing operational issues and *not* strategic ones. They always address the *how* of running the business, not the *what*.

There are usually a lot of fires that need putting out, and those are the urgent issues that attract everyone's attention (Figure 3-2).

OPERATIONAL

STRATEGIC

Figure 3-2. Operational concerns get in the way of strategic thinking.

Strategy Is Reactive, Not Proactive

As a result, there is a tendency to slip into a *reactive* management mode rather than a *proactive* one. The corporate profile starts being shaped by outside forces rather than by management. These forces can be governments, competitors, unions, and even customers. The environment or competitors, not management, molds the company's direction and strategy (Figure 3-3).

Figure 3-3. Corporate profile is shaped by outside forces.

We once worked with a large utility company that perceived their business and strategy to be completely shaped by the rules and regulations of the government. They were convinced of this because they were spending some 60 percent of their time in front of various government agencies and committees, trying to answer questions coming from a variety of different pressure groups. The other 40 percent of their time was spent reacting to these pressures.

The U.S. automobile industry has been in the same state for most of the last 20 years. During this time, their strategy has been set and managed by the Japanese. Many outside forces will gladly take over the direction of your company should you abdicate your right to do so yourself.

No Crisis...No Strategy!

Good times are another obstacle that impedes strategic thinking (Figure 3-4). When times are good, who needs to think about where they are going?

Figure 3-4. Good times ahead...No need for strategy.

The need to think about direction usually surfaces *after* a crisis. General Electric, which is highly regarded for its strategic planning process, did not become concerned about this kind of thinking until the disaster they had in the computer business in the early 1970s when they wrote off several hundred million dollars.

Bill Gates, one of the country's foremost strategic thinkers, is of this opinion as well:

> My success in business has largely been the result of my ability to focus on long-term goals and ignore short-term distractions. Taking a long-term view does not require brilliance but it does require dedication.
>
> When your business is healthy, it is difficult to behave as if you are in a crisis. That is why one of the toughest parts of managing, especially in a high-tech business, is to recognize the need for change and make it while you still have a chance.

Short-Term versus Long-Term Thinking

A fifth obstacle is that many executives associate strategic thinking with *long-term* planning and consider operational planning as *short-term*. Our work indicates that neither type of thinking is time-related (Figure 3-5).

Figure 3-5. Strategic thinking should not be time-related.

There are some strategic decisions that can be made which will have a short-term impact, and there are operational decisions that can have long-term effects.

The nature of the industry determines the time frame of both the strategic and the operational thinking. In the oil industry, one must look ahead 40 to 50 years, because the development of energy resources is a long process.

In the garment industry, on the other hand, one may not want to look further ahead than the next fashion cycle—six months or less!

A bias that our firm has developed, vis-à-vis operational planning systems used in many organizations, is against the adoption of the five-year business plan approach to determine the future of the company. Somehow the business community has developed a fixation around a five-year planning cycle. What is so special about five years? Shouldn't our planning be more related to our strategic time frame? All that is done with the five-year plan anyway is to update the first year and guess at the last four years. Strategy development and review is not amenable to an annual cycle because the environment is not that predictable. Tying strategy formulation to annual budget exercises ensures failure.

Planning Is Bottom-Up

Most "strategic" or operational planning systems are bottom-up. Every department head is asked to make a recommendation of revenues and expenses for the next year. These systems start in the bowels of the organization and work their way up through vertical or functional silos (Figure 3-6).

Figure 3-6. Strategic thinking should be top-down, not bottom-up.

The strategy of a company, in our opinion, must come from the top and go down. The only people who have a right to articulate the direction of the corporation are the people who have a real stake in that organization and have to live with the results of their choices and the direction in which they take their company. By using a bottom-up approach, top management abdicates its prerogative to develop an integrated corporate strategy.

Thinking Is Quantitative, Not Qualitative

The foundation of most corporate planning systems in place today is internally generated data—highly *quantitative* and historical in nature. Most long-range planning systems look back at five years of numbers (history) and extrapolate for the next five years. This kind of planning does nothing to change the "look" or the composition of a business in terms of products, markets, and customers. It also assumes that outside influences will remain the same in terms of competition, government, labor, and resource availability.

As such, management fails to take the whole picture into account. These systems are typically accompanied by a need to do a lot of analysis, usually requiring graphs, forms, bar charts, matrices, and volumes of numbers.

Management Uses Rose-Colored Glasses

Another difficulty created by long-range operational planning systems that are bottom-up exercises, is that most of the numbers that come to senior management are highly optimistic. When management is finally faced with all the numbers, the world looks very rosy and the only thing top management does is shave the numbers a bit.

In fact, what happens is that at every level of management, another degree of optimism is added on. Everybody has to make it better, each adding x percent to the forecast. Planning systems can't help set direction because they start from the bottom. Top management gets involved last in the process. When the numbers hit them, that's it. All they can do is react.

Numbers Planning Discourages Risk Taking

An article in *The Academy of Management Executives* quite clearly brings home the idea that numbers planning discourages risk taking. The authors—Charles Hill, Michael Hitt, and Robert Hoskisson—point out that America's declining competitiveness compared to Japan, Germany, Italy, and even the United Kingdom, in the 1970s and 1980s was due to a decrease in both *product and process innovation.* They attribute this decline to the quantitative management systems espoused in the United States, such as ROI-based financial controls and portfolio management concepts. These principles, they argue, "give rise to a short-term orientation and risk avoidance."

> The argument to this point has been that reliance on tight financial controls by the corporate office encourages decision making at the divisional level consistent with short-run profit maximization and risk avoidance. The result is lower innovative activity and declining competitiveness.
> Many market losses experienced by American firms can be attributed to a *lack of emphasis on product and process innovation. Product innovations* create new market opportunities, and in many industries are the driving force behind growth and profitability. *Process innovations* enable firms to produce existing products more effi-

ciently. As such, process innovations are one of the main determinants of productivity growth. In this technologically dynamic era, without a continual stream of product and process innovations, firms soon lose their ability to compete effectively.

The "risk avoidance" style of management in existence today in many U.S. companies has already cost America dearly. Many inventions, born in America, have seen the light of day as innovative new products abroad. One example is the transistor, invented by Bell Laboratories but exploited by Sony of Japan. A second is the videocassette, invented by California-based Ampex but exploited by Sony and JVC.

Reliance on Strategic Planning, Not Strategic Thinking

Most organizations we have worked with have very elaborate strategic *planning* systems in place. Strategic planning, however, does not strategic *thinking* make! In an article entitled "How to Prepare for 1995," *Fortune* (December 31, 1990) stated:

> At too many companies, strategic planning has become overly bureaucratic, absurdly quantitative, and largely irrelevant. In executive suites across America, countless five-year plans, updated annually and solemnly clad in three-ring binders, are gathering dust—their impossible specific prognostications about costs, process, and market share long forgotten. Asks John Walter, ex-CEO of R.R. Donnelley & Sons, America's largest printer: "Do I have the books in my closet with all the numbers in them? Yes. Do I look at them? No."

Organizations embark on time-consuming planning systems imposed on them by management, insisting that these "strategic plans" be addressed every 12 months. Because of the "fire drill" orientation of strategic planning systems, strategic thinking in many major organizations has come to a standstill. *There simply isn't time to think strategically.*

America's obsession with the "fire, ready, aim!" syndrome led to the country's decline during the 1970s and 1980s. Even Michael Porter, in an interview in *The Economist*, admitted that "strategic planning in most companies has not contributed to strategic thinking. The need for strategic thinking has never been greater." The irony of this statement is that Porter's own techniques have been contributing to the erosion of strategic thinking.

If the preceding techniques are not conducive to setting strategy, what is then? And how does a CEO go about developing and implementing a successful strategy?

The process needed to determine the future direction of an organization is not strategic planning but rather, *strategic thinking.* Strategic thinking is a process that enables the management team to sit together and think through the qualitative aspects of its business and the environment it faces. The team can then decide on a *common and shared* vision and a strategy for the future of the company.

The Process Itself Is an Obstacle

Although most companies have very sophisticated operational planning processes and systems, they do not have a *formal process* of strategic thinking (Figure 3-7).

As a result, even when they do wish to spend some time at the "mountaintop retreat" to think through "where they are going as a company," they usually do not have a process or methodology for

Figure 3-7. Most organizations lack a formal strategy process.

thinking strategically. Hence early into their discussions they are back to discussing operational issues. Some companies have attempted to develop a process, but they usually combine strategic and operational issues, thus making the exercise laborious and confusing. Our suggestion is that the processes are *different* and therefore should be *separated.* The factors and elements studied and evaluated in the strategic thinking process are not the same as in the operational planning process. For this reason, different time slots should be allotted to each process. Milton Lauenstein, a strategy guru, concurs.

> Management should understand that strategic planning encompasses two distinct functions: long-range planning and strategy formulation. Confusing these two activities has contributed to the sorry record of strategic planning. They are better performed separately.

The comparison of the two processes in the accompanying table should help to bring the differences into sharper focus. The remainder of this book is intended to give you an in-depth understanding of the key concepts and processes of strategic thinking that will enable management to change the rules of play.

A Comparison of Strategic Planning and Strategic Thinking

Strategic Planning	Strategic Thinking
Extrapolation This process extrapolates the organization's future by adding estimates of growth. It does nothing to change the nature or direction of the company.	*Framework* This process establishes a framework or profile against which ongoing decisions are tested. It reviews and questions the direction of the business.
Bottom Up This process usually starts in the lowest departments of the organization and works its way up.	*Top Down* Only one group of people has the right and the obligation to shape the company's future direction and that is top management.
Usually Optimistic A bottom-up process produces numbers and assumptions that are usually optimistic. Managers faced with such presentations find it difficult to assess or evaluate the meaning of these plans and end up shaving or trimming the numbers rather than contributing any meaningful input.	*Realistic* A framework or profile developed with the full participation of management and their knowledge and expertise becomes a better test bed for the allocation of resources.
Sometimes Erroneous No one in his right mind will project himself out of existence! This is human nature. Let us assume you have four divisions. Two are doing well and two are not. You have set a goal of 8 percent real growth. Here is what a bottom-up process will produce: The two divisions that are doing well will come in at 7.7 percent and 7.9 percent, respectively. They will shave their estimates knowing that you will be back for more. The two that are doing badly will come in at 8.1 percent and 8.3 percent, justifying their existence. And guess what year of the five-year plan that will be achieved in? Right! The fifth year. This is known as "hockey-stick planning."	*Guidelines for Emphasis* A good strategic thinking process will produce a profile for the company that can then be used to determine which areas of the business will receive more and which areas will receive less emphasis. The process, therefore, needs to be interactive between levels of management, so that managers whose areas will receive fewer resources in the future are still committed to the direction chosen by management.
Nothing Is Eliminated Many of our clients who rely heavily on a bottom-up process tell us quite candidly that they have difficulty "pruning" or eliminating product lines or services. This is due to the pressure toward "justification" that this process encourages.	*Better Balance* This process produces a clear list of products and markets that need to be trimmed together with a clear rationale as to why this needs to be done.

A Comparison of Strategic Planning and Strategic Thinking (Cont.)

Strategic Planning	Strategic Thinking
Internal Data	*Internal Plus External Data*
This process uses primarily internally generated data, most of it historical in nature. As a result, the process is objective and based on projections. It requires long and exhaustive studies with a heavy numerical base. It is a quantitative evaluation of the business	This process incorporates an assessment of both the internal and external environment. It is highly subjective since it is the personal perceptions of each member of the management team. Most of the information required is simple and easy to retrieve since it is stored in each person's head. The key is to tap that knowledge and bring these perceptions into an objective forum. This process is a *qualitative* evaluation of the business and its environment and is thus both *introspective* and externally focused.
Quantitative Analysis	*Qualitative Synthesis*
The input data is numbers based on historical performance. Skill required, numerical analysis.	The input data consists of opinions and perceptions regarding future trends. Skill required: synthesis.

ⓑ BEKAERT

Rewiring a
Global Strategy

Rafaël Decaluwé
Chief Executive Officer

When you got up this morning, took a shirt off a wire hanger, drove your car on steel radials across a suspension bridge, came home, rode your bike, and popped a champagne cork to celebrate your anniversary, you probably used Bekaert products at every turn. This Belgian manufacturer is a world leader in the steel wire and steelcord business.

With headquarters in Kortrijk, Belgium, the company has 60 plants in 20 countries, employing nearly 18,000 people worldwide. In 1995, Bekaert turned out about 1.8 million tons of wire which sold for just under three billion dollars. Its wire finds its way into a surprising array of products including most of the steel-belted radial tires made today, concrete reinforcing wire, steel rope for bridges, coat hangers, fencing, bicycle spokes, staples and, yes, even 5000 tons of wire annually for champagne cork cages.

In steel wire, the company has basically three areas of business. The industrial wire business has a high-volume, commodity orientation and competes primarily with steel companies. The specialty wire business makes custom special purpose wire products for specific customers. Another group produces wire fence—from cyclone fence to heavy welded security fence.

The steelcord division holds a significant share of the steel-belted radial tire market worldwide. The typical car tire contains one or two pounds of this reinforcing material, a truck or bus tire as much 20 to 45 pounds. In this part of the business, its main competitors are also its customers—the major tire companies who also make steelcord.

"We are truly a global business," says CEO Rafaël Decaluwé (pronounced de-cal'-oo-way). "It's a diverse business with various types of products that all come out of one raw material—wire that we source from the steel companies. We have businesses that are global, regional, or local and therefore have very different forms and shapes of management. And I should add that because we have had a very long association with Japanese companies, we have a very strong TQM culture."

He became CEO in October 1994, having been one of Bekaert's division managers. His first task was to define his role as CEO, and formulate an approach to the job.

"After interviewing and debating with a number of people, not the least of which were the people on the board—who look at my rating sheet and my pay every year—I came to the conclusion that my primary task is shaping the vision of the company, communicating it, and getting it implemented. Now those are three things that are easily said, but not so easily done," he explains.

His perception at the time was that the company was strong operationally, yet needed a vision of the future to drive its performance in the future. He looked at the three basic approaches: existing "excellence" models, such as Deming, Baldrige, and others; "solution-driven" consultants; and "methodology-driven" consultants. The first, he felt, are good tools for implementation, but don't address vision. The second, he believed, would run the risk of not understanding the business, jumping to conclusions and, most importantly, achieving low credibility with management. He settled on the third—in the form of the DPI *strategic thinking process.* "What I wanted is a methodology that involved the thinking of our own people. I would hope that the people who were working in this business for 20 and more years would have a better view and understanding of what this business is capable of doing and where it should go than an outside consultant, who comes in for three to six months, reviews and interviews in your organization, and then comes up with a so-called magic solution of what you should do for the next *X* number of years."

As the CEO looking at the organization, Decaluwé could see that "strategic thinking" was not a priority and had to sell the concept. "We made long-term plans that were mostly done by each business. They were number exercises without much *qualitative* thinking and analysis in my view."

"I felt that the numbers usually do not turn out anyway because they're fairly straightforward extrapolations based on existing assumptions. They really don't give you a lay of the land of where you are with your business versus competition versus the environment outside.

"What I was trying to get out of this process was really shortening the chain of the thinking within the group. Then from a group perspective and within our different businesses, we would start from a fundamental analysis of the environment. We were looking to get a feel for strengths and weaknesses, and to have a much clearer, qualitative picture of the road ahead."

He chose to use *strategic thinking* largely because of prior positive experiences with the process.

"It goes back a little bit in history. I had used the DPI process when I was division general manager, to help the business climb out of the clouds. If I could compare it to an aircraft, it enabled us to make sure we had a clear sense of direction and continued momentum and drive in that direction, as we were entering blue sky," he states. "I was most happy with that process in my divisional responsibilities. I then took over as CEO of the group and felt that was one of the things we were lacking.

"To me, the first challenge was overcoming the skepticism of my own management that there was a need to go through a conceptual strategic exercise. These are mainly engineers and they deal with numbers. To do a qualitative assessment, to many of them, seemed unnecessary.

"So the first challenge was to convince the management team of the need for a strategic assessment.

"There was some question as to 'Why do we need to do this? Aren't we doing well anyway? What's the point of starting this sort of exercise?' So there I had to argue, preach, and reason with them to get them to believe that a strategic thinking exercise is important. After a while I was successful in convincing them to go through the process, when they came to understand that it does not present them with a solution, but *that they are part* of the solution. So once we got into the process, the skepticism went away because they felt that they all had a part to contribute in it. And at the same time, once we had gone through the three-day session, what I call 'taking everybody through the funnel of the process,' not everything was smoothed over. But we had a chance to come back and refine what was said, and deepened the consensus and the commitment along with it."

Selecting a Driving Force

The nature of Bekaert's diverse businesses presented a challenge in the selection of a driving force. Some of its units sell industrial products serving again as "raw materials," such as tire-reinforcing cord, while others, such as the fence group, sell a finished product to consumers. Resolving the differences took some time.

"There were several driving forces tried out," he remembers, "there were differences of opinion around the table. But then in the first three-day session, in subteams we each developed a possible driving force and then analyzed whether each was sensible as we looked at the various outcomes of pursuing that driving force. It led to a conclusion that two out of the three we were looking at were not the right answer. We were looking at capacity-driven, technology-driven, and product-driven.

"By process of elimination, clearly product could not be it because we have a wide range of products. And we cannot picture ourselves as being like the example Mike uses of cars. He says a product-driven company makes cars and the next product will be another car, and another car. That's certainly not the case for us. It's wire, but the applications are so diverse that you can hardly say that they're the same product in the end."

The group finally settled on technology as its uniting driving force.

"We call it cold metal transformation and surface treatment, in the broad sense of the word," Decaluwé explains. "And for this technology we have over 10,000 applications."

The driving force then gives rise to areas of excellence and a set of critical issues. "Critical issues were the most important results. One of them that was important to us was deepening and leveraging our technology across the businesses much better than we had done in the past. Another was focusing our international expansion much more in terms of geographic areas. And at the same time we came to understand that we needed to develop certain new competencies that we did not have up till now, and would be important for success in the future. So, together with a never-ending cost reduction focus, at least it gave us some clear, critical issues that have been driving quite a bit of the thinking and the actions that we have developed since that time."

Specifically, the management of the group overall identified five basic critical issues that would be essential to supporting the bridge between the present and future "pictures" of the company. They were: developing greater depth in wire drawing technology; leveraging that technology development; building its capabilities in marketing, application development, and innovation (the areas of excellence associated with a technology-driven company); and developing a greater presence in Far East markets. And at the center of all of those, enhancing the skills of the people and structure of the organization would become a priority.

In the Steelcord Division, three critical issues were identified: TQM with customers, cost reduction, and internal functioning. Each of these were broken down into several component parts—nine goals—as action items, and a triangle "logo" created as a communication vehicle. This and other logos were created to symbolize the vision and goals and are used extensively as a means to keep attention focused on these initiatives.

"Twenty people signed off on that. It's a tremendous bond between them," says Decaluwé. "And we would never change that unless those same people were back around the table. Today, I can walk into any plant in the Steelcord Division, point to that triangle logo and ask any of the people working on the quality teams how what they're working on is related to the company's goals, and they will know."

From Concept to Implementation, Step-by-Step

Rafaël Decaluwé and his team have been careful to ensure that the strategy not only is articulated, but also continuously carried out and *refined*.

"Let's look at each of the steps. First, shaping the vision. I think of this as having three important pieces," says Decaluwé. "First of all, you have to understand where you are—what are we and where are we today? And you need also to draw a picture of the future. And that is your vision of what and where you want to be X number of years from now—you can say two years or five years or 10. And then I think the most critical part to it is, when you've painted the picture of where you want to be—how do we bridge the gap? We have actually created a bridge logo to symbolize that. And on top of formulating the steps of how we will get there, you also need a *clear sense of direction* of how you're going to move from where you are to where you're going.

"The next step—communicating the vision—has a lot to do with making sure that there is a clear sense of direction. You will, as a CEO, have to communicate it again and again—convincing, preaching, telling, arguing. That has been the most important challenge to me. You have to keep doing it—fifty, a hundred times—and you have to do it each time with enthusiasm even though it may be becoming repetitive to you.

"The next step involves what I call deployment at lower levels—getting all the noses pointing in the same direction. Now deployment to me has to do with systematic translation of the general goals into concrete terms understandable to the level of the organization that you're addressing.

"If you go to one of your machine operators and you say, 'Your responsibility is processibility at the customer's plant,' if he's polite he'll say, 'Well what does that mean to me?' And if he's that polite to ask, then I think you ought to at least do one thing—bring the message to him in understandable terms. What I would say to him is, 'To you it's the diameter consistency and the coating consistency of that wire. And that's how you can measure your contribution to the goal.' It's very important that you don't leave them with lofty sorts of objectives that they cannot identify with or can do nothing about."

Bekaert's long-standing commitment to TQM is a very significant part of the execution of goals such as cost reduction and performance for customers.

"We have the example of wire breaks—this is part of the cost reduction goal. Wire breaks in our process are very expensive because the weld in the product will give you more trouble in the next step, and of course your machine uptime drops."

Just as the management team uses a rational process to formulate the strategy, teams at various levels use critical thinking tools, such as systematic problem solving, which are appropriate to their needs. They are then able to complete the tasks which make up the critical issues—in this case reducing costs by identifying and eliminating specific causes of problems such as wire breaks.

"Putting a chart next to their machine where they can put another dot showing what they had accomplished is extremely powerful in terms of getting their commitment and ownership," Decaluwé believes.

"The progress that we've made on the critical issues is the result of assigning each one to a task force that will design answers to solve it, and a number of steps have already been taken. They're by no means finished, but at least I know that I'm now driving the business and progressing the business starting from those critical issues. And I can, at fairly regular intervals, gauge to what extent we are answering and continuously enhancing our response to those critical issues.

"It's taken hold. I wish we would be further down in terms of the steps of implementing the critical issues, but a number of them have developed well. We have understood very clearly, for instance, why there were barriers built into leveraging technology across the businesses, and we have taken the necessary steps in order to get there much more rapidly than we would have otherwise done."

Keeping the Flame Alive

Once the critical issues begin to take hold, the CEO's role shifts to keeping the organization's attention and enthusiasm trained on those goals. And he must continue to monitor and test and reevaluate. Bekaert's team has developed specific steps to ensure that this continues to happen.

"First of all, to ensure that the strategy is still correct, we've already done an update. So every other year you should go to a short form reassessment, and see if any of the key variables that are in the process have changed. We repeat the basic profile and continue to update through communication where we stand on the development and the implementation of the critical issues. I do that twice per year based on my communication with all the management employees in the group," Decaluwé explains.

This component is necessary for setting milestones and following up on the progress on critical issues. To "keep the flame burning," Bekaert uses a variety of other tools. Surveys of workers are used to gauge the level to which *they* think progress is being made. "TQM visits" to business units or plants by management keep the focus of problem solving on key processes and therefore, key goals. "You start with mutual listening," he says. "You give the opportunity for feedback and they get a clearer sense of direction and progress.

"I was a firm believer after my previous experiences that a team comes up with better answers than an individual, and therefore, if you can involve a team in that sort of thinking about strategy, your commitment from the group, having contributed to it, will be far larger and will make the implementation easier. I would certainly stand by that. So it starts from a philosophy of a CEO. In my own view you must feel that, yes, you are CEO, but you also realize that as one individual, given the size of the company, you're in no way physically capable of managing and directing strategy and all the operational issues yourself. So I recognize my own limitation from a physical and intellectual point of view as my starting point on building an organization with a team. In that context, I have found the *strategic thinking* approach extremely helpful.

"If you ask me now what were the advantages of the *strategic thinking process,* I was really looking for something that would force our people to think and come up with some answers," says Decaluwé. "It did bring us much closer and the team definitely functioned much better. It gave us consensus....It led us to focus on a few critical issues. We started out with a long list and got it down to five. It led the whole group to take on ownership. And on top of that, it is applicable to any level. Not only can you do it for the group, you can do it for business units.

"I call it a 'do-it-yourself kit' for managers in terms of coming to think about where you are with your business and taking hold of it.

"The last two and a half years have not been easy, but it has been a tremendously rewarding experience."

4
Crafting the Future Profile of the Organization

Strategic thinking, as we have defined it, is the thought process used by a CEO and the management team to "draw" a picture of what they want their organization to "look like" at some point in the future. This profile (Figure 4-1) is then intended to serve the company's employees

Figure 4-1. The vision as a strategic profile.

as a filter or test bed to help them make consistent and intelligent decisions on behalf of the organization over time.

The next question that surfaces, then, is: What does a CEO paint in the profile to help the employees make the right decisions? In other words, what is the *content* of a strategic profile? Still another way to pose the question is: What is the reflection (Figure 4-2), in physical terms, of an organization's strategic profile?

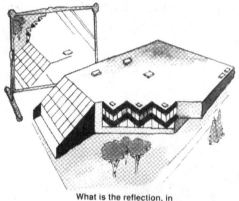

What is the reflection, in physical terms, of an organization's strategic profile?

Figure 4-2. The profile of a company has physical or tangible elements.

If someone asked me to invest a million dollars in his or her company on the basis that it would be a "good bet," I would certainly ask myself:

- Where is this company going?
- What will it "look like" down the road?

The answers would help me to determine, in advance, if it really would be a good bet!

Therefore, I would start looking for physical indicators of that company's direction and its eventual look. The elements that would serve as physical indicators of the company's strategy, direction, and eventual look include:

People/Skills	Suppliers
Buildings/Facilities	Geographic Markets
Plants/Factories	Technologies/Expertise
Products/Services	Dealers/Distributors
Market Segments	Processes/Capabilities
Customers/Users	Balance Sheets
Competitors	Advertising/Promotion

In fact, there are numerous things I could look for at this company, or at any other company—each of which would serve as an indicator of the direction and eventual look of that company. However, from this long list, four items are the true reflection of a company's strategy, direction, and eventual look (Figure 4-3).

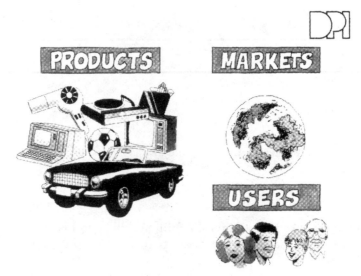

Figure 4-3. The principal areas that reflect a company's vision and profile.

1. The nature of its products
2. The nature of its customers
3. The nature of its market segments
4. The nature of its geographic markets

Everything else that goes on in an organization is either an input to these or an output from these four items. Capital, people, skills, facilities, and technology are all inputs. Profit, earnings, and dividends are all outputs.

Thus, the most important questions management must ask, and answer, if they want to shape the look of their company over time are:

- Which products do we offer? But more important, which products do we *not* offer?

- To which customer groups do we offer these products? But more important, to which customer groups do we *not* offer these products?

- Which market segments do we seek? But more important, which market segments do we *not* seek?

- Which geographic areas do we pursue? But more important, which geographic areas do we *not* pursue?

To us, it is more important for management to understand what the strategy *does not* lend itself to. Why is this so?

The management of a company conducts two activities that will contribute to altering the look of that company over time. First, every year through the budgeting process, management allocates resources. Unless they have agreed to a profile such as the one illustrated in Figure 4-4 (p. 62), it will be very difficult for them to allocate resources logically and strategically. Instead, the organization usually ends up in a tug-of-war over resources. This happens because each business unit manager promises more results if given more resources. If management takes away resources, however, each manager will then request a reduction of the results he or she will be asked to produce. Plans will then be compared, and usually the most loquacious manager wins. Our view is that plans should *not* be compared to other *plans*, but rather to the *vision* or *profile* of the future organization management is trying to build. Actions and programs contributing to this vision obtain resources, and actions or programs not contributing to this vision do not. Thus the strategic profile becomes a *tool to allocate resources strategically.*

The second management activity that will alter the look of the company over time is deciding which opportunities to pursue and which ones not to pursue. There are always opportunities facing any organization, but as we all know, some opportunities are much better than others. Therefore, management must have a tool, or filter, to discriminate between opportunities. Again, the strategic profile fills this void. Opportunities that have characteristics designated to receive more emphasis in the future will be pursued, whereas those items designated as needing less emphasis will not be pursued.

Figure 4-4. To shape a strategic profile, management must ask the right questions.

The result of a sound strategic thinking process must, in our view, produce a very clear profile not only of the kinds of products, customers, market segments, and geographic areas that the strategy of the business *lends* itself to and that *will* thus receive emphasis, but also and even more important, the kinds of products, customers, market segments, and geographic areas that the strategy of the business *does not lend* itself to and, thus, *will not* receive emphasis in the future.

How does management go about determining where the line of demarcation is so that when an event occurs they can quickly judge whether or not it fits their strategy and vision? What is it that drives the strategy of a business and, thus, the decisions of management, for determining what to emphasize or deemphasize?

The Strategic Heartbeat of the Business: The Driving Force

What is it that determines the nature of the products, customers, market segments, and geographic areas that a company pursues and those that it does not? How does management decide which of these it seeks to pursue and not pursue? The answer to these vital questions is the most important element of thinking strategically. It is a concept we call *driving force* (Figure 4-5).

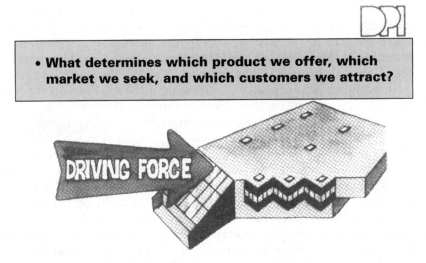

* **What determines which product we offer, which market we seek, and which customers we attract?**

Figure 4-5. Driving force gives a company its momentum.

In order to explain this concept, one must look at an organization as a body in motion. Every organization has momentum, or motion. Every organization is going forward in *some* direction.

Our contention is that there is something pushing, propelling, or *driving* it in that direction. The concept of driving force or *strategic drive* is that one element or component of a business drives the organization toward certain products, markets, and customers, thus determining that organization's look or profile. The concept of driving force is synonymous with a similar idea from *Shepherd's Laws of Economics:*

Behind each corporation must be a singular force, or motive, that
sets it apart from any other corporate structure and gives it its particular identity.

It is the identification of what drives and gives an organization its
momentum in a certain direction that is the key element of strategic
thinking. It becomes imperative, therefore, for the top executives of a
company to have a clear understanding of the concept of driving force
if they wish to better manage or even change the direction of their
organization.

One test of a company's strategy comes when management is assessing future opportunities. While working with the CEOs of many corporations, we observed that new opportunities were always put
through a hierarchy of filters. The final filter always seemed to be the
search for a "fit" between the opportunity and one key component of
the business. Some CEOs looked for a fit between the products the
opportunity brought and the organization's current products—
Chrysler's acquisition of American Motors is a good example. Others
looked for a fit in the similarity of its customer base or the markets
served. Still others looked for a fit of technology. Some companies
looked for a fit to their selling method. If a close fit was found, then
the opportunity was considered. However, if the relationship was not
seen as a close enough fit, then the opportunity was abandoned.

The search for an area of strategic fit varied from one company to
another. But it was always the same one in each company. In other
words, *one* element of the organization was driving its business strategy. The more successful the company, the more the CEO recognized
that the organization's strategy was anchored around a key component
of its business. It is this *strategic area* that is the heart of a company's
business and what gives it an edge in the marketplace.

What are some of the key components of a company that drive the
strategy of the business and thus the decisions of management as to
what they choose to emphasize or deemphasize?

Every organization, we found, is composed of 10 important strategic
areas:

1. Product/service concept
2. User/customer class
3. Market type/category
4. Production capacity/capability
5. Technology/know-how
6. Sales/marketing method

7. Distribution method

8. Natural resources

9. Size/growth

10. Return/profit

Although all 10 of these components are present in most organizations, only one of these is *strategically* most important to a company and is the engine that propels, or drives, the company forward to success. Unfortunately, in many companies, the key area that gives a company its strategic edge is not always understood by management itself. Once a company's management understands which driving force is at the root of the company's strategy, decisions about the types of products, markets, and users that will bring competitive advantage are made more successfully.

Depending on which of these 10 strategic areas is most important to a given organization, the decisions it makes about future products, users, and markets will vary greatly. Because each of these strategies can lead the organization in a different direction and greatly alter its future profile, management must choose which *one* it will pursue in order to gain competitive advantage (Figure 4-6). To illustrate the effect of each strategy, we offer the following definitions.

The Concept of Driving Force and/or Strategic Drive

Product-Driven Strategy

A product-driven company is one that has tied its business to a *singular* product. As a result, this company's future products will greatly resemble its current and past products in look and function. Future products will be modifications, adaptations, or extensions of current products: that is, derivatives of existing products. In these companies, there is a "genetic" linear relationship among past, present, and future products.

The automobile industry is a good example. The look and function of an automobile has not really changed for 100 years and probably will not change for the next 100. It moves people forward and backward; thus General Motors', Daimler-Benz's, and Volvo's business concepts represent product-driven strategies. Boeing also follows this type of strategy. Its business is built around the concept of an airplane, and the next product from that company will probably be another "flying machine." IBM is yet another company that is product-driven—the

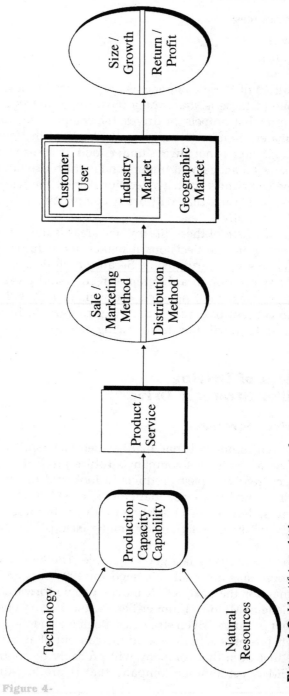

Figure 4-6. Identifying which component of an organization is its driving force is a key element of strategic thinking.

Figure 4-

product being computers and various derivatives, including mainframes, minis, micros, PCs, and laptops.

User/Customer Class–Driven Strategy

A user/customer class–driven company is one that has deliberately anchored its entire business around a describable and specific category of end users or customers. The company then tries to satisfy a range of related needs that stem from that class of end user. And it responds with a wide variety of unrelated products that are always aimed at the same group of end users/customers.

Playboy, for instance, is a good example of a company pursuing a user class–driven strategy. The phase "entertainment for men" on its magazine cover spells it out quite clearly. As such, Playboy is into magazines, hotels, casinos, cable television, video cassettes, calendars, and so on. These are all genetically unrelated products that are managed in very different ways. What they have in common is that they are geared to the young, single, affluent male.

Johnson & Johnson, whose strategy of making products for "doctors, nurses, patients, and mothers," is another such company. Its entire business strategy is driven by the health-related needs of these four categories of people. All of J&J's products—from Band-Aids to sutures to shampoo to talcum powder—are all genetically unrelated, but they are all aimed at these four classes of individuals. J&J could easily tweak its Band-Aid technology to make electrical tape, for example, but it would never do that since the buyers of electrical tape are electricians—not a class of users that J&J wants to serve.

Market Type/Category–Driven Strategy

A market type/category–driven company is similar to the user/customer class–driven company except that, instead of having its business limited to a set of end users, the market type–driven company has anchored its future to a describable market category.

An example is American Hospital Supply. The company's name identifies the *market* to which its business is anchored—the hospital. The strategy of the company is to respond to a variety of needs coming from that market. As a result, the product scope of such a company ranges from bedpans to sutures to gauze pads to electronic imaging systems and anything else a hospital might need.

Disney's concept of "wholesome entertainment for families" is another example of a market/category–driven strategy.

Production Capacity/Capability–Driven Strategy

The company that is production capacity–driven usually has a substantial investment in its production facility, and the strategy is to "keep it running" or "keep it full." Therefore, such a company will pursue any product, customer, or market that can optimize whatever the production facility can handle. Paper mills, hotels, and airlines are good examples of *capacity*-driven organizations. Keeping the facility at full capacity is the key to profits. Print shops are another class of business pursuing this strategy. A printer will tend to accept any job that the presses can handle, and optimizing the use of those presses leads to profit.

A production *capability*-driven company, on the other hand, is one that has built special capabilities into its production process that allows it to make products with features that are difficult for its competitors to duplicate. It then looks for opportunities where these capabilities can be exploited. Job shops, converters, and specialty printers are examples.

Technology/Know-How–Driven Strategy

Technology/know-how–driven companies are companies that have some distinctive technology at the root of their business. They have the ability to enhance or acquire new complimentary technologies or know-how for which there is no immediate product available. These companies will then seek out applications in the marketplace for the use of this new technology and then transform it into products.

Over time such a company gets involved in a broad array of products, all of which stem from the technology, and serve a broad array of customers and market segments.

This organization uses technology to gain competitive advantage. It fosters the ability to develop or acquire hard technology (e.g., chemistry) or soft technology (e.g., know-how), and then looks for applications for that technology. When an application is found, the organization develops products and infuses into these products a portion of its technology, which brings differentiation to the product. While exploiting this edge in a particular market segment, the company also looks for other applications in other segments. Technology-driven companies often are "solutions looking for problems" and usually create brand-new markets for their products. 3M, Sony, DuPont, and Polaroid are examples of technology-driven companies. DuPont's invention of nylon led it to market segments as diverse as nylon stockings, nylon carpets, nylon shoes, nylon thread, nylon sweaters, nylon fishing line, nylon tires, and nylon-laminated packaging materials. The only link between all these diverse businesses is that they all stem from one technology—nylon.

Sales/Marketing Method–Driven Strategy

A sales/marketing method–driven company has a *unique* way of getting an order from its customer. All products or services offered *must* make use of this selling technique. The company does not entertain products that cannot be sold through its sales method, nor will it solicit customers that cannot be reached through this selling or marketing method. Door-to-door direct-selling companies such as Avon, Mary Kay, Amway, and Tupperware are good examples. Other examples are catalog sales companies and the QVC Home Shopping Network. Whatever QVC can demonstrate on a TV screen, it will entertain as part of its strategy.

The direction of these companies and the products and markets they pursue are determined by the selling method. Amway or Tupperware would never operate in an area where door-to-door selling is prohibited. Their decisions regarding future products are also determined by their selling method. Whatever their salespeople can place in their carrying bags will determine the nature of the product these companies promote.

Avon, the preeminent example of the classic sales method–driven company temporarily lost sight of its driving force back in the early 1970s. With its army of door-to-door salesladies, Avon had become a dominant force in the cosmetic industry. However, conditions changed and the company found that a large number of its customers were no longer at home but in the workplace. Instead of adjusting its call site, the ex-CEO decided to go on an acquisition binge that included the purchase of companies such as Tiffany's and Medical Devices, which drained Avon of all its cash while its stock dropped from $140 to $18.

In 1989, a new CEO, James Preston, was appointed, and he very quickly decided to revert Avon back to its roots and driving force. "We're a direct-selling machine," he said. He then "undiversified" and sold off all the acquisitions to concentrate on what Avon does best. Today, Avon's two million salesperson army makes 50 percent of its calls in the workplace, and the company has regained its luster.

Distribution Method–Driven Strategy

Companies that have a *unique* way of getting their product or service from their place to their customer's place are pursuing a distribution method–driven strategy. Telephone operating companies, with their network of wires from their switches to the outlets in the walls of your home or office, are an example. A telephone company will only entertain products or services that use or optimize its unique distribution system. Food wholesalers are another example. Department stores such as Sears, Wal-Mart, Kmart, and J.C. Penney are a third.

Natural Resource–Driven Strategy

When access to or pursuit of natural resources is the key to a company's survival, then that company is natural resource–driven. Oil and mining companies are classic examples: Exxon, Shell, Newmont Gold, Anglo-American.

Size/Growth-Driven Strategy

Companies that are interested in growth for growth's sake or for economies of scale are usually pursuing a strategy of size/growth. All decisions are made to increase size or growth. LTV and Gulf & Western in the 1960s and 1970s were examples of companies following this strategy. Peter Grace's philosophy of size and diversification, often at the expense of earnings, made W.R. Grace & Company another example.

Return/Profit-Driven Strategy

Whenever a company's only criterion for entering a marketplace or offering a product is profit, then that company is return/profit-driven. Conglomerates are usually good examples. They are often organized along the lines of a corporate control body with fully autonomous subsidiaries. There are usually few links between these subsidiaries except a certain level of profit. Subsidiaries are bought or sold on this criterion alone. ITT, under Harold Geneen, had such a strategy. His dictum of *an increase in quarterly earnings, regardless what,* and the subsequent acquisition of some 275 unrelated businesses, showed strategic disregard for all other criteria. Other examples are General Electric, Allied Signal as are Hanson Trust and GEC in the United Kingdom.

The Strategic Heartbeat of the Enterprise Determines What Kind of Company You Become

One of 3M's largest businesses is its tape division. When 3M first developed masking tape and all its other derivatives, it discovered an enormous market, to the degree that to this day this division is still considered to be its "crown jewel." My friends at 3M told me that soon after the discovery of this product, there was a heated debate among 3M executives as to whether 3M should stay focused on this single product or whether it should diversify into other arenas. One group claimed that 3M was a "masking tape" company, a product concept–driven strategy, and should not deviate from this product and market. Another group claimed that 3M was a polymer chemistry–based company, a technology-based strategy, and should explore other applications for that know-how. Luckily for 3M, the latter group won and 3M went on to find numerous other successful applications for its polymer chemistry expertise in the form of other products such as audiotape, videotape, diskettes, all the way to Post-it notes. Had the product concept–driven strategy group won, 3M would be a substantially different, and smaller, company today.

Another example is B. F. Goodrich. Once a dominant player in the tire business, the company viewed itself as a tire company—a product concept–driven strategy. Because of its inability to compete in this business in the 1970s, the company sold off its tire business and redefined itself. Fortunately, the CEO, John Eng, decided that Goodrich was not a product-driven business but rather a technology-driven one based, again, on its knowledge of chemistry. The company had a long history of chemical innovation going back to the 1920s when it first developed PVC, one of the world's most-used plastics. Eng decided to bring the company back to its roots, and today Goodrich is into a broad array of chemical applications from cosmetics to pharmaceuticals and is a much healthier company.

Strategic Questions

Some key *strategic* questions for the CEO and each member of the management team at this point are:

- What is your current driving force?
- What should your future driving force be?

- What impact will your driving force have on the future look of your products, markets, and customers?

The answers we have received from the management teams of client organizations have been varied and frequently surprising, even to the executives themselves. Our view is that until there is unanimity among the management as to which component of the business is the driving force of its strategy, management will have great difficulty making consistent and intelligent decisions on the proper allocation of resources and on the choice of future products, customers, and markets that will shape the "look" or profile of the organization over time.

GATX

Trains, Planes, and Strategy

James Glasser
Chairman of the Board, President & CEO

Traditional wisdom says, if it ain't broke don't fix it. But in today's business environment of intensifying competition and accelerating change, even highly successful companies are surveying their strategic landscapes, looking for ways to build greater competitive advantage for the future.

Such was the case when James Glasser, CEO of GATX, decided to examine the company's strategy using DPI's *strategic thinking process.*

GATX was founded as General American Transportation Company, with its business concentrated in railroad tank cars. Over time, the company grew and diversified, developing bulk storage, manufacturing, and a broad range of capital equipment leasing businesses, including rail cars, ships, and aircraft. A holding company was eventually formed to manage these diversified businesses. Today, GATX is a prosperous $3.6 billion company.

"The company was in excellent condition," says Glasser. "We had gone through a restructuring in the early eighties. At that time we had both manufacturing operations and service-based subsidiaries that provided assets and financing to our customers. The manufacturing and asset/service businesses were two very different and incompatible cultures, and we decided at that time to exit all manufacturing businesses. So when we engaged this *strategic thinking process,* we had already restructured. We were enjoying record earnings, and our individual businesses had leadership positions in their various niches."

Mr. Glasser describes GATX as a "service-based asset corporation." The company provides equipment and financial services both nationally and internationally, primarily for the transportation and distribution of its customers' products.

GATX, for example, owns the largest tank car leasing company in the United States, the world's largest bulk liquid storage capacity, and the largest capacity of any self-unloader vessel float on the Great Lakes. And its leasing expertise extends into a variety of assets, with a heavy concentration in railroad and aircraft equipment. A recent acquisition has now taken them into distribution logistics, which includes warehouses, trucking, and value-added services.

With the company doing so well, why would the CEO want to look at refocusing its strategy?

"Well, we were not trying to 'fix' the company. The fixing had been done," Glasser recalls. "Our concern at the time was that we saw increasing competition coming on in the future, and we wanted to be sure we were positioned to capitalize on our strengths and core capabilities. We wanted to ensure that we could leverage our existing strengths to achieve sustainable growth in cash flow, earnings, market share and customer service."

The strategy team included the CEO, the heads of the five subsidiaries and several corporate staff people.

"We are a holding company with five divisions," Glasser explains. "We thought we knew our strengths overall, but we went through this process with all of these people present, arguing back and forth about what our strengths and weaknesses were, and achieved a much better definition.

"The wonderful thing about this process is that a consultant didn't come in and tell us what our strengths and weaknesses are, what we ought to capitalize on, what our driving force or strategy should be. Mike Robert, the facilitator of the process, didn't tell us anything. He just kept directing our thinking, asking questions. And the great thing was, he would never give up. Even when we were getting tired or ducking an issue that was unresolved, he wouldn't let us duck. He just kept on directing us to get to a conclusion using this rational process.

"Return on assets, it turns out, is our driving force, the primary mover in all our decision making" says Glasser. "We always talked about ourselves as an asset-based service company, and, as a result of the *strategic thinking process,* we've changed that.

"Now we see GATX as a service-based asset company. Although we have only flipped two words around, it's a very important distinction. We are primarily holders, owners, and managers of long-term, long-lived assets. A significant aspect of our business is to increase the return on those assets by increasing the services we provide with them.

"When we look at it that way, it ties together all of our operations."

To arrive at a clear business concept, and a coherent strategy that management can agree on, is an important hurdle to clear in any company. It becomes even more critical in a "holding company" situation when the operating units ordinarily have only sporadic contact with each other. In this kind of environment, managements in the operating units naturally concentrate on running their specific businesses. The bigger picture of the entire corporation, and its collective strength, can be obscured. Possibilities to jointly exploit expertise and create new business opportunities can be lost simply because commonalities go unrecognized. In the process of hammering out their new strategy, however, GATX subsidiary presidents were able to open up new lines of communication and gain fresh understanding of each other's businesses as well as the overall goals of the organization.

To assure that the emerging strategy is effectively implemented, a list of critical issues was developed as part of the *strategic thinking process*. In creating this list, a variety of possibilities arose, not just to recognize joint opportunities, but to act on them.

GATX established critical issues task forces—intersubsidiary/cross functional task forces—chaired by a corporate vice president or a president of one of the subsidiaries.

Each task force is charged with resolving a specific problem or implementing an initiative that is critical to making the strategy successful. At quarterly review meetings with each subsidiary, the activities of the task force are discussed, reviewed, measured, and revised where necessary.

"We talk about what we're doing to resolve such issues as enhancing information technology or building on our environmental capabilities. People in the company knew about these issues before, but they didn't know how they affected the other subsidiaries. Now as a result of these task forces, each of our subsidiaries has a much better feel for them and can work together to get them accomplished."

GATX has established task forces in several critical areas, including information technology, environmental capabilities, manpower planning and development, marketing, and others. Through the increased interaction and communication, new joint initiatives have emerged.

"We've tried joint marketing, for example, for a long time, and it never worked until we had this cross-marketing task force. We are starting to see subsidiaries making joint calls. We're learning how to approach a common customer in a more cohesive way and to introduce one GATX subsidiary to the customer of another subsidiary on a better, more organized basis. It's not being directed from the top down, but really from two or three levels into the organization—closer to the service we provide; closer to the customer. Throughout our organization it's getting enthusiastic support of the subsidiaries and their middle managers."

As most CEOs find as they watch the results of *strategic thinking* unfold, a new depth of understanding and communication between operating units and departments is an invaluable and long-lasting benefit.

James Glasser concludes that tangible results are being seen, and "the communication that has developed through this process has great value. Because of it, we're making progress on critical issues that we had tried for a long time to resolve. The DPI process is not only such a great communication device, but also it is a tool for integrating new thinking and processes in an established culture. Increasing the level and quality of communication is particularly tough to achieve when you're running a holding company.

"The most beneficial output has been the increased communication and cooperation among our subsidiaries toward improved customer service, employee involvement and satisfaction, and achieving sustainable growth in shareholder value." GATX's stock price has increased from $26 to $65.

5

Questions Often Asked about the Concept of Strategic Drive

In strategy sessions with the top management of many companies in North America, Asia, and Europe, several interesting questions have been asked when discussing the notion of what is driving their strategy. Here are some of those questions and our answers:

Are there not multiple driving forces present simultaneously in a company?

I call this the "Sybil" syndrome. Sybil was, as the movie of the same name depicted, a woman with multiple personalities who had great difficulty living with herself. The same is true in business. A company cannot be something one instant and something different the next. Each company, like an individual, has a unique personality based on one element of the business that dominates over the other elements of that business when nutcracking decisions are made about allocation of resources or choice of opportunities.

In a single-product, single-market, single-customer-base company, that single driving force is clear and permeates the entire company. It is in a multiple-product, multiple-customer, multiple-market-type company that we see the blurring of driving forces and accompanying business concepts (Figure 5-1).

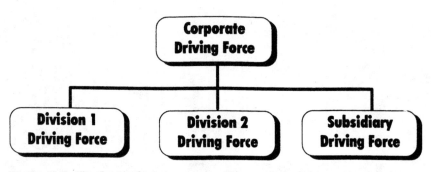

Figure 5-1. The driving force in a corporation.

In these types of companies one finds a hierarchy of driving forces and accompanying business concepts being practiced simultaneously. It becomes important for management to understand what this hierarchy is because some configurations can coexist well, while other configurations are inherently incompatible. Take, for instance, the case of a company whose corporate driving force might be that of a certain *technology,* while one of its divisions might wish to pursue a *user class*–driven strategy. These two strategies are inherently incompatible. The corporate body is saying that it wants all its divisions to pursue opportunities around applications of its unique technology regardless of customer segments, but the division is pursuing a strategy anchored to a restricted class of end users with products that do not necessarily stem from the corporation's key technology. No degree of management skill will ever resolve this inherent strategic incompatibility.

Another example is Johnson & Johnson. Although J&J has a number of divisions with driving forces differing from each other—such as the Band-Aid division, which is product-driven, the Tylenol division, which is product-driven, and the sutures division, which is technology-driven—none of these divisions would be allowed to offer products that did not cater to the needs of "doctors, nurses, patients, and mothers"—the user classes that *drive* the strategy of J&J.

It is important to note what the driving force is at the root of each organizational unit in order to:

1. Ensure that divisional strategies are compatible with the parent's.
2. Prevent any overlaps between the division's strategies.

> If not multiple, can there be two areas of the business working in tandem, driving the company forward?

I call this the *schizophrenic* strategy. One day you're this, next day you're that, and you zigzag your way forward.

Continental Airlines is a company that went through this adventure. In 1993, in an attempt to protect itself against Southwest, it separated itself into two airlines—regular Continental with full-service fares and Continental Lite with discount fares. In no time, this had all the customers confused. Some would fly from Los Angeles to San Francisco in the morning on a discount fare and come back in the evening on the "other" Continental at full fare. Red ink started flowing profusely and 12 months later the CEO was dismissed.

Our view is that there is only one component of the business that dominates its strategy and drives the company forward giving it a distinctive advantage against its competitors in the pursuit of certain products, customers, and markets. Until management clearly understands what that *one* component is, they will have difficulty making intelligent and consistent decisions as to the allocation of resources and the choice of opportunities.

Another company that suffered a massive bout of schizophrenia in the 1980s is Baxter Laboratories. Baxter has historically been a *technology-driven* company and, as such, invented a number of medical devices such as the first intravenous solution, the first artificial kidney, the first portable dialysis system, the first heart-lung bypass oxygenator, and so forth. Again, in an attempt at diversification in the 1980s, Baxter acquired American Hospital Supply, a wholesaler of a wide range of products to hospitals. American Hospital had a very different driving force. It is *market category–driven*, which causes that company to make very different choices in the types of products, customers, and markets that it pursues from that of Baxter.

As such, it requires different selling approaches, different manufacturing systems, different forms of R&D, different methods of warehousing and distribution, different forms of marketing, different types of people with different skills, and different information systems. Never the twain shall meet!

Finally, after 12 years of agony, the two entities decided to divorce and divided themselves into two independent companies. One will remain as Baxter and the other renamed itself Allegiance.

> Is not, then, profit the only strategic driving force for a company?

This is a legitimate question because one cannot survive in business without profit. However, unless the company is a financial conglomerate à la ITT, the driving force is usually not profit. The analogy I use to explain this conclusion is that of eating. In life, one must eat to live. That's a given. If one does not eat at least once or twice a day, one will die—guaranteed! The same is true in business. Every business must be profitable to survive—that is a given of business life, otherwise the company dies. But surely the purpose of life is not eating! There must be another purpose to life, although one must eat each day to live. The same is true in business. Surely there is a purpose to a company other than that of making a profit, although it must produce a profit in order to survive. Profit is the *result* of strategy, not its objective. Profit tells one how well or how badly the strategy is working, but usually there is another purpose behind the existence of each company. In other words, some other driving force is at the root of the company's existence.

If it is not profit, then should every company be customer-driven?

Every organization must be *customer-sensitive*. The rationale of this statement is that if your products do not fill certain user needs, the products will not succeed. Every organization, regardless of which driving force propels it, must make products that satisfy the needs of its customers. However, that alone does not make the company *user class–driven*. In other words, every corporation must be *user-sensitive*, but not all corporations are *user class–driven*.

Depending on which driving force it is pursuing, each organization is user-sensitive, but in a different manner. Here are some examples:

- *Product-driven.* This organization is user-sensitive in that its people are looking for new users of its current products, or else it is looking to satisfy new needs within its current user group with slightly modified products.

- *User class–driven.* This organization is user-sensitive in that its people are in a continuous dialogue, usually with a well-known or captive user, to try to identify the user's unique new needs that can be satisfied by totally new or different products.

- *Technology-driven.* This organization is user-sensitive in that its people looking for users that have applications for a technology which the organization has or is willing to acquire. Once applications are found, then products are designed and developed.

- *Production capability/capacity–driven.* This organization is user-sensitive in that its people are looking for users who offer products or services with components that can be substituted, replaced, or supplemented with their own so that they can optimize the capacity of their production facility.

- *Sales/marketing method–driven.* This organization is user-sensitive in that its people are looking for new products/services that can be sold to existing users through its current selling method or new users that can be reached through the same selling method.

- *Distribution method–driven.* This organization is user-sensitive in that its people are looking for new products/services that can be sold to existing users or new users who can be reached through its current distribution system.

> Is there not a natural evolution from one driving force to another over time for any company?

Another very good question. Again, however, the answer is no. Furthermore, if you feel that the driving force of the company is constantly changing, you have a clear indication that the company is drifting. In other words, there is *no* strategy. A good strategy stays in place over a long period of time. Constancy of purpose is the key to strategic success.

> Are there not some legitimate instances when one wants to deliberately change the strategic drive of the company?

The answer, obviously, is yes. One such instance is when the current strategy runs out of growth. Growth is another given in business because every company needs growth to perpetuate itself. Therefore, when the strategy runs out of growth, management should deliberately seek to change the driving force and, thus, the strategy and direction of the company.

One such example is Playboy Enterprises. Playboy's strategy of "entertainment for men," particularly young, single men, is not growing any more because the absolute number of men that fit Playboy's profile is diminishing. As a result, Playboy has been struggling and looking for another strategy for several years now, but has yet to find one as successful as the one it had for some 30 years.

A second legitimate instance when management should rethink the driving force of its strategy is when there is something so threatening on the horizon that such a threat might completely invalidate the existing strategy. A case in point is Exxon. In the mid-1970s, Exxon ventured into arenas outside its traditional business—namely, the purchase of Reliance Electric and several emerging office equipment companies. My view about these ventures is that Exxon, at that time, was deliberately looking to change its strategic direction. And with good reason. It saw its driving force—access to natural resources—threatened. One only needs to remember what many countries were doing with their oil reserves back then—nationalizing them! If I had been in the shoes of Exxon's CEO, I also would have come to the conclusion that if this trend continued around the world, there would be no Exxon down the road. Therefore, I would have embarked on a course to change the direction of Exxon away from its dependence on oil. However, finding a new strategy as successful as the one already in place might require a long time and several attempts.

Why do I postulate that such ventures have been conscious attempts to change the direction of Exxon even though the company lost $600 million on Reliance and over $200 million in the office equipment companies? The reason is simple. No one was fired! What usually happens to a division manager who loses $600 or $200 million? Right. But not at Exxon. And for this reason, this author contends that those were deliberate decisions made because Exxon management felt its strategic heartbeat was threatened and it was consciously looking to replace it. What happened then in the 1980s? The answer, again, is simple. The governments that had nationalized their reserves found out that reserves underground are not worth very much unless one knows how to bring them above ground. And who do you think does that best? Exxon. With the threat gone, Exxon in the mid-1980s rededicated itself to its first love—oil and gas—and sold off its nonstrategic ventures.

A third instance when the driving force of a company changes by accident and not by design is called "seduction." This occurs more often than not in companies because management gets *seduced* by opportunities!

Seduced by Opportunities

The best time to detect whether or not a CEO has a strategy is to observe the management team at work when trying to evaluate opportunities, especially those somewhat remote from the current business. On these occasions we noticed that, when faced with unfamiliar opportunities, management would put these through a hierarchy of different filters. The ultimate filter was always a "fit" between the products, customers, and markets that the opportunity brought and one key element, or driving force, of the business. This is a clear signal that management had a sound filter for their decision. In other instances, when there was no such filter in place, management would only look at the "numbers" and, if these looked reasonable, would jump aboard, only to find out later that the opportunity had something else at the root of its business, which was its driving force. Gradually the opportunity would start pulling the entire company off course.

We also found that seduction is at its highest when the current strategy is producing more cash than the business requires. Such has been the case with Daimler-Benz in recent years. After pursuing the strategy of making the "best engineered car" for over 100 years and making money every single year, Mercedes found itself in the mid-1980s sitting on a hoard of cash—$10 billion—which it did not need to run the car business. It was at this point that the finance person recommended the purchase of a number of companies in totally unrelated fields. Over the objections of the CEO (who later resigned), but with the approval of the major shareholder (Deutsche Bank), the company made a series of acquisitions from household appliances to airplanes. As we predicted in 1992, Daimler-Benz is currently struggling for the first time in its long history. Worse still, while the management of Daimler-Benz is preoccupied with these unfamiliar businesses, BMW is making significant inroads at its expense and has displaced Mercedes as the top selling car in Germany—its home market!

A more recent example is Seagram's. A few years ago, because of the death threat it saw to its liquor business, management changed the strategy of the company away from liquors into wine coolers, sodas, juices, and wines. More recently, the company extended its strategy again to enter the film business with its purchase of MGM Studios. Although the first change in strategy still limited the company to beverages, how does a movie making business fit under this umbrella? Is seduction at work here? If I were a Seagram's shareholder, I would be very nervous about this change in direction and I would be asking management some tough questions about the rationale behind their decision.

The lesson? Beware of seduction. Management skills are not always easily transferable from one business to another. In fact, each driving force brings with it the requirement to develop a different set of key skills, as will be seen in Chapter 7.

Seduction causes a change in strategy by *accident* and not by *design*. As a result, management is not conscious of the change in direction and keeps bumping into unanticipated, unpleasant "surprises" that it is unprepared to deal with properly and develops a "ready, fire, aim" syndrome.

> Do all the companies in the same industry have the same driving force?

The answer is no. Different companies in the same industry are often there because of a different "propeller" or driving force. The insurance industry is a good example.

Aetna and CIGNA are probably pursuing a product-driven strategy—insurance and different flavors of insurance such as life insurance, health insurance, car insurance, property insurance, etc.

The Association of Retired People (AARP) is also in the insurance business, but for a very different reason, or driving force. AARP's strategy is "services for individuals 55 and over"—a customer class–driven concept. As a result, insurance is but one service the organization offers its members. It is also in the travel business, the magazine business, the mutual fund business, the brokerage business, the lobbying business, the catalog business, etc.

USAA is in the insurance business for yet another reason. Its strategy of "services for the military market" is exactly that—a market type/category–driven strategy. As a result, insurance is also but one of many services this organization offers to that market.

Lloyd's of London is in the insurance business for a completely different reason. Lloyd's is probably technology or know-how–driven. Lloyd's, historically, has applied its *actuarial* know-how to just about every conceivable application it has been able to find, from merchant ships to Betty Grable's legs.

> Aren't all 10 areas equally important and can't they be fueled with resources proportionately?

In other words, isn't it as important to concentrate resources proportionately to customer service as it is to reduce our manufacturing costs? An astute question. However, a concept that could lead to detrimental results.

In the last 20 years, with the advent of European and Asian competitors and increased competition in the American market, a number of elements of business have become "givens" in order for any organi-

WHICH COMPONENT GIVES YOU STRATEGIC LEVERAGE
VIS-À-VIS YOUR COMPETITORS?

DRIVING FORCE/STRATEGIC HEARTBEAT

- Product/Service Concept
- User/Customer Class
- Market Type/Category
- Production Capacity/Capability
- Technology/Know-how
- Sales/Marketing Method
- Distribution Method
- Natural Resources
- Size/Growth
- Return/Profit

GIVENS

- Quality
- Customer Service
- Low Cost Manufacturing
- Growth
- Profit

Figure 5-2. One component of the strategic drive of a business goes beyond the expected conditions.

zation to survive over time (Figure 5-2). The following are a few examples:

- If your company is not involved in an aggressive program to continuously improve the *quality* of your *products*, I guarantee that your company will meet a certain death. Caterpillar learned this lesson just in time. Why is continuous quality improvement so critical to survival? Simply because, since the early 1980s, the Japanese manufacturers have made this a given to stay in any business in which they compete. In other words, the gap in the quality of your company's products and that of your competitors' will grow so large that your customers will bypass yours for theirs and you will disappear as a viable business entity.

- If your company is not involved in an aggressive program to continuously upgrade the level of your *customer service*, I guarantee that your company will meet with certain death. Why? For the same reason. The gap in the level of customer service between your competitors' and your company will be so wide that your customers will eventually disappear. It becomes extremely difficult to survive and prosper as a business entity without customers!

- If your company is not currently involved in an aggressive program to reduce its *manufacturing costs* by some 8 to 15 percent per year (dependent on the industry), I guarantee that you will die as a business entity. Why? Again for the same reason. All our clients around the world are engaged, and achieving, such results. Eventually the gap in the cost of your company's products and that of your competitors' will be so large in an era of diminishing prices that you will die as a business entity.

- If your company does not grow and produce a *reasonable profit* each and every year, I guarantee that your company will meet a certain death. Why? Once more for the same reason. No company can survive without growth in revenues and profits.

These, and other functional areas of any business, have become givens in today's competitive environment. They have become, in Las Vegas parlance, "chips" required to stay "in the game." Every business entity must have aggressive improvement programs in *each* operational area of its business, on any given day of the year, in order to stay in the game.

However, what you are trying to do in defining your *driving force/strategic drive* is to answer the following question:

Which component of the business goes beyond the givens and represents our area of *strategic advantage* and *strategic leverage* against our competitors?

Is it...

Our *product* concept?

The *class* of *customer* or *user* we serve?

The *market category* we target?

The *technology* at the root of our business?

Our *production capacity* or *process capability?*

Our *sales* or *marketing* method?

Our *distribution* method?

Our pursuit of a certain type of *natural resource?*

Our pursuit of *size* and *growth* for its own sake?

Our desire for *profit* or *return* for its own sake?

A Fundamental Concept of Business

The concept of driving force/strategic drive—to us at DPI—is one that is *fundamental* for any successful CEO to understand. It is the recognition and understanding, by all members of the management team, of that *one* predominant component of the business which will allow them to formulate a strategy that will give the organization a *distinctive* and *sustainable advantage* that can make competition almost irrelevant.

NorAm

Reenergizing after Deregulation

Milt Honea
Chief Executive Officer

When Milt Honea became CEO of Arkla several years ago, it was a company verging on bankruptcy. Deregulation was wreaking havoc in the natural gas business, and basic changes were urgently needed to turn the business around. In this interview Honea explains how he and his management team transformed the company into an aggressive, growing enterprise.

"We started as a gas company which had been completely integrated from the wellhead to the burner tip, but we're now out of the exploration and production side," says CEO Milt Honea. "When we got in trouble, we sold out of that area. So we are now integrated in gathering systems, interstate pipe lines and distribution. We are in six states, and cover more geography than any other gas distribution company. We're the third largest in terms of number of customers at 2.7 million."

Selling its exploration and production business was only the beginning. Through a series of other bold initiatives, the company, now called NorAm Energy, has successfully reversed its downward skid, and its financial results for the past couple of years have been exceptional. But of course, this didn't occur overnight. It took some fundamental changes, such as a sweeping culture-change program, and the creation of a completely new strategy with the help of DPI and its *strategic thinking process.*

"We were a company that had gotten in a lot of trouble and we were undertaking a turnaround," says Honea. "We had gotten close to bankruptcy. We were divesting assets, and sold about 700 million dollars worth of assets in the first year, primarily gas assets. We were trying to fix a balance sheet that had gotten damaged badly. Eventually, we decided we had sold everything that made any sense to sell. Our balance sheet was still weak, but we were alive. Then we said, 'Where do we go from here?'

"Our industry was in the midst of dramatic change from a regulated to a largely deregulated industry, similar to what had already happened in the airline and telecommunications industries. The question now was, 'How could we best position NorAm to grow, not just survive, in a rapidly changing and increasingly competitive market environment?'"

An important first step was a massive, companywide "culture change" program called *Operation Breakthrough.* Designed to find new life in the company's existing assets with its own people, this initiative involved a number of task teams.

"One of the first significant contributions was that one task team said we really didn't have a strategy. Particularly, we didn't have one that could be explained clearly to the employees so that everybody could rally behind it. We didn't have one that the investment community could buy into. They couldn't see our strategy. I had been working so hard at trying to patch things up, it was an awakening for me to realize that we really didn't have a strategy."

So, one of the task teams was charged with searching the U.S. for a strategy creation process or methodology. They came back with DPI's *strategic thinking process.*

"We needed to develop and, perhaps equally important," the CEO recalls, "to effectively communicate a clear vision of what we wanted NorAm to look like 10 years or so into the future, and what we as a company needed to do in terms of investment priorities and development of new competencies to achieve that vision.

"We liked the DPI approach, because it draws on the knowledge and experience of our people rather than attempting, as some consulting firms tend to do, to convince us of their view of the future and how they would position the company. By using our own people and our ideas, we have been able to achieve a total 'buy in' by those responsible for implementing the strategy—our own team."

A team of about 20 management people went through DPI's *strategic thinking process.* In the course of the sessions, it came time to select a *driving force*—a set of assets, skills, and competencies—that will drive the company's growth in the future. The group was leaning toward maintaining its distribution-driven strategy, in which the company's activities would all be based on the capabilities of its "pipes in the ground."

"We had said that wherever we have pipe in the ground—whether it is interstate pipelines or distribution systems that run through the cities of Minneapolis, Houston, Little Rock, and Shreveport—we probably ought to hang our hat on that. That is where we had been leaning, but we decided that was very defensive. If the world deregulates and unbundles to the point where you at your home can choose your gas supplier, your electric supplier, your telephone supplier and lots of other choices, for us to say we are going to hang on for dear life to those customers that are on our piece of pipe and that is *all* we are going to do, would be a very defensive and very negative strategy. So, the big enlightenment and the thing that opened us up to become a growth company was the decision, 'No, we won't do that.' The world *is* unbundling. We are not constrained to just sell gas to people that are at the end of our pipe. We can sell other products and we can sell them to off-system customers. Making that decision was a key turning point. We said, 'We are going to change this thing.' We decided to change our driving force to what DPI calls the *customer class-driven strategy.*"

In a radical shift, the company's future was transformed from simply a gas distribution company to one that is leveraging all of its skills and strengths to take advantage of a drastically changed future landscape.

"We have moved aggressively to implement our new retail marketing strategy and have reorganized to include our unregulated retail marketing activities in one business unit, rather than being spread out as relatively minor parts of three business units," Honea states. "We have also formed an international group, and we have a number of teams addressing critical strategy issues that were identified in the process."

The company is now bidding on projects in Mexico and Colombia and has created three new business units as a result of its new strategy. One of these units will make about $25 million in operating income this year with about $350 million in revenue. Not bad for a start-up. And the overall results are impressive.

"We now have an alignment in which all of the people in the company are pointing toward the same strategy and goals," Honea states. "Secondly, we have a strategic screen or filter, that enables us to make decisions. What businesses are we going to get into and what ones are we going to get out of? Where do we invest the limited funds that we have? How much do we use our funds to continue retiring debt to improve the balance sheet, versus investing to grow the company? So, once we identified our new strategy, this all became much clearer. The result was that the stock price doubled from $5⅜ to $11 in 15 months. Our earnings have gone up 30 to 40 percent a year now for the last three years. So our stockholders are happy, and our employees are enthused."

What will sustain this kind of success is the ability of NorAm's people to think strategically over the long term.

"As a company, we have clearly become more strategic-minded in our decision processes," Honea says. "We are now integrating our strategy deeper into the organization. All of our employees are beginning to look at their jobs differently and ask how their individual work supports and furthers NorAm's progress toward achieving its future strategic profile.

"The DPI process emphasizes strategic thinking and its integration into the decision-making process. Other strategy-development processes can generate a lot of paper, but they often have little or no impact on management decision making. Also, we needed a clear overall vision for NorAm. The DPI process provided a concise method for developing and clearly articulating that vision.

"We owe a debt of gratitude to DPI. DPI had the right process at the right time for NorAm. NorAm is not the same company it was two years ago when we began the DPI process. The future is bright and we have a clear understanding throughout NorAm of how we can grow and thrive as a company in that future."

6

Articulating the Business Concept of the Enterprise

"Follow me," Lawrence of Arabia shouted to his Arab troops as he led his army's charge into battle.

Although the term "leadership" is frequently used, few executives in business today can be considered true leaders. The ultimate test of a leader is whether he or she will be followed, as Lawrence of Arabia was followed by an army of people who were not of his race or religion. For the followers to allow themselves to be led assumes their implicit belief in the leader's ability.

Many books have been written on leadership, but few have been able to describe it in comprehensive terms except to attribute it to a "trait of personality," nor have they been able to describe the skills of leadership in any detail. John P. Kotter, in his book, *The Leadership Factor*, explains that leadership can be defined, analyzed, and learned. He also points out that it is not taught in business schools. Unfortunately, he did not articulate how leadership can be attained. Jack Welch, the CEO of General Electric, views it this way:

> A leader is someone who can develop a vision of what he or she wants their business, their unit, their activity to do and be. Somebody who is able to articulate to the entire unit what the unit is and gain through a sharing of the discussion—listening and talking—an acceptance of that vision. And then can relentlessly drive implementation of that vision to a successful conclusion.

This definition of leadership is probably as close a definition as we could conjure up ourselves. However, we have found that many CEOs have great difficulty articulating their vision to their people. Their strategy and/or vision is usually *implicit* and resides in their heads. Unfortunately, as long as the strategy of an organization is implicit and resides in one or two people's heads, it is very difficult for others around these one or two individuals to implement a strategy that is not clear to them. Followers want to know where they are being led. General Motors' former CEO, Roger Smith, said that the only thing he would do differently if he started his term as CEO over again would be to communicate his vision of General Motors (GM) earlier and more frequently than he did. He cited this failure as the major reason for his inability to turn GM around more quickly.

As a result, most CEOs realize that it becomes important to make the strategy, or the business concept, *explicit.*

Meaningless Mission Statements

Over the last few years we have noticed a substantial increase in the number of corporations attempting to construct mission or vision statements that articulate the organization's business concept. Unfortunately, their efforts are often fruitless because of the lack of a structured process to help them. As a result, they end up with statements that are so "motherhood" in tone that everyone can agree with them, but useless as guides to help people make daily operational decisions. Over time, the statement is quietly ignored.

Here are a few examples:

> We are a successful, growing company dedicated to achieving superior results by assuring that our actions are aligned with shareholder expectations....Our primary mission is to create value for our shareholders.

or

> The mission is to provide products and services of superior competitive quality and value, to achieve strong growth in sales and income, to realize consistently higher returns on equity and cash required to fuel our growth, and to have people who contribute superior performance at all levels.

or

Our primary enterprise objective is to increase the value of share-owners' investment by managing our resources and servicing our customers better and more efficiently than our competitors.

Why do I call these statements meaningless? These are statements put together by a group of people in an attempt to gain consensus. They contain words that are nice-sounding and that everyone can agree to. However, when used as a filter to make decisions, they fall apart because they allow everything through. Nothing is eliminated.

Increasing shareholder value...by doing *what?* By making *what* products? By selling to *which* customers? By concentrating on *which* market segments? By pursuing *which* geographic markets?

Without answers to these questions, how can someone be expected to allocate resources properly and choose the appropriate opportunities to pursue?

And then, along comes the *Sybil syndrome!*

ETHYL CORPORATION
"Strives to be a profitable and growing global manufacturer and marketer of value-added chemicals, an innovative supplier of niche life insurance and annuity products, and an increasingly significant force in the pharmaceutical industry."

This company had such difficulty living with itself that it recently separated into four independent public corporations.

Even Dilbert has taken a swipe at useless mission statements: "A mission statement is defined as 'a long, awkward sentence that demonstrates management's inability to think clearly.'" And he gives an illustration (Figure 6-1).

Figure 6-1.

No wonder so many of the *Fortune* 500 companies have lost large chunks of their markets and have had to engage in massive downsizing programs. The above are fairly representative of the kinds of meaningless mission statements in use in hundreds of corporations, which have led to the "hollowing" of America.

The Need for a Concise Business Concept

To us, the words *strategy, mission, charter, mandate, business purpose,* and *business statement* are all synonymous. If one were to browse through the annals of business history books, one is told by author after author that on any day of its existence, every corporation is practicing a *concept of conducting its business.* In other words, there is an underlying concept of business being practiced by the management of any organization although that concept may not be apparent to the members of the organization. Thus, the reason for the term *business concept.*

"Every practice rests on theory, even if the practitioners are unaware of it." So says management guru Peter Drucker in his book *Innovation and Entrepreneurship: Practice and Principles.* Another expert on the subject, Albert Sloan, who was CEO of General Motors in the first half of this century, put it this way in his book, *My Years with General Motors:*

> Every enterprise needs a concept of its industry. There is a logical way of doing business in accordance with the facts and circumstances of an industry, if you can figure it out. If there are different concepts among the enterprises involved, these concepts are likely to express competitive forces in their most vigorous and most decisive forms.

Yet another guru, Henry Mintzberg, has also made a similar observation, as reported in a 1980 article in *Harvard Business Review:*

> Strategy is the organization's conception of how to deal with its environment for a while. If the organization wishes to have a creative, integrated strategy...it will rely on one individual to conceptualize its strategy, to synthesize a 'vision' of how the organization will respond to its environment. A strategy can be made explicit only when the vision is fully worked out, if it ever is. Often, of course, it is never felt to be fully worked out, hence the strategy is never made explicit and remains the private vision of the chief executive.

Peter Drucker, the guru of all management gurus, calls it the "theory of the business." In a 1994 *Harvard Business Review* article, he outlined his thesis:

Every organization, whether a business or not, has a *theory of the business*. Indeed, a valid theory that is clear, consistent, and focused is extraordinarily powerful. These are the assumptions that shape any organization's behavior, dictate its decisions about what to do and what not to do, and define what the organization considers meaningful results. These assumptions are about markets. They are about identifying customers and competitors, their values and behavior. They are about technology and its dynamics, about a company's strengths and weaknesses. These assumptions are about what a company gets paid for. They are what I call a company's *theory of the business*.

Our view on the subject of mission statements is simple:

- A good business or strategic concept should not be longer than a paragraph or two. There is no need to have pages and pages describing what the business is about. However, every word, modifier, or qualifier must be carefully thought through because each moves the line of demarcation between the products, customers, and markets that will receive more emphasis and those that will receive less.

- It is our opinion that the ability of people to execute a CEO's strategy is inversely proportionate to the length of the statement.

Therefore, the statement must be precise and concise.

The driving force concept is a tool that allows management to identify which area of business is at the root of the company's products, customers, and markets and is strategically more important to that company than any other area. However, it is also a tool that allows management to articulate its concept of doing business in that mode.

How to Construct a Meaningful Business Concept

A *business concept* that can serve executives of a corporation as a test bed to make consistent and intelligent decisions on behalf of the company must contain the following elements:

- The first sentence must clearly describe *the* driving force of the organization. In other words, it must isolate that specific component of the business that gives the company a *strategic and distinctive advantage* over its competitors. If one is product-driven, then what is the specific product that drives the business? If one is technology-driven, then which specific technology is at the root of the business? If one is production capability–driven, then which specific production capability drives the business?

- The second part of the statement should contain words—nouns, adjectives, qualifiers, modifiers—that will delineate the line of demarcation between the "nature" of the products, customers, market segments, and geographic markets that the driving force lends itself to and those to which it does not.

- The statement should have a "tone" of growth to it since growth is a given in business. Every business must grow in order to perpetuate itself.

- It must have a tone of success to it as success is, naturally, implied from a sound strategy.

- Finally, it must reflect *future intent* and present condition. The statement should give people a feel for what it will be in the *future,* not what it is today.

Depending on the choice of driving force, each business concept will be dramatically different.

Examples of Strategic Business Concepts

The following are examples of business concepts that we have helped our client organizations to construct. For reasons of confidentiality, the names of the companies involved have been omitted. In each instance, the driving force and the strategic heartbeat appears in italics.

The first two examples are from product-driven companies—one in the manufacturing sector, the other in the service industry.

"Our strategy is to market, manufacture, and distribute *saw blade products* made from strip metal stock that provide exceptional value.

"We will concentrate on high performance, material separation applications where we can leverage our integrated manufacturing capabilities to develop customized, innovative, consumable products with demonstrable advantages that bring premium prices.

"We will seek out customer segments and geographic markets where the combination of superior distribution and technical support services will give us an additional competitive advantage."

"Our strategy is to provide *reinsurance* products to assist organizations in managing life, health, and annuity risks. We will differentiate ourselves by leveraging our mortality and morbidity risk management expertise.

"We will concentrate on market segments where we can establish and maintain a leadership position.

"We will concentrate in growth-oriented, 'free' geographic areas with reliable databases and predictable risk patterns where we can achieve critical mass and a balanced portfolio."

The next two are user class-driven concepts:

"We proactively seek out the building, repair, and remodeling needs of *professional trades people and DIYers* in the commercial and residential construction industry.

"We respond with cost effective, differentiated staple products that enhance the performance or ease the installation of key building materials and are category leaders.

"We concentrate in geographic markets with a significant and/or a growing construction industry and an adequate distribution infrastructure to reach a critical mass of end users.

"Our intent is to be the recognized leader in the products we offer."

"Our strategy is to fulfill the complete spectrum of health care needs of *cancer patients* and their families.

"We respond with treatment options that truly 'make a difference,' delivered by the ablest professionals in a seamless and sensitive manner that empowers patients to make coherent decisions.

"We will concentrate on geographic markets in which we can develop competitive advantage with all constituencies involved in the continuum of cancer care.

"Our intent is to be the recognized leader in providing positive, measurable outcomes."

The following statement is from a market category–driven company:

"We will proactively seek out the professional information/education needs of the *health science market.*

"We will respond with added-value content that maximizes the development of valuable copyright materials through multiple formats, languages, and/or distribution channels to capitalize on profitable customer segments in English-speaking countries."

The following two examples are those of production capability–driven companies:

"Our strategy is to leverage its cutting edge, integrated *specialty textile manufacturing capability* to exploit interior service applications for which we can develop customized, differentiated products.

"We will target and strive to dominate market niches that offer above average margins/profit.

"We will seek geographic markets with high growth potential where our superior sales, distribution, and service skills bring an additional competitive advantage."

"We will continue to be the leading international producer and marketer of metal-based specialty chemicals and powders that leverage our *process capabilities* to produce high added-value products.

"We will seek high volume, high quality, value-added industrial applications in market segments in which we can have a major presence through our ability to customize and differentiate our products/services to specific customer requirements.

"We will do this in geographic markets which have multiple market segments where manufacturing proximity can be an additional competitive advantage."

Then there is a production capacity–driven concept:

"Our strategy is to market transportation fuels through our own and other value-added distribution systems to optimize our *refining capacity.*

(Continued)

"We will stress end-user sales to high-volume customer segments and geographic markets where location provides a competitive advantage.

"Our intent is to gain enough critical mass to dominate the niche markets we operate in or enter."

The next two statements are examples of technology-driven concepts.

"Our strategy is to proactively exploit our proprietary *biomedical technologies (materials/electronics)* to satisfy therapeutic and diagnostic extension applications in the fields of cardiovascular and neuromuscular science to alleviate pain, restore health, and extend life.

"We will respond with differentiated, ethical medical devices distributed through a highly trained sales force focused on discrete customer segments.

"We will concentrate on geographical markets with a critical mass of applications, an established base of medical expertise, and an adequate health care infrastructure."

"Our strategy is to leverage our know-how in the *formulation and manufacturing of 'polymer' based composites.*

"We will seek growth opportunities and niche applications in market segments for which we can design differentiated value-added, consumable products.

"We will concentrate in geographic areas with growing demand where we can provide superior technical support."

The following two statements represent distribution method–driven concepts:

"Our strategy is to provide the most efficient *distribution network to serve the tire and wheel industry.* We will tailor our products, services, and facilities to satisfy the evolving needs of our customers and suppliers and respond with a proprietary advantage in the areas of cost, cycle time, or product diversity.

(Continued)

"We will continually extend our network to provide more reach and/or penetration than our competitors.

"We will concentrate in geographic areas with sufficient vehicle infrastructure where we can match our source of supply with a critical mass of independent resellers to justify optimum volumes in order to dominate the niches we enter."

"We will be the premier owner/operator of international *wireless networks* that deliver differentiated and value added products to businesses with mobile workers.

"We will concentrate on customer segments that require multiple services customized to various applications which create recurring revenue streams.

"We will focus on metro adjoining areas and connector corridors in North America and other countries with emerging infrastructures and above average profit potential."

Exotic? Definitely not! Sexy? Absolutely not! Powerful? You bet! The purpose of a clear business concept is not to arouse people but to provide them with a clear sense of direction and equip them with an easy tool to make intelligent and consistent decisions on behalf of the organization. In the next section we explain how the business concept is used to screen opportunities.

Turning the Business Concept into a Strategic Filter

The following statement is the business concept of another one of our clients.

"Our strategy is to leverage our *multipurpose, continuous process capability to combine metals and polymers to produce and market multilayered structures.*

"We will proactively seek out applications where we can respond with differentiated products that add value, are tailored to the spe-

(Continued)

cific needs of customers and end users, and bring cost, performance, and/or quality competitive advantages.

"We will concentrate in growth-oriented industry segments in which we can be a leader and in geographic markets where there are multiple applications available to us."

Although this business concept sounds highly technical, here is how it can be transformed into a very effective and simple *binary* filter (Figure 6-2) to screen opportunities that come to the business. One simply takes an opportunity through a series of questions which demand a yes or no answer.

Figure 6-2. The business concept is used as a filter to screen business opportunities.

Strategic Filter

Does the opportunity...	Yes	No
■ Leverage *and/or enhance* our multipurpose, continuous process capability to combine *metals* and *polymers?*	☐	☐
■ Produce *multilayered* structures?	☐	☐
■ Provide an ability to respond with *differentiated* products that add value?	☐	☐
■ Provide products tailored to the specific needs of customers?	☐	☐
■ Bring: —Cost advantages? —Performance advantages? —Quality advantages?	☐ ☐ ☐	☐ ☐ ☐
■ Target a growth-oriented industry sector?	☐	☐
■ Bring geographic markets with multiple applications?	☐	☐
■ Allow us to be a leader?	☐	☐

The more "checks" the opportunity receives on the "no" side of the ledger, the larger and larger the red flag should become, because that opportunity is violating major aspects of the strategy of the business.

The more areas of the strategy it violates, the more it will be an "exception to the rule" and exceptions always end up being problem areas.

What Is the Strategic Quotient of Your Organization?

If you are interested at this point in assessing your organization's strategic position, you may wish to answer the questions in Figure 6-3 and have your direct reports do the same. If all the answers are similar and each person's business concept is identical, then you are in good shape. The wider the discrepancies in their replies compared to yours, the less clear your strategy is, and you may wish to call DPI for assistance.

Figure 6-3. Questionnaire to determine understanding of an organization's business concept.

1. Do you have a well-articulated, clear statement of strategy and business concept?

   Yes ☐   No ☐

2. Could you write a one- or two-sentence statement of that strategy/business concept?

   Yes ☐   No ☐

3. Do your key subordinates understand that strategy/business concept?

   Yes ☐   No ☐   Somewhat ☐

4. Could each of your subordinates write a one- or two-sentence statement of that strategy/business concept without consulting you or each other?

   One person could ☐   Some could ☐   None could ☐

5. Do they use this statement as a guide for the choices they make in pursuing new products, markets, and customers?

   Use frequently ☐   Use sometimes ☐   Never use ☐

6. Is it used as a filter to choose or reject products, markets, and customers?

   Yes ☐   Sometimes ☐   No ☐

(Continued)

Figure 6-3. Questionnaire to determine understanding of an organization's business concept. (*Continued*)

7. Have you ever sat down as a management team to try to obtain consensus as to the future direction of your firm?

   Yes ☐   No ☐

8. Was consensus obtained or are there still different visions of what the organization is trying to become?

   | Total consensus (single vision) ☐ | Some consensus (single vision) ☐ | Little consensus (different visions) ☐ |

9. Is the organization moving in a clear direction?

   Yes ☐   Not sure ☐   No ☐

10. Do you have a separate process of strategic thinking to determine *what* you want to become as opposed to *how* you get there?

    Yes ☐   No ☐

11. What is your strategic business concept?

    _____

    _____

    _____

    _____

    _____

    _____

Union Pacific Resources

Bucking the Traditional Wisdom

Jack Messman
Chief Executive Officer

From its beginnings, Union Pacific Resources (UPR) was not your garden-variety oil and gas business. Created as a unit of the Union Pacific Railroad, the company's purpose was to develop mineral resources on land given to the railroad by Abraham Lincoln. Over the course of time, it has evolved. Today, the company is America's number one independent oil and gas exploration and production company and drills for natural gas in many locations that have no relationship to the railroad. It has become a formidable competitor in the natural gas market. And in October 1995, the company was taken public, as UPR completed an initial public offering of approximately 17 percent of the company's common stock. It also intends to distribute pro rata the remaining 83 percent in a spinoff to Union Pacific stockholders.

Union Pacific Resources is different from most gas producers in another very important way. It makes a lot of money, even in an era when natural gas prices are depressed—down 20 percent last year—a year that saw the company's operating income increase 34 percent to $470 million on a gain in revenue of 9 percent to $1.46 billion.

The question is, how do they do it?

The simple answer is efficiency and an innovative approach to drill site management. But the story goes much deeper than that. And part of it lies in Jack Messman's innovative strategic approach.

CEO Jack Messman had experience in many businesses, the most recent of which was the computer industry, and bucks many of the traditional assumptions about the gas industry.

Rather than banking gas reserves and waiting for prices to rise as many competitors do, UPR follows a different philosophy. UPR strives to minimize reserves, which they regard as unnecessary inventory.

As he states, "If I told you that Ford Motor had 14 years' worth of cars on its lots, you'd think it was a bad idea. Why should oil companies be any different?"

Their strategy is not to drill single well sites. They believe that sustained success comes from drilling exploratory wells that will lead to multiple drill sites and new potential core areas. This takes smart use of advanced exploration and drilling technology as well as exceptional efficiency. This approach enables UPR to limit reserves and make money even when prices are low.

Jack Messman also believes that the efficiency necessary to achieve sustained success comes from a management structure that allows management decisions to be made as far down into the organization as possible. But those decisions must be consistent with the strategy. In order to do that, the management must understand the strategy and how their responsibilities fit into it.

Enter Decision Processes International, and its *strategic thinking process*. This critical-thinking process enables the management of a company to reason out the strategy together. With the resulting clarity of understanding and "buy-in," managers can then make day-to-day decisions, assured that they are consistent with the organization's overall purpose. CEO Messman brought in DPI to facilitate the process in hopes that a clear strategic understanding would speed decision making and enable the company to achieve a higher level of focus and flexibility.

"We were a functionally oriented company with top-down decision making," says Messman. "Our cross-functional processes were not broken, but highly bureaucratic. People wanted to be told what to do. No one felt we had a clearly articulated strategy."

Over the course of the initial three-day session, which forms the core of the process, the management team was able to debate the key issues shaping UPR's future in a structured and timely fashion. By participating in the process, the team was able to construct a strategy that all could understand and implement.

One of the results of the strategy refocusing was that the company changed from a traditional functional hierarchy to a business unit organization. "The business unit organization results in faster and more informed decision making throughout all levels of the company," says Messman.

The CEO now feels that the DPI process made it possible to "create a profit center organization with P&L responsibility pushed farther down the organization. Each profit center needed to know its own strategy and how to make it consistent with the corporate strategy."

Yet Jack Messman was skeptical of the need for such a process before going through it.

"Our company sells a commodity product," he says. "We had doubts about the applicability of the DPI process to a company which did not have an industrial or consumer product. Commodity products are not managed in the same way. For example, we do not advertise and it's tough to differentiate ourselves from our competitors. However, we found the DPI process did apply to our company, despite a commodity orientation. Using DPI's *strategic thinking process*, we developed a very effective strategy."

His point of view about the process began to change after experiencing the initial three-day session.

He now recalls, "It basically showed us that if you follow the DPI process, the answers to your strategic questions exist in the minds of your own management team. The process helps you get it articulated and decided. It's a systematic approach which, when properly facilitated, makes you focus on all the elements necessary to determine corporate strategy, such as internal and external environment, weaknesses, competitive threats, strengths, critical needs for success. It gave us a unified strategy against which we could test our tactics on a day-to-day basis."

This "filtering" effect assures decisions consistent with corporate goals. This has contributed significantly to UPR's ability to stay focused and achieve the efficiencies essential to its unique mode of operation.

The results to date have been impressive. Some key initiatives emerged from the process which have made the organization leaner and more effective, such as its new drill site inventory system.

"We know, for example, that the key element of our business is to create drill sites," Messman explains. "Knowing this, we developed a method to measure our inventory of drill sites which we did not previously have. This allowed us to plan our capital expenditures for plants

to coincide with the completion of new wells. It allowed us to anticipate when we might be in danger of not having enough drill sites to
feed our drilling machine."

The company has even changed its geographic objective as a result
of the new strategy.

"By agreeing to a strategy, you also agree as to what you are not
going to do," says Messman. "This avoids wasting time and resources
on activities which do not support the strategy. Our people have
become more focused on achieving success and stopped debating alternatives. Being more focused and efficient, we have more activities
directed at the strategy. We decided we are a North American company,
so we dropped international activities. Going overseas is just another
way of saying you're out of ideas. We just have too much to do here."

Today, UPR is the number one driller in the nation and continues to
turn out exceptional financial results in a business where such gains
are uncommon.

For example, UPR has managed sales volume gains for six consecutive years. And it is number one in the United States in profitability
measured by return on equity, number one in operating income, number one in hydrocarbon sales volume.

As Messman states in the company's 1995 annual report, "We are a
recognized leader in our industry. Devising ways to apply technology.
Challenging conventional wisdom....Getting to the future first."

7

Nurturing
Key Strategic
Areas of Excellence

As we worked with more and more companies over the years, we noted that there were some that could perpetuate their strategy successfully over long periods of time, like IBM or Daimler-Benz. Others, however, had great difficulty doing that, and their performance over time was akin to a yo-yo. What, we asked, made for the difference?

Over time, the strategy of an organization, like a person, can become stronger and healthier or it can get weaker and sicker. In our opinion, what determines which way the strategy will go are the *areas of excellence* (Figure 7-1) that a company *deliberately cultivates* over time to keep the strategy strong and healthy and give it an edge in the marketplace. An area of excellence, another key concept of strategic thinking, is a *describable skill, competence, or capability* that a company cultivates to a level of proficiency greater than anything else it does, and particularly better than any competitor does. It is excellence in these two or three key areas that keeps the strategy alive and working. Bill Marriott, of the hotel chain, stated that "It took the company over a decade to figure out that it had special expertise in running hospitality and food service operations...." This "special expertise" or capability is what we call an *area of excellence*.

The deliberate cultivation of strategically important capabilities, usually two or three of them, keeps an organization's strategy strong and healthy and gives it an edge over its competitors. Losing these

Areas of Excellence (Strategic Capability)

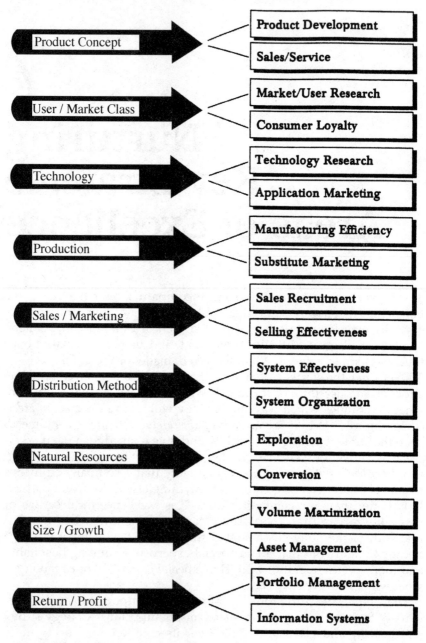

Figure 7-1. Determining the strategic capability of an organization is a key concept of strategic thinking.

two or three skills weakens the strategy and eliminates the organization's competitive edge.

Depending on which of the 10 driving forces is being pursued, the areas of excellence required to succeed, however, will greatly change.

Determining the Strategic Capabilities of the Business

Product/Service Concept–Driven Strategy

A product/service–driven company survives on the *quality* of its product or service. Witness the automobile wars. Who's winning? The Japanese. Why have Americans been buying Japanese cars and even been willing to pay premium prices for the last 40 years? The answer is simple: The Japanese make better cars. The bottom line for a product-driven strategy is: Best product wins!

One area of excellence, therefore, is *product and process development.* Compared to U.S. cars, Japanese cars of the late 1950s (when cars from Japan came onto the market) were far inferior. But Japanese car manufacturers understood well that pursuing a product-driven strategy required product and process development. And they strove to improve the product—to make it better and better—to the extent that Japanese cars eventually surpassed the quality of U.S. cars.

For many years Fujitsu (through its U.S. subsidiary, Amdahl) was satisfied with making copycat versions of IBM mainframes and had mediocre results. In 1991, the company decided to stop matching IBM and to start making better computers than IBM. This strategy is bound to produce better results, as its record 1995 and 1996 earnings showed.

A second area of excellence is *service.* IBM, which also pursues a product-driven strategy, is well aware of this requirement. Ask IBM clients what they admire most about IBM, and 99 out of 100 will say they admire its service capability. IBM deliberately invests more resources in its service function than any of its competitors, and thus has a considerable edge in response time and infrequency of product failures.

In a product-driven mode, you maintain your competitive advantage by cultivating excellence in *product development* and *product service.*

Market Category/User Class–Driven Strategy

An organization that is market/user class–driven must also cultivate excellence to optimize its strategy, but in dramatically different areas.

A market/user class-driven company has placed its destiny in the hands of a *type of market* or a *class of users*. Therefore, to survive and prosper, it must know its user class or market category better than any competitor. *Market or user research,* then, is one area of excellence. The company must know everything there is to know about its market or user in order to quickly detect any changes in habits, demographics, attitudes, or tastes. Procter & Gamble, which is consumer-driven, interviews consumers (particularly homemakers) over two million times per year in an attempt to anticipate trends that can be converted into product opportunities. *Playboy* does the same thing by monitoring changes in its subscribers through its magazine surveys each year.

A second area of excellence for a market/user class-driven company is *user loyalty.* Through a variety of means, these companies, over time, build customer loyalty to the company's products or brands. Then they trade on this loyalty. Over time, Johnson & Johnson has convinced its customers that its products are "safe." And it will not let anything infringe on the loyalty it has developed because of this guarantee. Whenever a Johnson & Johnson product might prove to be a hazard to a person's health, it is immediately removed from the market.

Production Capacity/Capability–Driven Strategy

When there is a glut of paper on the market, the first thing a paper company does is lower the price. Therefore, to survive during the period of low prices, one has to have the lowest costs of any competitor. To achieve this, *manufacturing or plant efficiency* is a required area of excellence. This is why paper companies are forever investing their profits in their mills—to make them more and more efficient. An industry that has lost sight of this notion is the steel industry in the United States and central Europe. By not improving their plants, they have lost business to the Italians and Japanese, who have done so. One notable exception in the United States is Allegheny Ludlum, which has done very well because it has the lowest costs of any steel mill, including the Japanese and Italian mills. As a result, Allegheny's revenues and profits have consistently improved. Its managers are unique in that they know the cost of each of perhaps 30,000 coils of steel floating around the company's seven plants at any given stage of production. "The thing that scares me now is that we know our true costs, but competitors don't," says CEO Richard Simmons. "How can they make logical pricing decisions?"

A second area of excellence for the production capacity–driven strategy is *substitute marketing.* Capacity-driven companies excel at substituting what comes off their machines for other things. The paper people are trying to substitute paper for plastic; the plastic people are trying to substitute plastic for aluminum; concrete for steel. The same is true in the transportation industry where bus companies are trying to replace trains, train companies the airlines, and so forth.

A production capability–driven company is one that has built special capabilities into its production process which allow it to make products with features that are difficult for its competitors to duplicate. It then looks for opportunities where these capabilities can be exploited.

Job shops and specialty printers are examples. As a result, these companies are always looking to add to or enhance these distinctive production capabilities, because herein resides their competitive advantage.

Technology/Know-How–Driven Strategy

A company that is technology-driven uses technology as its edge. Thus, an area of excellence required to win under this strategy is *research*, either basic or applied. Sony, for example, spends 10 percent of its sales on research, which is 2 or 3 percent more than any competitor. Its motto, "research is the difference," is proof that the company's management recognizes the need to excel in this area.

By pushing the technology further than any competitor, new products and new markets will emerge. Technology-driven companies usually *create* markets rather than respond to needs, and then usually follow their technology wherever it leads them. Merck is a good example of a company whose ex-CEO and chief strategist, Ray Vagelos, knew precisely what area of excellence had to be fueled to deliver new products. Merck, at Vagelos's directive, poured hundreds of millions of dollars into research, as a technology-driven company should. This investment has enabled the company to generate an ongoing stream of new products in an industry that introduces a new drug about as often as an aircraft manufacturer introduces a new airplane. It has consistently spent a greater share of its revenues on research than the rest of the industry. In 1986, the amount was $460 million, and it was increased to $1.5 billion in 1995, which was 12 percent of sales—more than any competitor over that time frame. Its research teams *excel* and are on the leading edge of science in biochemistry, neurology, immunology, and molecular biology. Few other drug companies can match the breadth and depth of expertise Merck has in these areas. Vagelos's successor, Ray Gilmartin, also knew what fuels Merck's growth when he declared that "Merck would remain a research-driven pharmaceutical company."

Another CEO who realized the importance of research as an area of excellence for his company was Edmund Pratt, Jr., ex-CEO of Pfizer, Inc. From 1981 through 1990, he spent 8 percent of sales on R&D. In 1990 alone, the amount was $602 million, or 14 percent of revenues. Pfizer is in the process of launching nine new drugs, which could have a potential of over $2 billion in sales for the company. "We've got new drugs coming out our ears," said a pleased Pratt shortly before his retirement.

His successor, William Steere, comes from the same mold and is perpetuating that investment. In 1994, the amount was $1 billion, and the 1995 budget was increased to $1.3 billion, which might surpass even Merck. As a result, the Pfizer new product hopper is brimming over.

Also in the pharmaceutical industry, yet another CEO clearly understands the relationship between his company's driving force and its areas of excellence. This is Robert Bauman of SmithKline Beecham in the United Kingdom. Bauman articulated the relationship in this manner: "The unifying theme of the company has always been a science based strategy [technology driving force]." As such, he allocated 80 percent of the firm's $800 million budget to six therapeutic areas of excellence. These are anti-infectives, biologicals, cardiovascular, central nervous system, gastrointestinal, and inflammation and tissue repair. Bauman expects that the company will be generating 25 percent of its revenues from these strategic capabilities.

A second area of excellence for technology-driven companies is *applications marketing*. Technology-driven companies seem to have a knack for finding applications for their technology that call for highly differentiated products. For example, 3M used its coating technology to develop Post-it notepads and some 60,000 other products.

Sales/Marketing Method–Driven Strategy

The prosperity of a sales method–driven company depends on the reach and effectiveness of its selling method. As a result, the first area of excellence that companies such as Avon and Mary Kay must cultivate is the ongoing *recruitment* of door-to-door salespeople. Mary Kay had tremendous success in the 1980s because it was able to draw several hundred thousand women to sell its products. Avon's fortunes suffered because its sales force had dropped considerably during that same period.

The second area of excellence needed to succeed with this strategy is improving the *effectiveness* of the selling method. Door-to-door companies are constantly training their salespeople in product knowledge, product demonstration, and selling skills. Growth and profits come from improving volume through the diversity and effectiveness of its sales methods.

Distribution Method–Driven Strategy

To win the war while pursuing distribution method–driven strategy, you must first have the *most effective* distribution method. As a result, you must offer products and services that use or enhance your distribution system. Second, you must always look for ways to optimize the *effectiveness,* either in cost or value, of that system. That is your edge. You should also look for any form of distribution that could bypass or make your distribution method obsolete.

Both Federal Express and Wal-Mart are good examples of distribution method–driven companies. They are constantly striving to improve the efficiency of their respective distribution systems—the heartbeat of their businesses. As David Glass, CEO of Wal-Mart, stated: "Our distribution facilities are one of the keys to our success. If we do anything better than other folks, that's it." Knowing that, Glass invested $500 million in a computer system that links the company to its suppliers in order to lower costs even further.

Fred Smith, CEO of Federal Express, also knows what the strategic heartbeat of his business is when he says, "The main difference between us and our competitors is that we have more capacity to track, trace, and control items in the system" (*Journal of Business Strategy,* July/August 1988).

Natural Resource–Driven Strategy

Successful resource-driven companies excel at doing just that—*exploring* and finding the type of resources they are engaged in. Exxon considers itself to be the best at "exploring for oil and gas," and it does this better than any competitor. It was the recognition of this fact that led Exxon to drop its office equipment division. There's not much oil and gas to be found there, plus that kind of venture requires excellence in areas Exxon does not possess.

John Bookout, ex-CEO of Shell USA, is a good example of a strategist who understands his company's areas of excellence. Shell's particular expertise is "enhanced oil recovery in offshore waters deeper than 600 feet." In this area, Shell has few rivals, as Bookout explained. In 1983, Shell drilled a project called Bullwinkle in the Gulf of Mexico at a depth of 1350 feet. Outsiders thought the project was too risky, particularly since Shell did not spread the risk by taking other partners in on the deal. "You can't believe how easy that decision was," he says. "It took us 30 minutes in the boardroom." The reason? Bookout was banking on Shell's area of excellence in deep water recovery.

This area of excellence has enabled Shell to paralyze its competitors. Shell recently announced major discoveries in the Gulf of Mexico that are estimated to contain a minimum of four billion barrels of oil. Its current CEO, Philip Carroll, thinks that the real number is somewhere between 8 and 15 billion barrels, a number greater than Alaska's Prudoe Bay. Even its competitors recognize this superiority, as Amoco CEO Laurance Fuller admits: "When it comes to deep water drilling, Shell is out in front of the industry."

Shell has since nurtured that area of excellence to the point that they can now descend to 8000 feet—a capability no competitor will be able to replicate for years, if not decades, to come.

Size/Growth or Return/Profit–Driven Strategy

Companies that choose either a size/growth–driven or a return/profit–driven strategy require excellence in financial management. One such area is *portfolio management.* This means proficiency at moving assets around in order to maximize the size/growth or return/profit of the entire organization.

A second area of excellence is *information systems.* These companies usually have a corporate "Big Brother" group that constantly monitors the performance of its various divisions and as soon as a problem is detected, an attempt to correct or expunge it is made. Harold Geneen had such a group at ITT.

Importance of Areas of Excellence

Why are areas of excellence an integral part of strategic thinking? No company has the resources to develop skills equally in all areas. Therefore, another strategic decision that management must wrestle with, once the driving force has been identified, is to clearly identify those two or three skills that are critical and to give those areas *preferential* resources. In good times, these areas receive additional resources; in bad times they are the last areas you cut. For example, 3M, which is a technology-driven company, had a chairman, Alan Jacobsen, who clearly recognized this concept. When Jacobsen took over as chief executive, he set about to improve 3M's profitability. He asked all his division heads to cut expenses by as much as 35 percent, but he spared R&D expenditures. In fact, he *increased* R&D from 4.5 percent of sales to 6.6 percent. The reason: Research is a required area of excellence for a technology-driven company. Ever since then 3M has been on a roll, spitting out 300 to 400 new products each year, and its stock has more than doubled in the last five years. "Des" Desimone, 3M's current CEO, also understands this concept: In an attempt to rev up 3M's product creation pace, he has increased R&D's percentage another point.

A company, therefore, has two additional key strategic decisions to make if it wishes to succeed. First, it must determine which strategic area will drive the business concept and, thus, the direction of the organization. Second, it must decide what areas of excellence or competence it must cultivate to keep that strategy healthy. These areas of excellence should receive preferential treatment—fueled with more resources in order to develop a level of proficiency greater than any competitor. Once resources are diverted elsewhere, proficiency diminishes and the company loses its edge vis-à-vis its competitors.

Too often, organizations are distracted from what has made them successful. The most successful organizations are the ones in which the leader and senior management clearly understand their business concept and fuel the key areas of excellence required for success with more resources each year than they give to other areas. They then pursue this business concept with total dedication and without allowing any competitor to attain the same level of excellence in those few key capabilities. As Benjamin Disraeli so clearly noted many decades ago, "The secret to success is constancy of purpose." And, as Lewis Preston the ex-CEO of J.P. Morgan, one of the world's most successful banks, said about the firm he headed: "We aren't likely to deviate radically from the clear strategic path we have been on since the days of the first Morgan partners."

Sometimes, an area of excellence or strategic capability is one that has been cultivated over a long period of time. Pioneer, the Iowa corn seed king, dominates its rivals because it has deliberately cultivated the skill of gene juggling to a higher level of proficiency than any competitor. The company develops more than 20,000 hybrids per year, of which only 5 to 10 make it to market. And it has been doing this for over 65 years. The result has been an increase in farmers' yields from 40 to 110 bushels an acre.

Knowing what strategic area drives your organization and the areas of excellence required to support that strategy is akin to understanding what the strategic weapon is that will give you a distinct and sustainable advantage in the marketplace. Our experience has clearly shown that any strategy can work, but that no company can pursue two strategies simultaneously. No organization has the resources to develop excellence in several areas concurrently.

Understanding the concepts of strategic drive or driving force and areas of excellence makes life for the CEO and the management team much easier in terms of the decisions they make about the new products, markets, and customers that constitute the future profile of the organization.

Raytech
C O R P O R A T I O N

Creating Strategy with an
Albatross Around Your Neck

Craig Smith
Chief Executive Officer

"I became President of Raymark in September of 1985, before the for-
mation of Raytech in 1986," recalls Raytech President and CEO, Craig
R. Smith, "and at that time the business was in turmoil. There had been
a shareholder derivative lawsuit in addition to asbestos litigation--
there were a lot of distractions. The litigation was so overwhelming,
we had difficulty focusing on the business."

A subsidiary of the Shelton, Connecticut-based company, had for
many years been a leading producer of asbestos heat-resistant component parts used in construction, agriculture, and automotive applications. The asbestos-related litigation was a monumental obstacle—one
that threatened the company's very existence. Focusing people's attention on the future had become all but impossible.

The company was in desperate need of a strategy that would allow
it to build future performance even as it headed into Chapter 11.
Management had tried traditional strategic planning methods, but
results were less than satisfactory.

"We put together a huge effort in developing strategy-books, charts, financial information, and nothing was ever done with it. I've been involved with several strategic planning processes in my career and my objection has always been that it's a big production to put your strategy together, and all the charts look like hockey sticks with growth at the tail end of the planning period; but nobody works the plan. When the next planning period arrives, it's the same thing all over again. I told myself if I ever got the chance, I was going to change that process."

Given the unusual pressures on daily operations, Raytech simply could not afford to rely on ineffective strategy methods. "Decision making was paralyzed," he says. "We couldn't get anything done on a timely basis."

Then he ran across *Strategy Pure and Simple: How Winning CEOs Outthink Their Competition.*

"The thing I like about the DPI process is the strategic thinking. That, to me, is the key," Smith says. "You can identify your driving force and your areas of excellence in a few sessions. Mike and his people do a great job of facilitating that. The process allows you to take what you know about your business and organize it so that you come out with a strategy that reflects the way you think and in a way that you can act on it."

"It's not a complex strategic planning process," he continues, "it allows you to identify the critical issues in your business, it gives you a method of addressing them. You're dealing with the concept of your business and how you want to go about business, instead of all the numbers. It becomes a vital part of your operations. You don't just put it on the shelf and wait until the next planning period. You don't have to spend weeks crunching numbers. This process has great appeal to me because I am very comfortable with the rational concepts it's built on. It fits well with the way I think about the business."

Craig Smith is a believer in participative management and encourages his people to apply their knowledge and make decisions based on an understanding of the strategic direction.

"I believe that people have to learn to think strategically. You can learn the concepts of the DPI process, you can learn the techniques, but what I like about it most is that you have to learn to think differently."

Through the *strategic thinking process,* Raytech management has been able to reexamine its capabilities and point the company toward promising new opportunities.

Raytech has traditionally followed what DPI refers to as a product-driven strategy. "We thought in terms of more clutches and more brakes," Smith says.

In working through the process, it became clear that growth potential lay in the company's expertise in polymer matrix composites technology. By leveraging its composites technology the group reasoned that it could create a variety of new products, markets, and customers. In the parlance of the process, they would shift their driving force from product-driven to applied technology-driven.

"I happened to be in one of the groups with the director of technical development," Smith recalls about the three-day process. "We had been talking about products, but as soon as we said we were going to talk about building on our technology and forget our traditional products, a lamp came on in his head. He said we've got to think about our business completely differently.

"He started talking about places where you can use composites technology which had nothing to do with our current products. It had to do with wet laid carbon fibers, protective clothing, filtration systems, and a lot of other new areas."

This realization has led Raytech to pursue fresh directions in developing new applications. Today its business concept is substantially different from what it was only a couple of years ago. No longer just a maker of friction materials for clutches, the business concept is to "leverage polymer matrix composite technology for niche applications with differentiated, value-added products in geographic markets with growth opportunities."

"What this statement covers for us is that it defines our technology, talks about applications, tells what kind of products we'll develop— differentiated, value-added products—and it defines the kinds of markets we'll go after. Our people understand it because they worked on the strategy themselves," Smith explains.

This new strategy has enabled Raytech to focus its limited resources on capabilities that will enable it to realize this vision.

"We're now focused on areas of excellence where we have skills and abilities, expertise or areas of competence which we are developing to a level of proficiency beyond anything else we do. When we say application research, what does that mean? It means we're going to excel in understanding raw materials, product formulations, and manufacturing processes related to polymer matrix composites, to enable the development of superior products to meet market needs. We know about fibers, binders, additives, paper-making, bonding, and steel processing and how to combine two or more of these materials to create the desired performance characteristics in new products. We can use organic or inorganic fibers, rubber, resin or metallic binders, along with various additives—that's when I felt we were making progress— when we began to talk about our business in those terms. Now it's becoming a different business."

Smith now believes that the established direction has taken hold and that the focus of people's thinking has changed dramatically through the DPI process.

"We've got our operating people focused on strategy. They don't get involved in any of the problems associated with asbestos and bankruptcy. It has provided a future concept of the business. We know where we want the business to go and we've marshaled our resources to get there."

Today, the challenge is to select opportunities carefully, pursuing them without wasting precious resources. Strategic thinking among the people doing the work is critical to that effort.

"Our primary responsibility is to see that our existing business remains healthy and financially sound, which is a little difficult in bankruptcy. Most companies' performance declines in bankruptcy. So we've been very careful not to dilute our efforts, but since we've been in bankruptcy, we've grown our pretax earnings at a compounded annual growth rate of 22.6 percent, which is exceptional.

"We're going to stay with our basic business and employ an inch-out strategy, taking our technology into new niche applications."

Several new products have been introduced, and Raytech is moving ahead with innovative applications that would not have been possible to even think about a few short years ago.

8

The Concept of Strategic Leverage

"Corporations don't compete, business units do." So says Michael Porter of the Harvard Business School in his book, *Competitive Advantage*. This conclusion is based on the notion that as a company grows into an array of multiple products and customer groups, it ends up in a variety of different markets, each with a different group of competitors. Thus the need, and the Porter rationale, to separate the corporation into business units based on a product/customer matrix that places each unit "closer to the market" and increases its ability to compete successfully.

In our view, nothing could be further from the truth. Our own experience with all 300 of our clients clearly indicates the opposite phenomenon. It is *companies* that compete and *not* business units! In fact, what will determine a business unit's ability to compete (or not compete) is determined even before that business unit is formed.

Successful companies, in our view, are those that can *leverage their unique set of capabilities (driving force and areas of excellence) across the largest number of products and markets.* Companies that can spread the heartbeat of the business and their accompanying strategic capabilities across as many business units as possible are those that will assist that business unit in surviving and prospering. The opposite is also true. Business units that cannot use key corporate capabilities are often "orphaned" from the thrust of the corporation and will have difficulty making it on their own.

The Link Between Business Unit Success and Corporate Competitiveness

Sharp, of Japan, is an excellent example of a company that has leveraged its unique capabilities. Sharp is into LCDs for laptop computers as well as a large number of other consumer electronic devices, ranging from cordless phones, projection televisions, and fax machines to electronic diaries and calculators. It has recently introduced laser diodes for use in computers, laser printers, CD players, and videodisc players (Figure 8-1). It is working on photosensitive films that will

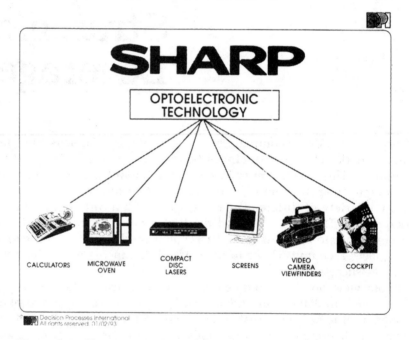

Figure 8-1. Sharp's strategic capabilities.

someday function as a self-contained image processing computer and eliminate the need for memory chips and microprocessors.

Why is Sharp engaged in all these diverse product, customer, and market areas? They all draw on Sharp's knowledge of optoelectronic technology. "We've been accumulating optoelectronics know-how for 21 years," says president Haruo Tsuji, which accounts for Sharp's success as the world's largest supplier of optoelectronic devices with sales of over $100 billion annually. Sharp, in our opinion, has mastered this concept of capability leverage to the nth degree. Figure 8-2 is a "family

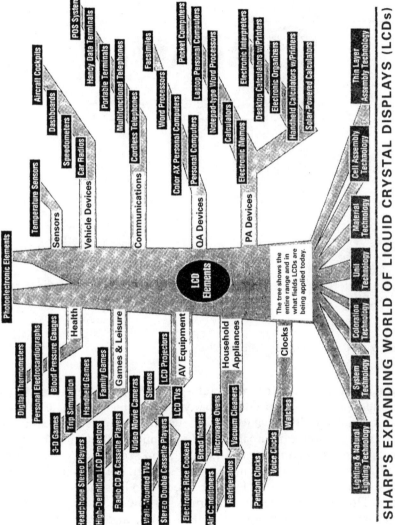

The tree shows the entire range and in what fields LCDs are being applied today.

SHARP'S EXPANDING WORLD OF LIQUID CRYSTAL DISPLAYS (LCDs)

Figure 8-2.

125

tree" that shows over 250 products that stem from Sharp's superior expertise in the area of liquid crystal displays.

Canon and Casio are two more examples of companies that have mastered the concept of strategic leverage (Figures 8-3 and 8-4).

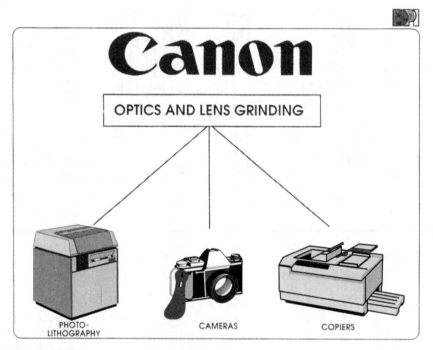

Figure 8-3. Canon's strategic capabilities.

Canon's wide range of products—copiers, cameras, and fax machines—all draw on that company's optics technology. Canon is also a good example of what happens when a company tries to innovate outside its strategic capabilities. In the mid-1980s, Canon made an enormous investment in the fast-growing and seductive PC market by introducing a PC of its own. Massive investment, massive failure. Why? Have you ever seen a PC with a lens? No lens, no probability of success. However, if Canon could figure out how to design a PC with a lens that makes it do things other PCs can't, like scanning, then it would probably have a winner.

The calculators, television screens, watches, and musical instruments that come from Casio all have the common trait of drawing on the company's expertise in the areas of semiconductors and digital displays.

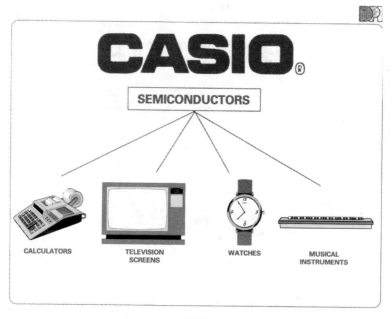

Figure 8-4. Casio's strategic capabilities.

A fourth Japanese company that clearly understands its heartbeat (driving force) is Honda. Although its most visible products are its cars, Honda also makes lawn mowers, motorcycles, and generators (Figure 8-5). All these products revolve around Honda's key expertise—engines—and the company is religiously following Honda's business concept of "engines for the world." When Honda entered Formula 1 racing, it went in with its engines. The car bodies were by McLaren, Lotus, and others.

Canada's Nortel is another company that clearly understands its strategic capability and has been exploiting it very successfully worldwide for a number of years. When Nortel developed the software for its first digital switch, it did so in a manner to ensure that it would be used in a wide range of products including hybrid analog switches, configurated central office switches, and PBXs (Figure 8-6).

There are some U.S. companies as well which clearly know where their strategic advantage lies. Hewlett-Packard and 3M are two good examples. Hewlett-Packard has exploited its knowledge of instrumentation technology into everything from scientific measuring devices to oscilloscopes (Figure 8-7).

3M is probably the best U.S. example of a company that has built an array of more than 60,000 products based on its knowledge of polymer

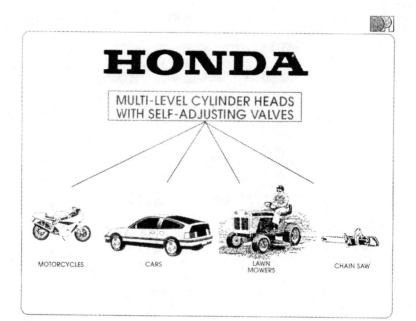

Figure 8-5. Honda's strategic capabilities.

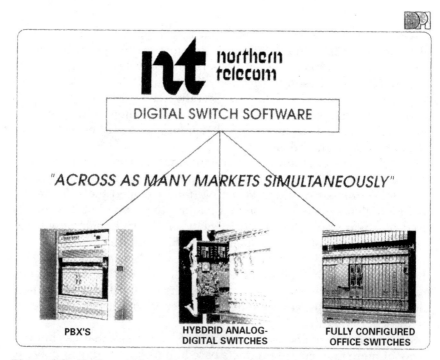

Figure 8-6. Northern Telecom's strategic capabilities.

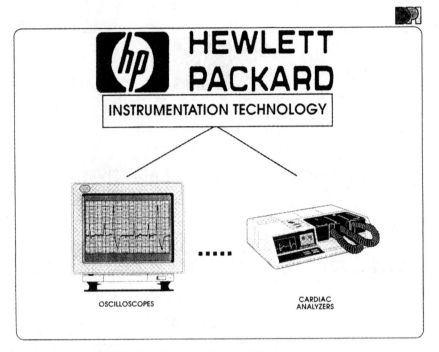

Figure 8-7. Hewlett-Packard's strategic capabilities.

chemistry as applied to coatings and adhesives (Figure 8-8). This strategic capability has led 3M into some 50 business arenas such as film, floppy disks, videocassettes, audiotape, sandpaper, adhesive tape, electrical tape, and computer wires—to their most recent success, Post-it notes.

Another CEO who clearly understood his company's strategic heartbeat, its corresponding area of excellence, and the advantage of leveraging these across all products and markets was Percy Barnevik of ABB, the electrical equipment company based in Switzerland. Although the company sells locomotives, robotics, turbines, and power generation equipment, at the root of all these businesses is ABB's expertise in electricity and electronics—a technology-based strategy. As such, Barnevik fueled and cultivated that expertise by investing eight percent, as compared with five percent by competitors, into R&D. "You have to be in command of your core technology," he says in an article appearing in *Fortune*. "For us, it's power semiconductors (electronic switching devices for high voltage transmission), and I wouldn't dream of buying them from the Japanese." He then ensures that this capability is spread across all of ABB's businesses, which is the leverage that the corporate parent brings to each of its business units.

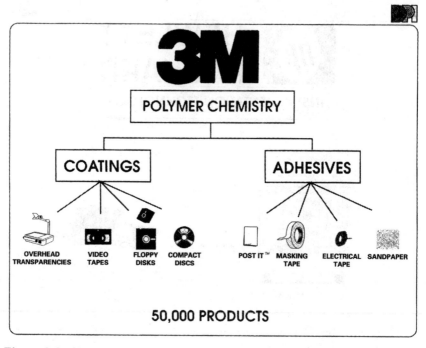

Figure 8-8. 3M's strategic capabilities.

There are also some examples of companies that do not understand what is at the root of their business. In the late 1970s and early 1980s Armco, up till that time a very successful steel company, decided to diversify. And diversify it did! Into everything from oil rigs, petroleum exploration, building products, strategic metals, and insurance. For a short time, the new strategy seemed to pay off with record profits. But in 1982 the company lost $342 million, and it is still trying to recuperate to this day. The reason: When these unrelated businesses got into trouble, Armco management, who were steel people, did not understand the unrelated businesses, and Armco itself was not bringing any strategic advantage to any of them.

Another example is United Airlines. Under its previous CEO, United negotiated cost-reduction labor contracts with its unions only to use the money to diversify into hotel and car rentals with its purchase of Hertz and Hilton—two businesses to which it brought little advantage. Even the union executive, Captain Jim Damron, understood this when he complained: "In two consecutive contracts, we gave concessions to the company, and we received nothing in exchange except seeing our company lose 25 percent of our market share. They took that economic leverage and used it to buy hotels and rental cars."

Leveraging Your Product Innovation Investment

As we worked with more and more companies over the years, we noticed that some got much more "bang for the buck" from their strategy efforts than others. For example, why is it that Merck can develop 12 new blockbuster prescription drugs in a 10-year period when the industry average is 1 every 15 years?

The answer is simple. Those that outperformed their competitors had clearly identified the *driving force* at the root of their strategy and had also clearly identified the corresponding *strategic capabilities* that the companies must excel at to make their strategies succeed over their competitors'.

The reason for Merck's success stems from ex-CEO Ray Vagelos's deliberate investment in four areas of medical science—namely, biochemistry, neurology, immunology, and molecular biology. All 12 of the blockbuster drugs derived from these four strategic capabilities deliberately cultivated by Vagelos to a higher level of proficiency than any of its competitors.

Thus, our advice to our clients is that the best product innovation is one that *leverages upon the company's strategic capabilities* and "fits" the strategy of the business.

We have also discovered that a company that attempts to innovate outside its strategic parameters (its driving force and accompanying areas of excellence) usually fails. And there is yet another good reason for that to occur: Most *innovations stem from prior knowledge.*

For example, it is not a coincidence that Edison and Siemens invented the light bulb, in different parts of the world, within hours of each other. Neither man would have done this if electricity and the conduction of electricity through wire had not been invented first. Mr. Daimler and Mr. Benz would not have developed the automobile if the combustion engine had not been discovered first. Steve Jobs and Steve Wozniak would not have developed the personal computer if someone else had not discovered the microprocessor first. And the list goes on.

Proof of this notion is Leonardo da Vinci. As brilliant a new product innovator as he was—he conceived the bicycle, the helicopter, and the submarine over 400 years ago—the fact remains that most of his ingenious inventions never saw the light of day. One cannot build a helicopter without the prior knowledge of shaping flat metal. One cannot build a submarine without the prior knowledge of providing oxygen to a vehicle submerged underwater.

The same is true of a company. Every company develops areas of knowledge and expertise that it adds to over time, and any new product innovation that draws on that knowledge has a high probability of success, whereas any that does not has a high probability of failure.

Thus, a company can leverage its new product innovation investment by favoring innovations that draw on the strategic heartbeat (driving force) and the accompanying strategic capabilities (areas of excellence) of the enterprise. In fact, *leveraging these across the broadest array of products and markets* is the key to a product innovation program that will outpace the competition. Successful new product creation works like a telescope (Figure 8-9). It produces the best results when it

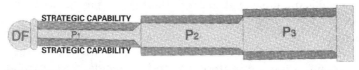

Figure 8-9.

derives from an extension of the company's driving force and areas of excellence to create new products for new markets.

Strategic Leverage

Understanding what component of the business is its strategic heartbeat and what your company's strategic capabilities are will greatly enhance your ability to succeed in your current markets. It will also open up other opportunities, in possibly unrelated product/market areas, that are strategically sound because they draw on the firm's strategic heartbeat and areas of excellence.

Honda recently announced the development of a new car engine that meets the 1999 California emission standards today—without the need to change anything about the gasoline. How long do you think it will be before Honda introduces this technology into its lawn mowers, chain saws, and tractors? Right! 12.5 seconds! Why? Simply because the competitive position of each of these business units will be enhanced by drawing on this corporate capability.

Strategic leverage means changing the equation that says $1 + 1 = 2$ into one that says $1 + 1 = 3$, sometimes 4, and sometimes 5. Decisions that affect only one product, one customer group, or one geographic area keep the organization running in place. To grow faster than competitors, one must make decisions and investments that enhance the competitiveness of multiple products, multiple customers, and multiple geographic markets—*simultaneously!*

A company that clearly understands its strategic capabilities and is leveraging these is Johnson & Johnson, the author's former employer. In the same week, the company announced that it was acquiring Neutrogena as well as the clinical diagnostic division of Kodak. Why these two seemingly unrelated businesses? Simply because both companies' products are aimed at the same class of users that J&J's other businesses target—doctors, nurses, patients, and mothers. As a result, J&J management feels confident that these new products fit the company's *heartbeat*. Its strategic capabilities will also be leveraged into these new businesses to make them even more successful.

Two other CEOs who understand this concept extremely well are Michael Eisner of Walt Disney and Ted Turner of Turner Broadcasting (now part of Time-Warner). Turner has built a number of cable networks that each utilize the others' programs. A news piece seen on *Prime News* on Tuesday evening is seen again on *The International Hour* on Saturday afternoon and then seen at some other time on *CNN Headline News*, a separate network. It eventually makes its way across all the Turner networks, such as The Airport Channel in airport gate areas to The Worldwide Hotel Channel in hotel rooms around the world.

At Disney, Michael Eisner has done the same type of leveraging to increase Disney's revenues from a few hundred million, when he took over, to more than $8 billion 10 years later. His leveraging concept is simple: Start with a character, Aladdin, and produce an animated film. Then leverage that character across a number of other products and markets. First, you have Aladdin look-alikes greet customers at Disneyland and Disney World. Then you sell Aladdin dolls at these parks, as well as in all Disney stores around the country. Then you show the film on your own Disney cable network. Then you license the Aladdin character for a host of other uses, from coloring books to hats and tee shirts. Finally, you sell a video version through video stores such as Blockbuster. And the business grows exponentially!

The essence of a successful product innovation program therefore is the CEO's and management's clear understanding of which component of the business is more important than all others and is the heartbeat of the business—and, as such, lends itself more to certain products, customers, market segments, and geographic markets.

A company has two key decisions to make if it wishes to have a successful product innovation program. First, it must determine which strategic area will *drive* the business and, thus, the direction of the organization. Second, it must decide what *areas of excellence* or *capabilities* it must cultivate to keep its strategy healthy. These areas of excellence should receive preferential treatment—fueled with more resources in order to develop a level of proficiency greater than any competitor and then *leveraged across the broadest array* of products, customers, and markets. Once resources are diverted elsewhere, proficiency diminishes, and the company loses its product innovation edge vis-à-vis its competitors.

The lesson to be learned from all these examples is obvious. The CEO and the management team must clearly understand what the driving force is that constitutes its strategic weapon and competitive advantage. As one Exxon executive told this author when explaining why Exxon eventually retreated from its disastrous foray into office equipment: "We did not understand the 'trivia' of those businesses and, therefore, could bring nothing to the table."

OM Group, Inc.

Winning the M&A Game

Jim Mooney
Chief Executive Officer

It's probably the greatest war game in the world," says Jim Mooney, chairman and CEO of OM Group. "You create a vision, develop a stronger army, bring on new weapons, bring on new growth. You don't let any of your people get hurt and it's all nonviolent. How much more fun can you have?"

Recent history is filled with companies that have tried, as OMG has, to grow with mergers and acquisitions as a key component. Many would not agree that, in the end, it's really not much fun. AT&T and RJR Nabisco come to mind. These companies failed to follow a principle that has been the guiding light at OMG. Have a clear, distinctive strategy, a differentiating set of strategic capabilities, and build on those—and *only* those.

By keeping a strategic focus, OMG has grown from $2 million in 1971 to nearly $500 million in 1997, with productivity and profitability that far outpaces the averages among its peers in the chemical industry.

The story began in 1946 when Mooney Chemicals was founded as a small family-owned producer of metal-based carboxylates—specialties used in the tire, paint, and petrochemical industries, among others.

When Jim Mooney's father retired in 1979, Jim became CEO. Jim is one of 14 brothers and sisters, and in the early 1990s his stockholder siblings decided to cash out and sell their equity. It was up to Jim and Mooney Chemical's management to come up with a way to satisfy the family's wishes—and set the company on a new plan to grow.

Fortuitously, one of its suppliers, Outukumpu, a Finnish mining concern, was planning to exit its business in cobalt, one of Mooney's critical raw materials. Jim Mooney saw in this the opportunity to provide a way out for the Finnish company, enhance Mooney Chemical's business, *and* raise enough cash to buy out the family's interests as well as Outukumpu's. A deal was hammered out to merge Outukumpu's Kokkola cobalt business, Vasset, a small French carboxylate company, and Mooney, to form OM Group. The plan called for OMG to go public, raising enough capital to buy out Outukumpu's and the family's interests in two years.

The elements of future success were clearly there: a strategic integration of a low-cost material supply, supported by international production, product development, and marketing. Yet some imposing obstacles to success remained to be resolved.

Despite complementary skills and capabilities, the companies appeared to be operating based on different "driving forces." More daunting was the fact that the companies had been operating in different economic systems. So some fundamental strategic, operational, and cultural conflicts needed work.

At the suggestion of one of OMG's directors, Markku Toívenan, Mooney decided to use DPI's *strategic thinking process* to help the management team work through the difficult issues it faced. In the course of the initial three-day sessions, several conclusions emerged.

"We thought we had two driving forces," says Mooney, "and we did. And there were also the conflicting cultures of a Finnish, a French, and an American company trying to do business together as one cohesive company.

"The Finnish operation, being part of a large mining operation, was clearly production-capacity-driven. And the people had always worked under a government-driven system. Mooney, on the other hand, had always been product-driven. It had 220 products, sold into 17 different industries. And the Americans were capitalist. So we had to come to some understandings about how we would put these companies together in a way that made sense to all of us."

After the three days, substantial progress was apparent.

"For one thing," Mooney recalls, "the top 20 individuals in the new company all came to have the same understanding of where we would take the enterprise. And it wasn't top-down or bottom-up driven. It was a consensus where the associates worked together in teams to see what we could do together, identify critical issues that would have to be resolved, and decide how we would work them out."

This consensus-building approach enabled the companies to look less at their differences, and more at the mutual capabilities they now command. Although cultural differences aren't likely to disappear entirely, they are much less of an issue today because an understanding has been reached as to the future direction of the company and the role each unit now plays in molding its future successes.

The concept behind the merger had been to combine the vertically integrated metal refining production strengths of Kokkola with the value-driven product expertise at Mooney and Vasset, and forge them into a single synergistic unit.

"We came to the conclusion that if we could take advantage of Kokkola's manufacturing capabilities and Mooney's marketing capabilities in metal-based specialties, we could make more products and provide greater geographic coverage. With this synergy we could be very successful," says Mooney. "We wouldn't be producing products just to fill capacity, but to create new high-quality, value-added products that would fulfill customer needs. Ultimately, our specialized production expertise and flexibility would lead us to be a production-*capability*-driven company."

"Today we see ourselves as transforming metals into specialty chemicals. Before, the Kokkola unit saw itself as refiners of cobalt and nickel metals and Mooney as a producer of metal-based specialty chemicals." The difference is subtle, but the key to OMG's strategy.

Four years and a major acquisition later, Mooney would say that the creation of this common strategic understanding "brings a unique culture to the organization. It's not an American culture, or a Finnish culture. It's not a Taiwanese or Zairian culture, but it *is* an OMG culture. No matter what nationality they are, the people understand it. They understand the vision of the company, that we are results-oriented people. They understand the successes. They want to buy into and want to be part of the successes. And that extends to the customer and the supplier and the shareowner. That carves out something that has lasting power."

But of course this didn't happen overnight. Another hurdle had to be cleared before any of this would be possible—the IPO, which was issued in October 1993. And largely because it had a well thought out plan, the stock opened at $8.50 and by 1997 had increased in share value more than threefold.

The successful IPO enabled OMG to follow through with its plan to buy out Outukumpu's interest in the firm and enabled the family to realize their equity.

How Vision Attracts Investment

"We've been well received by the markets for two reasons," Mooney continues. "The first is our performance which has been very good. The second is that we've been able to communicate our business in a way that the market can understand. Without the *strategic thinking process* helping us, that story would not have been as clear.

"For the first time we had a uniform identity for the company. Because of this, the Finnish owners were more comfortable that we were capable of bringing it to the marketplace. And it made the investment bankers more comfortable because they really understood our key drivers for growth and earnings.

"The easiest way to describe our business is with the concepts developed through the *strategic thinking process*," says Mooney. "The best thing about it is you don't have to give away your secrets, but you do let them know how you think. They know that they're buying a metal-based specialty chemical company with growth opportunities. It's real simple, that's what we are. We're nothing more than that. We're not going to look at anything else. They know that we have a global presence. They know that we have ongoing new product development, that we have an advanced and proprietary production capability. They know that we have long-term reliable supply relationships which feed that production capability. They know they're buying into a company with experienced management that understands the external environment as well as the internal environment. They understand how we focus on niche markets and what areas we want to go into, what areas we don't want to go into, based on our strategic focus and discipline. They know where we want to expand our existing product range. They know where targets are for new product development, and that strategic acquisitions have to fit the criteria that we just developed in front of them.

"The investors can see we have absolute discipline in our focus, and that there is no variation off of that.

"We're getting ready to do a secondary issue right now," Mooney explains. "We just filed today and if I didn't have the concepts developed through *strategic thinking*, I don't know how I would explain this thing. The first thing they always tell us about our business is it's too complicated, you go to 30 markets and you have 250 products. You have global capabilities. You're buying material out of Zaire and Zambia, which are politically unstable. And they can give you a million reasons why they can't buy our stock. But once we go through the operational strategy that we use to run our business, show them our vision strategy without giving away the secrets, address some critical issues, that simplifies the business real quick. Growth through metal-based specialty chemicals, period—nothing more than that. Niche markets, new product development, global expansion, acquisitions, it's pretty clear what we're going to do. They don't want a public relations firm telling them what OMG is doing, they want to hear it direct."

In Jim Mooney's view, too many companies suffer from a *lack* of vision or a distinctive strategy. This hurts their chances of growing *and* convincing potential investors and customers that they will grow. Relying on "spin doctors" to position the company's story is no substitute, he feels.

"I'll go to presentations and someone will be talking about how important their investor relations or public relations department is. And I'm sitting there thinking, 'My God, if you've got to talk about that, you've forgotten what you're in business for. You don't really have a vision. You're trying to create a vision where there isn't one.' Investors will support you with a clear vision. They won't support you if all you've got is a public relations manager. People see right through that. I can't tell you how many companies I see that have good operations people, but they have no vision as to where the company's going, what's driving it. They'll actually say, 'Well, you know, we had a bad quarter last one, we may have a bad quarter this one, but we're doing everything we can, we're going to fix it.' I'm sitting there thinking, 'Holy cow, how can you even go to work like that?'

"And you see good companies, good fundamental technologies, good fundamental production capabilities, good fundamental marketing skills, and they can't deliver a vision that will bring shareowner satisfaction, that will bring customer satisfaction. Even if you've got all those fundamentals going for you, if investors and customers don't *understand* your vision, they'll have trouble going along with you."

After the IPO: Acquiring to the Driving Force

Since the beginning, OMG has pursued a plan to grow in three areas: acquisitions, new products, and geographic reach. Guided by strategic filters, clearly agreed upon by the entire management team, OM Group appears to be succeeding in making the plan work. This built-in compass helps them target only opportunities that leverage their production capability.

"When our people develop products or look at markets or identify acquisitions, they know exactly where we're headed, they know what we're looking for," says Mooney. They know when they see an acquisition and they bring it to my attention whether this fits in, whether it's metal-based specialty chemicals, whether it's something we can leverage with our production. We don't want to get into a 'me too' application. We look for new product potential, whether it offers new niches, whether it fortifies the current weaknesses we have or builds on strengths. These are the critical issues we have to look at.

"That's the great thing about it. Based on our production capability, if we've identified a new product, we identify where the customer will use our product, we understand what the size of the potential growth is, we understand what the product return is, the profit, and we go after selected markets on a geographical basis. Everything is based on leveraging our production capability technology and the raw material resources within the product."

OMG's most recent acquisition is a good example of this line of thinking. And by initiating the new venture with the *strategic thinking process,* synergies and opportunities to leverage their driving force were recognized quickly.

"We just made a substantial acquisition. We bought a company called SCM Metals which expands our metal-based powder business into copper. Now we can leverage both the copper and the cobalt from a refining standpoint and pick up new niche markets where we can find new opportunities. We went in there and said, wow, they're in metal powders, so are we. They use smelting technology, we have smelting technology. They go into about 15 different markets, so do we. Their raw material costs are in copper. Lo and behold, over half the cobalt we refine has copper in it. We came in from a very different standpoint than they did. But together, we realized, hey, why can't we take that copper on a low raw material cost basis, utilize our production capability and take advantage of it. And our stainless steel powders, there's a lot of nickel in them. OMG has a vertical integration in nickel. So these are opportunities. And we talked about particle size of the powders. OMG has tremendous particle size technology. With SCM and OMG combined, we've even *enhanced* our technology, which is driven by our production capability, and we know how to make it happen. See how they fit in?"

As he builds OM Group, Mooney is adamant that the company will grow as a cohesive unit, interlocked by its driving force—its specialized production capability in metal-based specialty chemicals—and vision. To say it, though, is one thing. To do it, another. So the CEO goes into each acquisition using the same approach that has been successful for them to date.

"First item on my agenda in running the business is to look at their operational objectives and understand them," he says. "The second order of business is to put them through the *strategic thinking process.*

The pure reason why we do this is so that everybody understands where the company is headed. It builds trust, it builds confidence, it builds opportunities, it addresses weaknesses in a very positive way. This process has the unique capability of enabling you to look at your own plan and have bullets going through you and you don't feel bad about it.

"A good example is when we sat down with the *strategic thinking process* with SCM. There was an area of strength, or rather we realized there was a *weakness* that could be *developed* into an area of strength. Now, SCM operated with this weakness for years. And what we were able to do through the process was identify quickly this weakness that could be turned into a strength—so much of a strength that if we were successful at this, it would be a *unique* strength.

"They hadn't realized it was a weakness. Before, they didn't have the opportunity to see it that way. No one asked them to think differently. They were tied into thinking on a functional, quarter-to-quarter basis. Now we come in with this process and it gets them all stirred up and all of a sudden they're saying this can be a real strength to the company. This is something that we can change. Who doesn't want to change the place where they're working, where they can take a weakness and convert it into a strength? At first they were thinking, 'How are we going to grow 15 percent a year, 20 percent a year? We never did that before.' Now they're thinking, 'Hey, we can do it. And this is all we've got to do.'"

Grasping the Big Picture

"At first everybody thinks that they understand strategy," Mooney says. "Yet they confuse operations and the vision, and what the larger critical issues are that have to be addressed, and what you have to do in your strategic profile to get where you want to be. After that's all laid out and there's disagreements on it and it's hashed out, there seems to be a point of consensus. At that point of consensus the critical issues that need to be accomplished can be addressed very easily. In a matter of three days you can get a whole management group there. So at the end of the three days they understand what your driving force is, they understand what areas of excellence you have. And they understand another point, which is critical—timing. This method creates an *urgency*. And that urgency brings positive results.

"I think what happens is people identify the position the company is in and the opportunities they have. So there's a sense of urgency to accomplish these critical issues. This has certainly happened with OMG.

"And that's because they *were* the rationale. They're the ones saying, these are our strengths, this is what we do well, this is where we have the most opportunity, the external opportunities, the internal opportunities. What do we have to do? We have to leverage a production capability. And they were able to come to that conclusion themselves.

"If I had tried to sell my position, it wouldn't have the strength as if *they* came to that conclusion. And not only that, when you get done, there's the compelling logic as to *why* you're doing what you're doing.

"I've always liked this about the *strategic thinking process*. It brings a sense of ownership, it brings a sense of entrepreneurship, it brings a sense of teamwork, and consensus. The people become integrated in the process. That's what it comes down to. It diminishes egos. It diminishes ultimatums. It diminishes the possibility of the company getting off into something that we shouldn't be into. There are so many checks and balances. Turf issues are forgotten. You bring down the walls on egos."

In the end though, what really matters is results. And you don't have to look far to find them at OMG. Since 1993, sales have grown from $180 million to $388 million in 1996, with estimates as high as $500 million in 1997. The stock rose from $8.50 to $37 in three years for an increase in shareholder value of $627 million. Its "sales per associate" are at around $850,000, and operating profit is at approximately $115,000 per associate—2½ to 3 times the industry average.

"It's because we let everybody get involved with the results," Mooney states. "It's pride of ownership. Entrepreneurship. New product development. Geographic growth. Right down the line. They're part of it. They see it. They live it."

9

The Ultimate Strategy: Control of the "Sandbox"

There are a number of theories flourishing in the United States that revolve around competition and how one should deal with one's competitors. Here, again, we have some opposing, but logical, views. Most of the theories support a perspective that one must worry about all competitors simultaneously and try to be successful against all of them. Our view is that no company has the resources or ability to compete against all competitors and should not attempt to do so. Instead, a company should target a few key competitors and ensure success against these. In fact, we are also of the opinion that, sometimes, competition is irrelevant.

To Compete or Not to Compete?

The rules of competition described in this chapter are based on the premise that a company has made the decision to grow its business at some competitor's expense. That is not always the case. Some markets may be growing at a rate sufficient to satisfy everyone's appetite. An example is the PC market during the 1980s. During that 10-year period, how much time do you think Apple spent worrying about Compaq or Compaq about Apple? Right! Probably very little, because there was plenty of growth in this market to keep both companies churning out record-breaking sales and profits year after year. However, how do you think that will change in the next 10 years? Right again. As the demand for PCs plateaus, these companies will start competing with each other for growth much more than before. Therefore, a major caution is that the concepts in this chapter only apply if you have made a *conscious* decision that you have to increase your business at some competitor's expense.

Once the decision to grow is made, how does one go about doing it? Once again, we find that most gurus of competitive tactics who preach the concept of attacking a competitor's weaknesses are wrong. We believe that a better approach is that held by General Patton:

> I have studied the enemy all my life. I have read the memoirs of his generals and his leaders. I have even read his philosophers and listened to his music. I have studied in detail the account of every damned one of his battles. I know exactly how he'll react under any given set of circumstances. And he hasn't the slightest idea what I'm going to do. So when the time comes, I'm going to whip the hell out of him.

The following are, in our view, a set of rules that will produce better results against your competition.

Rule 1: Control the Sandbox

The mark of a successful strategy is that it allows you to *control*, or at least *influence*, the terms of play in the competitive sandbox. If you are not controlling or at least influencing the conditions of play in the competitive arena you have proactively chosen, your strategy is not working! Change it quickly rather than suffer a long, painful death.

For the last 40 years, IBM has controlled the terms of play in the worldwide computer sandbox. Has Unisys? Has Honeywell? Has NEC? Has Fujitsu? Has Wang? Obviously not! Compaq and Sun are currently trying to *influence* the terms of play. They are not yet in control, but their recent actions indicate an attempt to influence or even change the terms of play. Will they succeed? Time will tell. The remainder are not even in the sandbox.

The PC sandbox is another poignant example. Which company is in total control of the PC hardware sandbox currently? Another way to phrase the question is: Which company makes the decision as to when the next, more powerful PC will be introduced? Not Compaq. Not

AST. Not Gateway. There is only one and one company alone that makes that decision. That company is Intel. While pursuing Andrew Grove's so-called paranoia strategy of "doubling the power of their microprocessors every 18 months, Intel has achieved the ultimate goal in strategy: total and complete control of the PC hardware sandbox.

Intel's control has even changed the rules of the so-called PC manufacturers, such as Compaq, AST, and Gateway. These companies are no longer manufacturers. They have become *distributors* of Intel chips. Intel decides when and where the next generation of PCs will be introduced, and they do so at a time and place that suits their goals and objectives, and no one else's. Every other company in the industry *reacts* to Intel's every move. Microsoft does the same thing on the software side.

AT&T used to control the telecommunications sandbox. Does it today? Does MCI? Probably not. Does U.S. Sprint? Definitely not. Does anybody? Probably not. Who will eventually? Time will tell. In the meantime, several players will make attempts to control the industry, and several will come and go before a new sandbox with clearly defined terms of play emerges.

If your strategy does not allow you to control or at least influence the terms of play in the competitive sandbox in which you have chosen to play, this is a clear signal that it's not working! Change it because it's a reactive strategy. Otherwise you will always be reacting to events created by other companies.

Rule 2: Identify Which Competitors Your Strategy Will Attract

Once your strategy has been developed, look around to see which organizations will be attracted to it. If your strategy represents a change from the one you pursued in the past, the competitors it will attract will *not* be the same as the previous ones. Once you understand your strategy, and the sandbox you will be in, new potential competitors can easily be identified.

Rule 3: Anticipate Each Potential Competitor's Future Strategy

The next step is to anticipate each competitor's driving force and business concept. At this point, some might say that this cannot be done because we do not sit in on our competitors' strategy sessions. However, the strategy of any company ends up translating itself into physical evidence, such as products, geographic markets, customers, buildings, technologies, facilities, people, skills, and so forth. By looking at the actions of a competitor in these areas, one can identify what has *driven* the competitor to do what it has done—in other words, identify what was the driving force behind that competitor's strategy. In the same manner, by looking at a competitor's current actions, announced actions, or anticipated actions, one can identify the strategic heartbeat of that competitor's business. This can be done for each competitor that you think your strategy will attract.

Rule 4: Draw Competitive Profiles

You can now anticipate where each competitor will put its emphasis and deemphasis in terms of products, users, and geographic markets; therefore, you can now draw "pictures" of what each competitor will look like from the pursuit of such a strategy. One misconception exists, however, about competitive behavior. Many people assume that all the competitors in one industry behave the same way. Not necessarily so. Usually, each competitor's strategic heartbeat is different, so each competitor will act differently under a similar set of circumstances. However, if you detect what is at the root of a competitor's strategy, you can anticipate the various behaviors and put into place a different set of actions to deal with each competitor. For example, although Toyota and Honda are both in the car industry, each will react very differently under a similar set of circumstances, because each is pursuing a strategy that has a different driving force at its root. Toyota wants to become "the world's largest car company," whereas Honda's driving force is its engine technology; it is in the car business only because of Mr. Honda's concept of producing "engines for the world."

Other examples are Kimberly-Clark and Procter & Gamble. Both companies are slugging it out in the diaper business with their Huggies and Pampers brands (Figure 9-1). Although they find themselves fierce competitors in this arena, each is there for a radically different reason. Kimberly-Clark is there because the driving force of its strategy is to optimize the *capacity* of its paper mills. And one arena where this can be done is in the diaper market. Procter & Gamble, on the other hand, has a strategy with a very different driving force at its root: "Meeting the household needs of *housewives*" (a user class–driven strategy) has been at the root of the company since its conception. It is in the diaper market because diapers represent one such need.

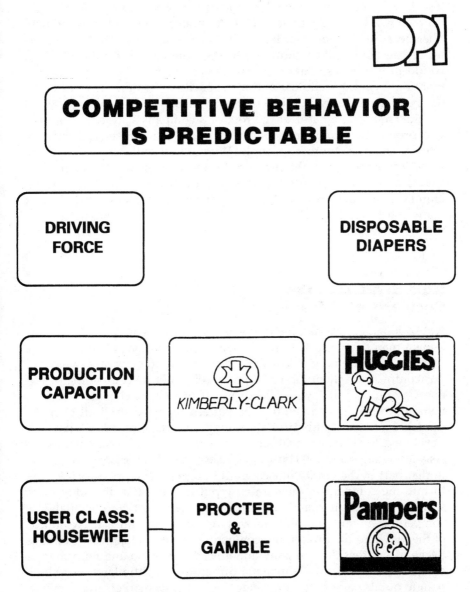

Figure 9-1. Understanding the root of a company's strategy can help predict behavior.

Under a similar set of circumstances, each of these companies will behave very differently. Let us suppose that a third company, such as DuPont, were to invent a synthetic fiber 20 times as absorbent as cellulose. How would Kimberly-Clark and Procter & Gamble behave?

Procter & Gamble would sell off its paper mills and buy the new fiber because it would not let go of its consumer and strategic heartbeat—the homemaker/mother. On the other hand, Kimberly-Clark would probably ease out of the business and seek other opportunities that might employ cellulose and the capacity of its mills. It would give up the homemaker rather than its paper mills.

Understanding what is at the root of a company's strategy can help you predict that company's behavior under a given set of variables. Honda, again, is another example. When faced with emission control standards imposed on the industry by the EPA in the 1970s, all other car companies responded with catalytic converters. Not Honda! Honda went back to work on what drives its business and what it knows best—engine technology—and it redesigned its engine to meet the EPA's standards without the need for a catalytic converter.

Rule 5: Manage the Competitor's Strategy

Not so long ago, we had the opportunity to work with one of the best-known manufacturers of buses. When we arrived, one competitor was identified as pursuing a "copycat" strategy. In other words, whatever bus contract our client bid on, a few weeks later its competitor would enter a similar but lower-priced bid. If our client chose not to bid, neither would the competitor. The pattern repeated itself all over the world. Once the competitor's strategy was recognized, a plan was developed to "manage" that strategy. A very large project emerged in Asia involving some 4000 buses. Because of a bad experience previously in that part of the world, our client did not want the project. However, to lure the competitor, the company put in a bid that included more services than required and at a price well below cost. Sure enough, the competitor submitted a bid and was awarded the contract. Two-thirds of the way into the project, the competitor ran into major cost overruns to the extent that the company announced it was looking for a merger partner to help it out of financial difficulties. A little later, our client bought out its competitor for a song, took over its market, and eliminated it from others. All actions were put into place *two years before!*

If one wants to identify a competitor's strategy, one needs to understand two elements about that competitor. These two elements are the competitor's driving force (strategic heartbeat) and the business concept that the competitor is practicing in that mode. Again, let us look at the car industry for examples (Figure 9-2).

Figure 9-2. A company's driving force and its business concept determine its strategy.

In the car industry, as noted before, several companies are pursuing a product concept–driven strategy. For example, Mercedes-Benz's concept of its product is the "best engineered car." This concept, articulated by Karl Benz some 110 years ago, has propelled this company ever since, resulting in uninterrupted profits year after year, in spite of what is happening in the automobile wars. This concept, therefore, determines how the car looks, whom it is sold to, how it is merchandised, how it is priced, and so on.

Then along comes Volkswagen, also a product concept–driven company—cars, more cars, and still more cars. However, Volkswagen's concept, as we all know, is slightly different from Mercedes'. As first articulated by Dr. Porsche, VWs are a "people's car." As such, Volkswagen goes down a slightly different road than Mercedes, starting with how the car looks, whom it is sold to, how it is priced, how it is merchandised, and so on.

Then along comes Volvo—again, a product concept–driven company. Its concept, "safe and durable" cars, is different still and is the concept articulated by the founders of the company, Gustaf Larson and Assar Gabrielsson, back in 1927. They believed that the most important thing a car maker could offer its customers was a safe trip. As a result, Volvo's product has a slightly different look, is sold to a slightly different customer, at slightly different prices, and so on. In other words, Volvo goes down yet another slightly different road.

Then along comes BMW, another product concept–driven company. Because of its slightly different business concept, the "ultimate driving machine," BMW's cars are sold on their performance capabilities.

Then comes General Motors. What is GM's business concept? In order to identify the business concept, it is sometimes necessary to go back into the company's history. In this instance, one has to start with Alfred Sloan, who articulated GM's concept in the 1920s as "a car for each income strata." The concept then stated: "As such, GM cars must look distinguishable one from the other" to justify a higher price as Americans migrated up the income scale and bought a higher-priced GM car.

Here is a good example of why it is important to understand the business concept of an enterprise. During the 1970s, GM was attacked by the Japanese. In response, GM management, faced with mounting losses of market share, took a quick look at Japanese car makers to determine what advantage they had and concluded that it was cheap labor—which resulted in a $1500 per car price advantage. GM said, "We must reduce our costs. Therefore, we must have all our cars go through the same manufacturing system. Therefore, what do we do with the design?" Right! We must make all of our cars' designs similar.

When GM went down the "look-alike" road in the mid-1970s, its management lost sight of GM's original business concept, which had contributed to its success through the years. Ford, on the other hand, had a "copycat GM" strategy from 1940 to 1975. Whatever models GM brought out, Ford would copy within a year or so. In the mid-1970s, however, when Ford executives saw GM go down the look-alike road, they finally said "Not this time. Then Ford—not GM—started making distinguishable-looking cars." In fact, Ford today is practicing GM's strategy. Ford, and lately even Chrysler, has inherited GM's strategy by default because GM management abandoned it by accident! And who has had more success against those same Japanese competitors? You're right! Ford and Chrysler...by billions of dollars. Which leads us to another conclusion about strategy: *The strategy of a business can change by accident when management loses sight of the underlying business concept of the enterprise.*

So far, the preceding examples are all related to companies that are pursuing a product concept–driven strategy. But, as you will have noted, each has a slightly different concept of its product that will lead the company to behave differently given the same circumstance.

Another error of the competitive gurus is preaching that all the competitors in a given industry behave in the same manner and, therefore, that the factors of success are the same for everybody. We have never found that to be true. Instead, our work indicates that although several competitors may share the same driving force, business concepts will be different enough for each company to behave in a slightly different manner given the same circumstance. *A competitor's behavior can be anticipated* if one understands the company's driving force and business concept and if one can manage that competitor's strategy to one's advantage.

To avoid another flaw in the competitor gurus' thinking, never accept that all competitors in a given industry have the same driving force. Here are two more examples.

Honda is in the car business. But what is Honda's driving force? As shown in the General Motors example offered earlier, identifying a competitor's business concept sometimes calls for one to look back into that company's history. On other occasions, however, one needs to look at what other product categories the competitor is into beyond those your division or company is competing with in the marketplace. Honda makes cars, but it also makes motorcycles, lawn mowers, and generators. What is common to all these products? *Engines.* And if one were to read *Memoirs,* written by the now-deceased Mr. Honda, one would find his business concept: "Engines for the world." Honda is only in the car business because cars require engines. If someone ever invented a car that did not require an engine, Honda would soon exit that business. This concept also explains Mr. Honda's refusal to follow the suggestion of Japan's MITI (Ministry of International Trade and Industry) in the 1960s not to enter the car business because Japan already had too many car manufacturers. Understanding the concept also helps one to understand Honda's behavior in the marketplace. It explains, for example, Honda's desire to enter Formula 1 racing—only the engine portion, mind you, not the body. One can then also explain Honda's behavior when faced with competitive threats.

In the 1970s, the EPA announced strict emission control standards for cars. What did all the product concept–driven companies do? Add a catalytic converter to the engine. Not Honda. Honda went back to its driving force—engine technology—and changed its engine to meet the new standards without the need for a catalytic converter. In 1991, Honda did it again. Threatened with a new set of standards in California in 1999, Honda has developed an engine that already meets those standards without the need for additional components. Rest assured that Honda will spread that technology across all of its other products quickly, thus leveraging its driving force and strategic heartbeat. To prove our point that competitive behavior is predictable, one could wonder where else Honda might apply its engine technology know-how. This author is prepared to predict Honda's eventual entry into aircraft engines. Watch out Rolls Royce and Pratt & Whitney!

A final example is Saab. Saab is also in the automobile business. But what is Saab's driving force and business concept? Again, in what other business is Saab? The answer—military aircraft. Saab's roots are based in this area and Saab's business concept, as articulated by its founder, is to prove to the consumer "what allied aircraft philosophy can do for your car driving." As a result, if a competitor attacked Saab, Saab would respond by putting a turbo engine in the back of the car, fins on the side of the car, and a cockpit in the driver's seat!

The thrust of all the preceding examples is simple:

- Each competitor within a given industry is there for a slightly different reason.

- To understand the competitor's strategy for being there, one needs to identify each competitor's driving force and business concept.

- Once that is understood, one can do things to manage the competitor's strategy to one's advantage.

Rule 6: Neutralize the Competitor's Strategy

A *proactive* strategy is one that allows you to control or influence the rules of play in the competitive sandbox. Some experts will tell you that the way to do this is to analyze each competitor's strengths and weaknesses and then to exploit those weaknesses. Time and again, while working in strategy sessions with successful CEOs, this did not usually hold much appeal. When asked why not, one CEO replied, "I'm not interested in spending *my* money to make any competitor stronger." When asked to clarify this statement, he went on to explain that attacking a competitor's weakness makes the competitor recognize this weakness and then do things to correct or eliminate it. You have awakened the competitor to that weakness, gained a competitive edge temporarily, but then given the competitor a long-term advantage. You now need to attack another weakness and the whole cycle starts over. If you carry this scenario to its logical but somewhat absurd end, eventually you will have strengthened your competitor so much that it might put you out of business.

Another school of management might propose that we identify that competitor's driving force and areas of excellence and then try to "out-excel" the competitor in the areas he is the very best at. As described in a previous chapter, this is called *imitation* strategy and *no significant shifts in market share occur by cloning the competitor's strategy.*

Compaq, for the last several years, has had a strategy of building PCs on the "Wintel" architecture—in other words, offering PCs that combine Intel chips with Microsoft Windows. Almost all of Compaq's competitors have come to imitate that strategy. Is any one of them gaining on Compaq? Absolutely not! In fact, Compaq is building more and more distance between itself and its competitors each year.

A better approach, in our view, is to go for the throat and attack that competitor's very reason for existence—its strategy. I call this the *Vince Lombardi school of management.* When Lombardi's football teams took to the field, the first six plays were directed not at the opponent's weaknesses, but at its strengths. Prior to each game, Lombardi analyzed his opponent and identified the best four players on its defense. His offensive plan was then directed at these four players—the heartbeat of the opponent's defense. The rationale was simple. If his team broke through in those first few plays, the game was over! By attacking a competitor's weaknesses, the game gets played between the 40-yard lines. Up 10 yards, back 10 yards. If one wants to get to the end zone to score, one needs to attack at the heart of the opponent's defense. The same is true in business. Attacking a competitor's weaknesses only leads to marginal changes in market position. Significant gains can only be made by attacking the heartbeat of that competitor's strategy.

Once you have identified your competitor's future driving force and translated it into a profile of products, markets, and customers resulting from that strategy, you need to identify the areas of excellence that each competitor is cultivating to support that strategy. These will be different from one competitor to another because each company is probably pursuing a different strategy. Once this has been done, you are ready to proceed to determining which sandbox you want to play in.

Managing a competitor's strategy and controlling the sandbox can only be achieved by attacking the driving force of the competitor's strategy and accompanying areas of excellence. Remember that an area of excellence is a describable skill or capability that a company deliberately cultivates over time, to a degree of proficiency not only higher than anything else *it* does but, more importantly, better than anything its *competitor* does. It is this higher degree of competence in a couple of key strategic skills that keeps the company's strategic heartbeat strong and healthy and gives it an edge against its competitors. Areas of excellence are to the strategy of a business what clean arteries are to the human heart. When the arteries get clogged, the heart stops beating. When one's strategic skills diminish, the strategy loses its strength and, thus, its edge against its competitors.

The strategy of any company is supported by the development of expertise or skills in a couple of strategic areas, and it is these areas of excellence that make that company's strategy work. Therefore, the same concept applies in reverse. If you want to weaken a competitor's strategy, attack that competitor's areas of excellence. Diluting, diminishing, or neutralizing those areas of excellence are the best ways to obtain a significant advantage and control or influence the sandbox. You attack the heart and guts of the business. You attack the strategic heartbeat and key strategic skills of that competitor. You go for the throat. There is no such thing as genteel competition. The Japanese, for example, attacked at the heart of American automobile companies' businesses—they made better cars!

When MCI decided that it needed to be more aggressive at AT&T's expense, it chose not to exploit AT&T's weaknesses, but to attack AT&T's heartbeat. "MCI is starting to hurt AT&T where it hurts the most: the Big Business customer" reported *Time* magazine. "MCI is determined to steal the giant's bread and butter accounts." MCI went after AT&T's largest account—Merrill Lynch—and won. Next on MCI's hit list: Chrysler, United Airlines, Westinghouse, and Procter & Gamble.

Rule 7: Choose Your Competitors; Do Not Let Your Competitors Choose You

To be proactive, each company must consciously choose in which competitive arena, or sandbox, it wants to be. The first step is to delimit the sandbox. You can make the sandbox as large or as small as you want. It's your choice. IBM has chosen to compete in all corners of the computer sandbox, from laptops to mainframes. Compaq, on the other hand, originally decided to limit the size of its sandbox to PCs (Figure

9-3). In fact, it even decided to divide this sandbox even further into home PCs and business PCs and to deliberately avoid the home PC market because of its volatility. Only in 1997 did Compaq decide to expand its sandbox to include the home PC market with the introduction of its $995 model.

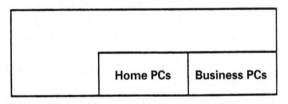

The IBM Sandbox

Mainframes	Micros	Minis
Laptops	PCs	Software

The Compaq Sandbox

	Home PCs	Business PCs

Figure 9-3.

Once you have delimited the sandbox you wish to play in, you need to ask: Who do we invite into the sandbox to have a good time with?

All successful CEOs we have worked with have always been careful not to be drawn into competitive arenas by mistake. In order to control the sandbox and the terms of play, two decisions must be made. The first is to decide which competitor to invite into the sandbox. Against this competitor, you now want to devise "offensive" tactics because you are confident that you can attack that competitor's strategic heartbeat and areas of excellence. We will discuss how to do this in Chapter 10. The second class of competitors to include in your sandbox are those that are in a position to attack your areas of excellence. You'll want to monitor these competitors very carefully because they could give your strategy difficulty. The rest of the competitors are probably not in a position to do much damage. If you don't disturb them, they probably will not disturb you. If any attack you, they will probably attack your weaknesses and only make you better.

In our view, one should practice the concept we call *single-target* competition. In other words, go after *one* competitor at a time. We all know what happens to someone who starts a war on two fronts! Again, the Japanese are masters of single-target competition.

Toyota, since its inception, has had only one competitor in its sight— General Motors. Toyota's stated strategy is to outsell GM worldwide and, eventually, in the United States. Komatsu has had only one competitor in its sight for over 30 years. Not Deere, not Fiat, not Volvo— but Caterpillar. Komatsu's strategic war cry is "Eat the Cat." At Honda, the war cry is "Beat Benz," not in terms of the number of cars sold, but in terms of the quality of cars built. And for the last three years, Honda has achieved its goal.

Subaru recently targeted Volvo. For many years, Volvo's strategy has been to build "safe and durable" cars, and for the last 30 years Volvo has been showing us pictures of its cars crashing into walls and the passengers walking away uninjured. Subaru has recently started an advertising campaign that, at the top of the page, shows the Volvo car crashed into the wall and, at the bottom of the page, a Subaru car stopped one yard away from the wall. The caption: "If you want to be in an accident, buy a Volvo. If you want to prevent an accident, buy a Subaru." Subaru has targeted Volvo and has decided not to attack Volvo's weaknesses, but rather the very heartbeat of its strategy. And Subaru has come up with a very ingenious way to do this. In just six months, Subaru started to make significant gains at Volvo's expense.

Changing the Rules of Play

Our experience with corporations has made us firm believers in General Patton's approach to competition. In fact, the concept is even older than General Patton. General Sun Tzu wrote in the fourth century that "what is of supreme importance in war is to attack the enemy's strategy." And the best way to neutralize a competitor's strategic heartbeat, in our view, is to *change the rules of play*.

Pulte Corporation

PULTE

Changing the Rules in a Chaotic Sandbox

Bob Burgess
Chief Executive Officer

Homebuilding, like many other industries, is in a state of transition. Large builders are being challenged to manage their companies as businesses rather than a loosely connected series of deals and transactions. Homebuilding executives are being asked to manage all aspects of their business more effectively and to become skilled in areas such as consumer marketing and shareholder returns, which previously were reserved to more traditional corporate environments.

Pulte Corporation, one of the nation's largest builders, is aggressively embracing this transition in management focus. Its success in large part is based on developing a strategic vision that can be communicated to all company employees as well as the outside world.

When Bob Burgess became CEO of Pulte a few years ago, he believed that the direction of the company was somewhat vague and confusing to both management and the investment community. "We were operating a number of unrelated businesses with over 70 percent of our profits derived from noncore homebuilding businesses," he says. "Although we were one of the largest builders, I don't believe

Wall Street or our employees truly understood what direction we were trying to achieve."

In order to bring needed focus to the business and improve the efficiency of its operations, Pulte's senior executives decided to try the *strategic thinking process*. The process, facilitated by the author, has enabled Pulte's management team to establish and build upon a new strategy based on the company's core homebuilding strengths.

"We brought our corporate and field management teams together to candidly assess our strengths and areas of competitive advantage," recalls Burgess. "We wanted the best input and complete buy-in from our entire senior management team." The *strategic thinking process* enabled all levels of management to develop a common understanding of the future direction of the company. Pulte's new strategy calls for a clear emphasis on its homebuilding strengths and a goal to become the best production homebuilder and supplier of related services such as mortgages and building supplies.

Based upon the results of the *strategic thinking process,* a new long-term business plan was developed, called *Plan 2000.* This plan clearly defined the company's operational, organizational, and financial goals for the next five years. After deciding on the company's strategic direction, management evaluated all existing businesses under the Pulte umbrella to determine their compatibility with the corporate direction. "It was obvious that many of our financial services operations did not fit our new strategic profile," says Burgess. Management then implemented a plan to divest these nonconforming businesses in an orderly fashion.

The underlying purpose of Plan 2000 was to ensure a leadership position for Pulte in all aspects of the homebuilding business. "At a critical step in our strategic discussions," says Burgess, "the process allowed us to confront ourselves with the realization that an 'industry leader' is a company that is able to change, control or substantially influence the 'rules of play' in the 'sandbox' in which it chooses to play. Pulte's Plan 2000 is designed to change many of the traditional rules of the homebuilding marketplace."

The *strategic thinking process* also forced Pulte's management team to identify and overcome significant barriers and obstacles to its aggressive growth plans. Prime among these concerns was the industry history of builders who had lost control of their businesses in the midst of major growth efforts. "To heed this historical warning and to stay attuned to local market needs," Burgess states, "Pulte reorganized its building company into four distinct operating companies, each with the core competencies, authority, and responsibility to operate effectively in its respective area of the country. As we approached $2 billion in sales, it was very evident we had to drive the decision-making process much closer to the customer. Our new organization accomplishes this and better positions us to achieve our goal of doubling the size of the company by the year 2000."

Pulte has also embarked upon an ambitious continuous quality improvement process called *Pulte Quality Leadership*, or PQL. Recently, Pulte has expanded its PQL process—originally an internal quality process—to include partnering efforts with many of its suppliers and subcontractors. This enhanced PQL process has earned Pulte the 1995 Quality Builder of the Year award from the National Association of Home Builders and, more importantly, has significantly improved customer satisfaction ratings. Burgess considers PQL and the resulting ability to truly "delight" Pulte's customers to be prime examples of changing the rules of the homebuilding "sandbox." This ongoing commitment to quality has also generated attractive dividends for Pulte's employees and shareholders. Over the past four years, operating profits have increased 200 percent.

DPI's *strategic thinking process* not only helped Pulte focus on growing its traditional homebuilding markets profitably, but also challenged the company to seriously examine new market niches and related businesses. The demographics of an aging U.S. population led Pulte to expand its housing products to meet the needs of the rapidly growing active adult and empty-nester market segments. They are buyers who are seeking a lifestyle centered on a secure community with little or no maintenance responsibilities. Another new market niche utilizes manufactured housing products in subdivision or community settings. Manufactured homes can be produced at lower costs, while achieving the quality and design characteristics of site-built housing. "By utilizing manufactured housing, we can provide an affordable product, maximizing the existing strengths of the Pulte organization and creating a true competitive advantage," says Burgess. Pulte is also studying various opportunities to leverage its homebuilding expertise internationally, a strategy that should bear fruit for Plan 2000 and beyond.

Pulte's strategic thinking sessions also identified opportunities to expand its home mortgage and building supply companies, both of which are strategically related to and supportive of its core homebuilding business. These expansion opportunities leverage off Pulte's strengths and at the same time strengthen Pulte's homebuilding capabilities. As Burgess pointed out, "Our Builders' Supply & Lumber Company executives truly understand the needs of the production builder. Their business, like homebuilding, is based upon excellent customer service and a real understanding of what it takes to make a builder more efficient. They are builders first and distributors second, and that expertise at Builder's Supply truly changes the rules of play."

Burgess credits Mike Robert's assistance in formulating coherent goals and directions for Pulte, adding: "Mike channeled our discussion toward a single focus for the company. While we started out with a multitude of approaches and ideas, we ended up very strongly in agreement." Burgess cautions, however, that "the initial three-day *strategic-thinking* work session is only the tip of the iceberg. The real benefit of going through the process is what happens in the weeks and months that follow. It has caused us to raise the level of our strategic thinking both in the field and at the corporate office."

Another residual benefit of Pulte's *strategic thinking process* was the creation of a "template" which enables the company to filter and access new business opportunities. "The emphasis in this portion of the process is as much on what you *shouldn't* spend your time on, as on what you *should* be doing," Burgess explains. "We have a very lean management team for a $2 billion company, and we can't afford to spend time on opportunities that don't clearly meet our strategic objectives. You can easily wander into many vertically integrated businesses which may be seductive but don't serve your core direction. With our strategic template, we're now able to eliminate almost immediately those opportunities which don't fit."

The results of Pulte's strategic-thinking efforts speak for themselves. "There's no doubt that we are now much more focused on long-term growth in shareholder value," Burgess says. "The entire organization is directing its attention on what it will take to reach the goal line." Pulte is clearly becoming the homebuilding industry leader and is playing an increasing role in the way the housing game will be played in the future.

10
Strategy Deployment

"It's easy to develop a strategy, it's the *implementation* that's difficult." This is a statement we have frequently heard over the years. Our own experience shows that the *formulation* of a strategy is as difficult as its implementation. However, many CEOs have difficulty getting people to implement their strategy for several reasons.

Why CEOs Have Difficulty Implementing Their Strategy

The Strategy Is Implicit and Not Explicit

In too many organizations, the strategy of the company is implicit and resides solely in the head of the chief executive. Most chief executives have a strategy. However, they have great difficulty articulating it to the people around them.

One senior executive of a *Fortune* 500 company once said to us, "The reason I have difficulty implementing my CEO's strategy is because I don't know what it is!"

> Lesson No. 1: People cannot implement what they don't know.

Because CEOs have difficulty verbalizing their strategy, most people are placed in the position of having to "guess" what the strategy is, and

161

they may guess wrong. Or else, they learn what the strategy is over time by the nature of the decisions they recommend which are either accepted or rejected. Gradually, a subordinate learns where the line of demarcation is between the things that are permitted by the strategy and those that are not. This is called *strategy by groping* because the strategy becomes clear or explicit only over a long period of time, during which people may have spent too much time pursuing and implementing activities that did not fit while not paying enough attention to opportunities that represented a better strategic fit.

The Strategy Is Developed in Isolation

A second reason the strategy may not be implemented properly is that it was developed by the CEO in isolation. Many CEOs have a strategy, but their key people are not involved in the *process* and therefore have no ownership. In such a case, subordinates usually do not understand the rationale behind the strategy and will spend more time questioning it than implementing it. The CEO becomes more and more impatient as subordinates question his logic more and more often. The CEO, on the other hand, can't comprehend why his people are not executing what, to him, is a simple strategy.

> Lesson No. 2: People don't implement properly what they don't understand!

Some CEOs might involve one or two people in the formulation of the strategy. This is better than doing it alone but is still not good enough. The *entire* management team must be involved in order to achieve accurate understanding and proper execution.

As Dale Lang, chairman of *Working Woman* magazine, noted as a reason for using our strategic process: "I could have dictated to the staff what I wanted to do, but it's a whole lot better if they reach the conclusion themselves. In that way, they're working their plan and know how and why they chose it."

The Strategy Is Developed by an Outside Consultant

The worst of all strategic crimes and the "kiss of death" for any strategy—even a good one—is to have an outside consultant develop your strategy. No outside consultant has the right to set the direction of your organization or knows as much as your own people about the business and the environment it is facing. Most strategies developed by outside consultants end up in the wastepaper basket for two reasons:

1. Everyone can quickly tear the conclusions apart because they are not based on an intimate knowledge of the company, the business, or the industry.
2. There is no commitment to that strategy by senior management because it is not *their* strategy.

Experience has shown that almost any strategy will work, unless it is completely invalidated by negative environmental factors. Experience has also shown, however, that no strategy will work if a couple or a few members of senior management are not committed to that strategy. In effect, if total commitment is not present, those uncommitted to the strategy will, on a day-to-day basis, do everything in their power to prove it wrong.

> Lesson No. 3: People don't implement what they are not committed to.

In order to obtain commitment, key managers must be involved at each step of the process so that their views are heard and discussed. Participation, although sometimes time-consuming, builds commitment. Key managers buy into the strategy because they helped construct it. It is as much their strategy as the CEO's.

Many CEOs have used our process knowing the outcome in advance. They did so anyway, using it as a tool to tap the advice and knowledge of their people and to obtain commitment to the conclusion, so that implementation of the strategy can then proceed expeditiously. The Japanese call this *nima washi*—bottom-up commitment.

Operational People Are Not Good Strategic Thinkers

Because most people spend their entire careers with an organization dealing exclusively with operational issues, they are not good strategic thinkers. With few exceptions, we have found that only the CEO or the general manager sees the "big picture" and views the business and its environment in strategic terms. There usually is only one strategist in any organization and that is the CEO. Most managers are so engrossed in operational activity that they have not developed the skill of thinking *strategically.* Therefore, they have difficulty coping with strategic issues, especially if these are sprung on them out-of-the-blue. "The problem," says Milton Lauenstein in an article in the *Journal of Business Strategy,* "is that many executives have only the fuzziest notion of the functions of strategy formulation."

Lesson No. 4: The CEO may encourage the participation of key subordinates in the strategic process for strictly educational value.

People will implement a strategy more effectively if they understand the difference between a strategic process and either long-range or operational planning together with the difference between strategic and operational issues.

The fact that *two-thirds* of the companies on *Fortune's* original 1955 list are no longer on it only 42 years later, and that *one-third* of those on the list in 1980 are also no longer there only 17 years later, says a lot about the *strategic thinking* ability of American executives. And all this has occurred during the emergence of so-called *strategic planning* systems that have enamored business executives for the last 20 years!

The Critical Issues Are Not Identified

One aspect of strategy is its formulation, another is thinking through its implications. Most strategic planning systems we have seen used in organizations don't encourage people to think through the implications of their strategy. As a result, they end up reacting to these events as they are encountered and many people start losing faith in the strategy. "There were so many holes in the CEO's strategy, I gave up trying to implement it," is how a senior vice president of a major organization put it. Every strategy, especially if it represents a change of direction, has implications.

Lesson No. 5: People give up on a strategy whose implications have not been anticipated.

A good strategic process should help management identify and practically manage the implications of a strategy on the company's products, markets, customers, organization structure, personnel, and culture.

Identification of Critical Issues

Critical issues are the bridge between the current profile and the future strategic profile of an organization that management has deliberately decided to pursue (Figure 10-1). The direction of the organization has

Figure 10-1. Critical issues are the bridge to the strategic profile of the future.

been decided, and managing that direction begins. Managing that direction on an ongoing basis means management of the critical issues which stem from four key areas—structure, systems/processes, skills/competencies, and compensation (Figure 10-2).

Structure

There was a fad in the 1970s and 1980s to reorganize and restructure companies. After the reorganization, the difficult question to answer became: "Now that we are reorganized, where are we going?"

In our view, structure follows strategy. The organization structure of the business must support of the direction of that business. We have further learned that each driving force requires a slightly different organization structure. A product concept–driven company (Figure 10-3) does not organize like a customer class–driven company (Figure 10-4).

A technology-driven company organizes around groupings of similar applications (Figure 10-5).

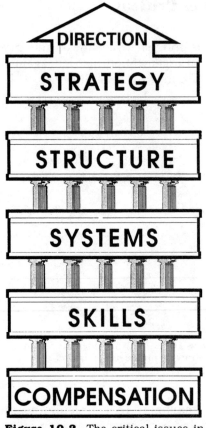

Figure 10-2. The critical issues in the strategy stem from the company's structure, systems/ processes, skills/ competencies, and compensation.

A return/profit-driven company's organization (Figure 10-6) is dramatically different from all the others. Each driving force brings with it a different organization structure.

Processes/Systems

The next discussion that leads to critical issues is one that revolves around the subject of "systems." Many companies today have purchased sophisticated and costly electronic information systems only to find out some time later that the systems are not supportive of the company's business strategy. Again, our view is that all information systems must be aligned with the direction of the organization and

PRODUCT / SERVICE-DRIVEN ORGANIZATION

SIMILAR PRODUCTS   SIMILAR PRODUCTS   SIMILAR PRODUCTS

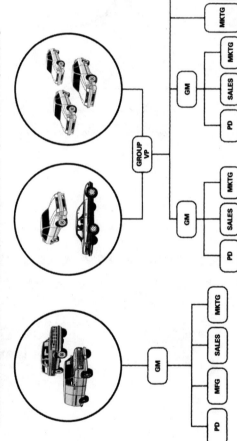

Figure 10.3

USER / MARKET CLASS DRIVEN ORGANIZATION

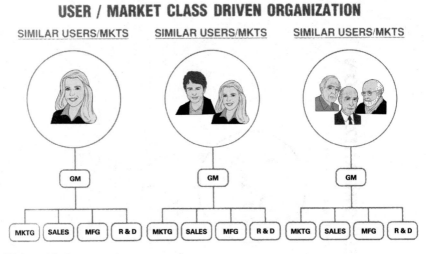

SIMILAR USERS/MKTS   SIMILAR USERS/MKTS   SIMILAR USERS/MKTS

GM   GM   GM

| MKTG | SALES | MFG | R & D | MKTG | SALES | MFG | R & D | MKTG | SALES | MFG | R & D |

Figure 10-4.

TECHNOLOGY-DRIVEN ORGANIZATION

SIMILAR APPLICATIONS   SIMILAR APPLICATIONS

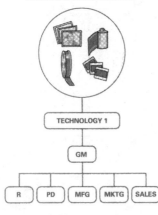   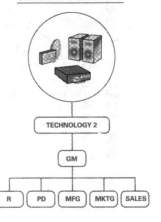

TECHNOLOGY 1   TECHNOLOGY 2

GM   GM

| R | PD | MFG | MKTG | SALES | | R | PD | MFG | MKTG | SALES |

Figure 10-5.

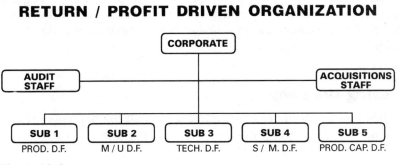

Figure 10-6.

that there are usually critical issues that surface in this area of systems or processes.

Skills/Competencies

When an organization changes its direction, this change will usually require the acquisition of a new set of skills. These can be developed, but frequently they do not reside in-house and must be acquired, thus giving rise to another set of critical issues.

Compensation

In spite of all the titles or power you might think you have over people, my experience has convinced me that people do not do what you want them to do; people do what they are paid to do. If your strategy says that you want your people to behave in a certain manner, but your compensation system rewards them to do something different, I can bet most anything that at the end of the year they will have done what they were paid to do and not what you wanted them to do.

As a result, another area of discussion that raises critical issues is one around the subject of compensation, to identify what changes need to be made to ensure that the compensation of key individuals is geared to support the strategy and direction of the business.

Around these four areas—structure, systems, skills, and compensation—a number of critical issues are identified and assigned to specific individuals for resolution. The results expected are articulated, the macro action steps are listed, other people that need to be involved are assigned to each team, and completion and review dates are established. These critical issues then become "the plan" for the organization, and it is the ongoing management and resolution of these issues that makes the CEO's vision a reality over time. It is how the strategy is deployed successfully.

Closing the Loop

At this point, you might be wondering how all the concepts presented tie together. Figure 10-7 attempts to link everything discussed previously into a cohesive whole.

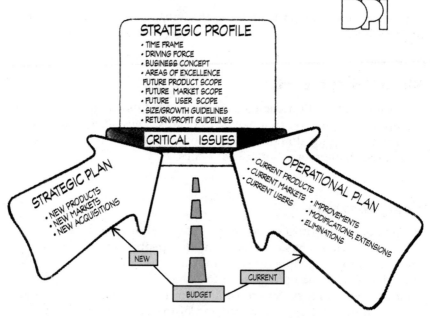

Figure 10-7.

The rectangle at the top of the graphic represents the output of our *strategic thinking process.* The strategic profile is a description of what an organization wants to look like at some point in the future. The inside of the rectangle contains the content of this picture. The critical issues are the bridge that needs to be crossed in order to go from what the company looks like today to what it wants to look like tomorrow. Now comes planning time.

The Operational Plan

At this point in the process, one needs to examine the organization's current activities and decide which products, customers, and markets need to be improved or modified. Moreover, one must identify those that need to be eliminated because they no longer fit the vision of what the company is trying to become.

One of the most difficult decisions we find management having to make is not what to do but rather what not to do anymore. This is because there is always someone telling management to "hang in" a little longer—that the corner is about to come but, in fact, it never does. During the operational planning stage, these decisions become easier to make, because all participants have agreed that those activities no longer fit the aspiration of the type of company they are trying to build.

The Strategic Plan

In our view, a strategic plan is one that will alter the "look" of an organization in the future. The key elements that will alter the "look" of a company in the future are the new products, new customers, and new markets that the company wants to add to that look. A plan now needs to be constructed to make these happen.

Our experience shows that if you want to give birth to brand-new activities (products, markets, acquisitions), it is wise to have people other than those who are running your current businesses midwife these projects. The rationale is simple: Those running your current businesses have a locomotive on their hands, and keeping that engine on track will require all their time and energy. As such, it is wise to have new activities managed outside the normal structure of the current business.

The Strategic Profile Is the Target for all Decisions

As Figure 10-7 clearly illustrates, the strategic profile becomes the target for all the decisions that are made in the organization. Plans and decisions that fit inside the frame of the profile are pursued, and those that do not fit are not.

Tools to Allocate Resources

The last piece in this jigsaw is the budget. And, again, the strategic profile is the anchor for these budgeting decisions. Management must now ensure that resources are allocated to all plans in order to guarantee their viability.

The Role of the CEO as Process Owner

There is only one person in any organization who can "drive" the strategic thinking process and that is the chief executive of the organization. *Strategic thinking must start at the top of the organization.* Strategic thinking is definitively a "trickle down" process and not a "bubble up" one. It is a very interactive process, but the CEO must be its owner. As such, the CEO must show commitment to the process by participating in all of its steps.

Because the process is highly interactive, it is not for the faint of heart. The process invites discussion, debate, and constructive provocation. Everyone, during the process, has the opportunity to express his or her views, have these challenged, and then challenge those of others. As a result, the process is ideal for CEOs who encourage frank, open discussion of issues and challenges. CEOs who are not comfortable with this type of management style should not use our approach.

The *strategic thinking process* leads to better implementation of the strategy. In our experience, there are only two ways to implement one's strategy—by compliance or by commitment.

Compliance is having the CEO tell his or her subordinates what the strategy is and how it is expected to be executed. The CEO then farms out different tasks to each subordinate. They, in turn, implement without questioning its rationale. In this world of increasing complexity, we have found that this approach is having less and less appeal.

The second, and more effective, method is through *commitment,* which comes through active participation in developing the rationale behind the strategy. As a result, we recommend that all key stakeholders be involved in each step of the process.

One role that the CEO should not attempt to play is that of process facilitator. One cannot have a foot in the process and another foot in the content. Attempting to guide the process while participating in the debate will give everyone the impression that the CEO is trying to manipulate the process to a predetermined conclusion. Therefore, it is wise to have an outside third party guide the process along.

The Role of the Process Facilitator

Many CEOs have attempted to use our process by playing the role of owner and facilitator, only to call us quickly after their first meeting. Each would then recite to us the difficulties mentioned in the previous paragraph.

Whenever a client hires us to assist in the strategy effort of the company, he or she wants to take several hours to indoctrinate us in the details of the business. After a few minutes, I diplomatically ask the client to stop. It is not an advantage to know the client's business in depth. In fact, it is a disadvantage. I tell my clients that getting to know their business too well might make us lose our objectivity because we might start to empathize with their problems. There are several pragmatic roles that a trained third-party facilitator can play.

First, a few thoughts on the word *facilitator*. Facilitators are not moderators. A moderator is a person who directs traffic as best as he or she can during a meeting, but without the use of any specific process. A process facilitator has a very different role. This is a person who comes to the meeting with a structured process together with specific instruments that keep the discussion moving forward in a constructive manner. The facilitator also keeps the process honest, balanced, and objective. The CEO of a *Fortune* 10 company used to say to this author: "You know Mike, you're the only one in this room who can tell me to sit down and I do. Nobody else in this room would dare say that!"

The question of using external or internal resources as facilitators of the process is an important one and usually comes up in all large companies with whom we work.

The Results

We have noticed a variety of results from the use of the *strategic thinking process,* and we make a point of asking each of our clients what value they received. Without exception, six items are always mentioned: clarity, focus, consensus, cohesion, commitment, and filter.

Clarity

Although not every client changes its direction as a result of this exercise, all clients have said that the process brought clarity to their strategic thinking. As a group, the management team starts the process with slightly different perceptions of the company's strategy or, in some instances, with a nonarticulated and somewhat fuzzy strategy. At the end of the exercise, however, the team has produced a crystal-clear strategic profile. Each member of the management team now shares a single vision of the organization's future.

The profile can also be used to bring clarity to other people in the organization. Some of our clients have published all or parts of the strategic profile to communicate the company's strategy to various interested groups—for example, in annual reports to inform shareholders of the company's direction. Others have used it as a discussion piece in internal forums with employees. Corporate beliefs usually get published extensively. As the driving force is the heart of strategic thinking, corporate beliefs are its soul.

Focus

Focus is another output of the process. The strategic profile produces a better tool to allocate resources and to manage the time and efforts of others. It enables managers to direct their efforts toward activities that complement the desired direction of the company and to avoid wasted efforts on nonrelated issues.

When we asked the chief executive of Alcan why the metal tent card with the inscription "Our product is aluminum" faces the visitor in his office, he replied, "I don't want any of our people talking to me about any other subject than aluminum." The metal used for the tent card is, of course, aluminum.

Consensus

The process brings about consensus at each step. The debates and discussions are conducted in such a manner that agreement is achieved systematically on each key issue before moving on to the next one. The assignments worked on during the work session are designed to place on the table all the key questions about the future of the organization. These instruments bring forward everyone's best thinking and provide an opportunity for each person to present his or her views, opinions, and rationale on every important issue. We have found that it is not sufficient to collect a person's perceptions only through a survey. A person also needs an opportunity to explain and elaborate his or her point of view.

A group vice president said of his superior, the sector vice president, at the end of one of our work sessions: "I have worked with this man for over 20 years, yet I found out more about his views on our business in the last three days." This feeling has been expressed in many of the strategy sessions with which we have been involved.

Because the process provides a forum to discuss issues in an orderly manner, there is never a dissenting voice at the end of the work session. This unquestionably contributes to a more harmonious organization.

Cohesion

"Hockey stick planning," one executive told us, "leads to hockey puck management." Without a clear strategic profile, the organization bounces from one seemingly good idea to another. It zigzags its way forward and expends valuable time, money, and effort leapfrogging from one suspicious opportunity to another. When there is no clear direction accompanied by a solid test bed to screen opportunities, management can often be seduced by the financial aspects of an opportunity, only to discover later that there is no fit with the rest of the organization's activities. The strategic profile becomes the bedrock or cornerstone of their actions and, when used in such a manner, results in a synchronization of resources instead of dispersion and fragmentation. Less time will be wasted exploring undesired options and fewer effort will be expended justifying the existence of the "sunset" portions of the business.

Commitment

At the end of the process there is absolute commitment from all management team members to the new direction. The reason is simple: It is their strategy. They participated at every step. All their views were heard and their inputs considered. This commitment sometimes comes from surprising quarters. The vice president of a division of a complex multinational, whose unit was going to be deemphasized in the future, said to us, "I recognize the fact that we're not going to be getting the same resources as in the past, but I'm totally committed to that decision. I now understand why those funds need to be given to other parts of the business." This is an important achievement. Every organization must discriminate between its various units when allocating resources, and it is important that the managers of the less fortunate units understand the reasons. These units still need to be managed well even though they may not be the "stars" of the future. In this instance, our process served as a unifying force within the organization.

"For any strategy to succeed, you need operating people to understand it, embrace it, and make it happen." says Roger Schipke, former senior vice president of General Electric. We couldn't agree more.

Filter

Probably the best use of the strategic profile is as a filter for the operational plans and new product or market opportunities. As an operational filter, the strategic profile can reduce and even eliminate "hockey puck" management. It clearly identifies the areas of more emphasis and less emphasis in the future. This knowledge should be "etched" on the brain of every key manager and used as a "working sieve to guide their daily operational decisions and actions," as a general manager of a client organization described the use he wanted his subordinates to make of this tool.

More important, the strategic profile is an excellent way to ferret out good from less promising products or market opportunities. When these opportunities present themselves, the answers to a few questions can quickly test their fit with the organization's strategic profile and direction.

- Does this opportunity complement or violate the driving force and business concept?

- Does this opportunity bring products that fit those that will receive more emphasis or less emphasis in the future?

- Does this opportunity bring markets that fit those that will receive more emphasis or less emphasis in the future?

- Does the opportunity bring users that fit those that will receive more emphasis or less emphasis in the future?

- Does this opportunity bring products, markets, and users that can be supported by the present areas of excellence? Or will it require excellence in areas beyond our current capabilities?

- Does this opportunity meet the size/growth, return/profit guidelines?

This quick test can help an organization in two ways.

1. If you receive negative responses to each of these questions, beware—it may be a good financial opportunity, but there may not be an appropriate fit with what you are currently doing. Experience has shown that there needs to be more reason than money to exploit an opportunity. In our view, those other reasons are a fit with the driving force, business concept, areas of excellence, and product's market/user scopes.

2. If there is no apparent fit but you still want to pursue the opportunity, it might be better to do so under some other form of organiza-

tion structure. Your present structure does not support the type of opportunity being considered. Another form might.

The value that a strategic thinking process brings to a company is hard to measure in tangible terms. We have been involved with clients that have made important strategic decisions during the work session which involved substantial sums of money and which had enormous impact on the company. The intangible rewards are much more discrete but probably have as much of an impact. These seem to be of as much value to clients as the more tangible ones.

The process of strategic thinking described in this book has been developed and refined while working with client organizations. It is not a theoretical approach to the subject; it is tested methodology, currently being used by a number of corporations. It places, in logical order, the various elements that management needs to consider in order to conduct its strategic thinking in a timely, efficient manner. It assembles and collects management's impressions and opinions about the environment in order to conceptualize or synthesize a collective vision to deal with that environment.

American Saw & Manufacturing Co.

Strategy on the Cutting Edge

John Davis
Chief Executive Officer

American Saw & Manufacturing Company, not surprisingly, makes saw blades. But not your ordinary garden-variety hand saws. American Saw's products are sophisticated cutting tools made using proprietary manufacturing technology and marketed to professional users. American Saw's Lenox brand blades are known for high quality in 55 countries around the world.

Under its third-generation family management, the company currently employs over 700 people.

"We make band saw blades for the metal cutting industry, as well as hacksaw, jigsaw and reciprocating saw blades for the professional tradesman," explains John Davis, American Saw's CEO. "We're similar to Gillette. We don't make the tools; just the blades. We sell to two separate markets: industrial users of band saws, and tradesmen like carpenters, plumbers and electricians who use our blades on power tools."

Business has been brisk for the past few years with record earnings. Yet Davis and his management team were convinced they could still improve performance dramatically.

"We got to a point where we wanted to expand. In fact, our goal was to double sales." recalls Davis, "and the question was 'How do we do it efficiently, and most important, profitably?' That's when I began to think about developing a strategy. I heard Mike Robert speaking about the *strategic thinking process* at a Young President's Organization meeting and the concept made sense to me. It's logical, and compatible with our basic business philosophies."

Armed with the book *Strategy Pure and Simple* the management team began to work on the *strategic thinking process* themselves.

"In the beginning we were skeptical of any consultant coming in. We tried doing the process ourselves and got frustrated with our progress, so we called in Mike Robert to facilitate. Mike brought a lot of structure to conversations we'd been having, and a lot of debates were brought to a conclusion.

"The facilitator probes out ideas and thoughts. Ordinarily, someone may have a good idea, but because of accepted paradigms, the person won't express it. This process gets everyone to think outside those limitations."

One of the fundamental issues the *strategic thinking process* helps to resolve is identifying the company's driving force—the one element of the business that is at the core of its success. The process identifies 10 possible driving forces. Each implies a set of *areas of excellence* that must be cultivated and given resource priority to support that particular type of strategy.

American Saw arrived at three driving forces as possibilities, and discussions around the issue helped to clarify the company's strategic options.

"It's difficult to decide on a driving force," says Davis, "because every company has all or most of these forces at work. It's a matter of deciding which one dominates. We got it down to product, technology, or market category. We, of course, make saws. And we have very good technology at the base of our company. And we serve our customers very well. But what it all boiled down to was that our product is our driving force."

The selection of a driving force is a pivotal point in the process. By playing out the implications of each possible driving force, the management team was able to visualize what the company would look like down the road under various scenarios. By pursuing its product-driven strategy, for example, the company would continue to develop, manufacture, and market saw blades. In a market category—driven mode, American Saw would begin to supply other needs of the markets it serves, diversifying beyond saw blades. To follow the technology track, the company's unique technology would be leveraged into new types of products and markets.

All three represent possible avenues for growth. But, in the end, American Saw management agreed that making and selling saw blades is the best course. Growth would come from making changes in its business approach to increase sales.

One of the initiatives created to accomplish this goal was an increased emphasis on product research and development. This, it became clear, was critical to the success of its product-driven strategy and would assure American Saw's leadership in product quality and performance.

Another initiative created two separate divisions which would each concentrate its attention on providing the right products and service to its two major market segments.

"One of the elements that this process helped us to look at was the structure of the company. Did we have the right management and marketing structure or was our structure hindering our growth?

"We decided to divide our company into two divisions, one to serve the industrial user, and the other to serve the tradesman, the user of power tools. With that divisional focus, we're better able to find out what the customer wants in the product. Now the R&D, manufacturing, and sales are all much closer to the customer. We're much more able to give that customer what he wants now and three years from now. And the new structure has already increased our sales and profits."

This major transition was eased, in Davis' opinion, by the fact that the management team participated in building the logic that led to this expected conclusion.

"I've read a number of strategy books, books on strategic planning, and I think too often strategies are made in a vacuum," says Davis. "Then the management is given a copy of the plan and asked to implement it. I'm not sure they always buy into that kind of plan. In going through this *strategic thinking process,* there's a lot of debate, and everyone sees the reasons why certain critical issues are identified and certain things get done."

This understanding has produced quick acceptance and implementation for a new structure that departs from a long-standing way of doing business.

"I think everyone really saw the logic to it," Davis says, "when we divisionalized the company, I don't think it was as big a shock as it would have been if we hadn't gone through the *strategic thinking process*. People in both divisions now see that they have a much clearer focus."

As American Saw works toward their ambitious new goals, management continues to use the process to identify new critical issues and press ahead.

"We're seeing better performance," Davis concludes, "there's certainly that feeling among all the people in the company."

11
Strategic Product Innovation

The Lifeblood of Corporate Longevity

There was a time, not so long ago, when one could walk into any office anywhere in the world—from Prudential Insurance to Siemens to General Motors to AT&T to Michelin Tires—and see hundreds of Friden calculators on row after row of wooden desks.

There was a time, not so long ago, when one could go into any office anywhere in the world and see several duplicating machines made by Addressograph Multigraph.

There was a time, not so long ago, when one could walk into any store in the world, large or small, and see one cash register, if not several, made by the National Cash Register Company.

There was a time, not so long ago, when one could go into any house in the United States, and some other one hundred countries, and find a Singer sewing machine.

There was a time, not so long ago when these four companies— Singer, Addressograph Multigraph, NCR, and Friden—were industrial powerhouses with worldwide brand recognition. However, just a few years later, two of these companies are almost extinct, and the other two do not command the market presence they once did.

On the other hand, there are companies that over the same time period have been able to maintain and even enhance their positions: companies such as 3M, Caterpillar, Coca-Cola, Johnson & Johnson, Merck, Marks & Spencer, Castrol, Hewlett-Packard, and Rubbermaid, to name but a few.

In every country, in every industry, one can identify two distinct types of companies: those that seem to have an ability to perpetuate themselves over long periods and those that do not. Once this discovery is made, one needs to then ask, as we did: What is it that companies with the ability to perpetuate themselves successfully know about business that the others either don't know or have forgotten?

The answer to this question, in our view, is the solution to the corporate fountain of youth. In our opinion, the companies that can maintain, and even enhance, their market positions over time have mastered the process of *strategic* product creation and innovation.

Strategic Product Innovation Is the Corporate Fountain of Youth

Without an aggressive product innovation program, organizations sputter and die. Every sane business executive will attest to this hypothesis. Not so long ago one of the most revered names in the bicycle industry was Schwinn, the 97-year-old company based in Chicago. Yet, in 1992, Schwinn declared bankruptcy. With the advent of a multitude of new bicycle designs in the 1970s and 1980s, Schwinn failed to see the changes sweeping the industry. According to *Forbes*, "Schwinn was obsessed with cutting costs, instead of innovation." Nonetheless, most organizations practice product innovation in a haphazard manner, apparently hoping that it will happen. In a DPI survey of 200 *Fortune* 500 companies, two-thirds said they had no formal manner by which to encourage the search for and the development of new products.

The innovative prowess of the United States has eroded in the last two decades. However, some U.S. corporations are still among the world's best. Caterpillar, Merck, 3M, Johnson & Johnson, Hewlett-Packard, Intel, PepsiCo, Rubbermaid, Procter & Gamble, and some others seem to have an infinite ability to churn out new products at a dizzying speed, which means that the skill is alive and well. In fact, in these companies product innovation is viewed as a paranoiac need. These organizations consider their abilities to continuously find opportunities for new products and markets as their "lifeline."

Why is it that 3M kicks out between 300 and 500 new products per year and has been doing so for many years without interruption? Why is it that Johnson & Johnson can continuously bring a stream of new health-care products to market in an industry that is "regulated"? Why is it that Merck can introduce new prescription drugs at a pace six times that of its competitors? Why is it that Rubbermaid can introduce new products with a success rate that is higher than 90 percent with no market testing, when experts tell us that 90 percent of all new products fail? Why is it that Intel can bang out new PC chips faster than PC manufacturers can assemble them? Why is it that Caterpillar can introduce unique new earth-moving machines with features, and at a rate, that no else can match?

Why is it that these companies, and a few others, can create and introduce a continuous flow of new products but their competitors cannot?

This is a question that has intrigued this author for the last 30 years. Finally, 10 years ago, I set out to find an answer. In an attempt to answer this question, we first studied the corporations that were not able to perpetuate themselves over time in an effort to uncover the reasons for this failure. Our conclusion: Failure was the result of a self-inflicted wound, because the companies were practicing one of the seven deadly sins that lead to corporate stagnation.

The Seven Deadly Sins of Corporate Stagnation

---

1. We must protect our cash cow at all costs, or else we perish.

Every company has a product or a market that is its cash cow. *Never worship at the altar of the cash cow.* You will inevitably perish. The reasoning is simple. For every employee that you train in techniques to protect your cash cow, there are one thousand people in competitive organizations thinking of ways to destroy your cash cow. And the odds are that they eventually will succeed.

IBM is a case in point. IBM's cash cow, as we all know, has been its mainframes—once the powerhouses of computing capacity. Over the years IBM has done everything in its power to protect that cash cow. Unfortunately, with the advent of smarter chips from companies such as Intel, Motorola, Fujitsu, and Advanced Microdevices, together with the development of smaller and smaller computers with increasing capacity by such companies as Apple, Compaq, Dell, AST, and Gateway, the mainframe's importance went on a downward spiral for the last 10 years, and so did IBM's economic performance.

The unfortunate element in this cruel scenario is that the first PC chip, RISC, was developed by IBM—in 1973! To this day, it is a chip more powerful than anything brought to market by anyone else. IBM made a deliberate decision not to introduce this chip because the company could foresee the devastating effects it would have on its mainframe business. In 1994—21 years later and maybe 21 years too late—IBM has finally introduced it under the brand-name PowerPC.

Another company, however, that has been thriving from these same changes is Hewlett-Packard. During this same period, HP has gone from seventh in the industry to second, and its stock has zoomed from $40 to over $90. Why? The reason is simple. In the words of its CEO, Lewis Platt: "The best defense is preemptive self-destruction and renewal. We have to be willing to cannibalize what we're doing today in order to ensure our leadership in the future. It's counter to human nature, but you have to kill your business while it is still working."

Once a company starts worshipping at the altar of the cash cow, its decision-making process becomes paralyzed. Once paralyzed, no new initiatives are undertaken in the debilitating interest of protecting the cash cow.

---

2. Our industry is mature; there is no more growth or innovation possible.

Some people would claim that the reason products become generic, prices come down to the lowest level, and growth stops is that the "market is mature." Mature markets, in our view, are a myth.

Consider some examples. Who would have thought 10 years ago that people would pay $300 for a pair of shoes? Running shoes at that! After all, everyone had a pair, and the market was mature. Then along came Nike and Reebok!

Who would have thought 10 years ago that people would be paying $3000 for a bicycle? After all, everyone had one, and the market was mature. Then along came Shimano and its "mountain" bikes with 21 speeds!

In yet another business, the former management of A.E. Staley thought that the corn milling business was mature and decided to embark on a diversification spree to become a consumer products marketer that nearly destroyed the company. Its new owners, Tate & Lyle, decided to rededicate the company to its previous core business with great success. Its CEO, Neil Shaw, expressed it this way, "The old management took their eyes off the ball. We got back to doing what we do best—we're corn millers." With its old strategy back in vogue, Staley introduced new products, one of which is a fat substitute made from corn that has reversed the firm's financial performance overnight and put it back on a highly profitable road.

Adolph Coors is another company that has managed to grow impressively in the beer business—an industry considered by Busch and Miller to be mature. This was achieved by introducing an avalanche of new products aimed at niche markets. Furthermore, while the large breweries are cannibalizing each other's markets to maintain their share and volume, a host of "microbreweries" have emerged to give birth to new, niche brands such as Samuel Adams, Sharps, and O'Doul's. The big breweries see the market as mature and have stopped innovating, and the only growth in the U.S. market is coming from these innovative, microbreweries which are thriving. Ten years ago, there were only a few; today, there are over 500!

Even in the liquor industry, probably one of the world's oldest industries, the mature market concept is a myth—decided not by us, but by the CEO of one of the industry's most successful players. In a market where consumption is dropping 1 percent per year on a worldwide basis, the CEO of Guinness argues, "Consumption is not actually a very good indicator in any business of whether there are any opportunities there." To prove this point, CEO Anthony Tennant defers to his company's performance—$1.2 billion of earnings on sales of $3.8 billion for an operating profit margin of 31 percent. Furthermore, all four of the major players in this field produced margins of over 25 percent. So much for mature markets.

The military truck industry is yet another market which most truck manufacturers view as mature and, as a result, hasn't seen any changes in truck design since the Korean war—45 years ago. That is, until Stewart & Stevenson, based in Houston, looked at the business and decided to do something about it. They have developed a new truck that can consistently outclimb its rivals on dirt as well as sand because of a system that automatically inflates and deflates the truck's tires to give the vehicle more traction on slippery or rough terrain. As a result, Stewart & Stevenson, unknown in the industry a few years ago, has won contracts for over 20,000 trucks against formidable competitors such as Volvo, General Motors, and Mercedes.

In yet another so-called mature industry—that of commercial buildings—one company has found growth. Honeywell, the manufacturer of temperature control devices, has found a new growth path. By combining its control technology with that of sensors, it has introduced a new product which controls lights, security, and temperature and shuts off the television and closes the windows. Michael Bonsignore, Honeywell's CEO, states: "And somebody says there's no growth in buildings. We just have to know where to look."

Ultimate proof that there is no such thing as a mature business or industry may be a recent study done by David Birch of Cognetics, a Cambridge, Massachusetts, research company. His study attempted to identify America's fastest-growing companies. These companies, referred to as "gazelles" by Birch, are companies that have doubled in size every year from $100,000 in revenues in 1989. The results are revealing. The industries with the most fast-growing gazelles tend to be the aged and moribund (Table 11-1). In fact, there seems to be an

Table 11-1. Industries with Fast-Growth Companies*

Industry	Percent of companies that are fast growers
Paper products	8.3
Chemicals	7.8
Instruments	7.7
Rubber, plastics	7.6
Electric & electronic equipment	7.2
Banking	7.0
Insurance carriers	6.8
Food products	6.4
Primary metal products	6.2
Wholesale trade (nondurables)	6.2

*Industries with the largest share of companies that at least doubled revenues between 1989 and 1993 from a minimum of $100,000.

inverse relationship between an industry's health and the concentration of gazelles. Of the 20 gazelle-friendliest industries, not one was in the top 20 in terms of growth.

Two CEOs who do not believe in mature markets are Jack Welch of GE and Lawrence Bossidy of Allied Signal. In 1996, GE's revenues grew 11.6 percent which is 50 percent better than the rest of the capital goods industry and more than 40 percent better than all industries as a whole. "Maturity is a state of mind," says Jack Welch.

When Lawrence Bossidy took over as CEO of Allied Signal a few years ago, he encountered a company that had not produced any growth in many years. As a result, he went to the general managers of each business and asked them why their businesses were not growing. General manager after general manager had the same answer: "We're in a mature industry. There is no more growth in our business." Bossidy's response: "There is no such thing as a 'mature market.' What we need are mature executives who can make markets grow." In the last three years Allied Signal has produced growth in excess of 10 percent. Same businesses, but probably not the same general managers!

The concept of a mature market, in our view, resides in the mind of the beholder. In other words, it is a state of mind. Management convinces itself that its business is mature and, as a result, two things start to happen. First, the company stops looking for opportunities because it has convinced itself there are no more. Therefore, it stops innovating. Second, the company starts diverting its resources to unrelated opportunities that take it way off course, usually with disastrous results.

There are always opportunities, particularly if one is practicing market fragmentation! D. Wayne Calloway, the CEO of PepsiCo, put it this way: "If the market you're in isn't growing, you'd better find a way to make it grow."

---

3. We're in a commodity business.

There is no such thing as a commodity business. There is always the possibility of differentiating yourself. Commodity businesses are a state of mind as well. Your company's products become commodities when management convinces itself that they are. It's a self-fulfilling prophecy.

When Stanley Gault took over as CEO of Goodyear after a long period of stagnation, he was stunned by repeatedly being told by his management team that "a tire is a tire is a tire is a tire" and that, as a result, tires were a commodity that could not be differentiated. Having spent many years as CEO of Rubbermaid, Mr. Gault knew differently, and he challenged his product development team to reinvent the tire. Within a few months, Goodyear introduced the Aquatread tire which eliminates "surfing" when driving through water. A few months later, it introduced an improved, dual-track version. As the sales of these two new products have soared, so has the value of Goodyear's stock.

Another of our clients trades in clay. That's right—wet mud—the commodity of all commodities! Still, that company has been able to find a wide range of product applications—from Kaopectate anti-diarrheal medicine to kitty litter.

Yet another example is baking soda—one of the world's oldest commodities, until someone at Arm & Hammer saw an application for it in refrigerators to absorb foul odors. This small breakthrough enabled the company to reconsider its conclusion about the commodity status of baking soda. Once the mindset broke, the company started looking for other potential applications and soon found one—toothpaste. Now there are over a dozen brands of toothpaste that contain baking soda— all selling at a premium! What will they think of next? How about Arm & Hammer antiperspirant—which the company just introduced. And this year? Baking soda gum! So much for commodity products.

Then, there is the "mother" of all commodities—water. Yet the French have mastered the marketing of this mundane commodity by branding it under a variety of names such as Vitel, Evian, and Perrier. They have been so successful that their success has attracted the attention of the product innovators/differentiators. And thus, the birth of Nordic, which took water and added fruit flavorings such as strawberry, raspberry, and lemon. And then along came Clearly Canadian, which added fruit flavorings and bubbles to give us fruit-flavored, bubbled water. And then another company decided to add tea to the mixture and—voilà!—Snapple was born.

The key to not allowing your products to become commodities is to practice a concept we call market fragmentation. More will be said about this important concept in Chapter 12.

---

4. Only entrepreneurs in small companies can innovate. Large companies stifle risk taking and new product creation.

The seductive fallacy that new products can be created only by entrepreneurs can quickly become an impediment to new product innovation. This is particularly true in the United States because of the large number of companies that have been started by entrepreneurs and the hero worship these founders receive. Henry Ford of Ford Motor Company, Thomas Edison of General Electric, Ray Kroc of McDonald's, Steve Jobs of Apple Computer, Bill Gates of Microsoft, and Fred Smith of Federal Express are but a few such "heroes."

Lesser heroes, however, seldom receive the adulation reserved for entrepreneurs, except from other employees of the firms they work for. This is regrettable, because most new product innovations are originated by people who work for someone else.

Some quick examples. All of 3M's 60,000 products are the creation of salaried employees. Post-it notes came from Spencer Fry, a 3M chemist, and his search for a method to keep track of certain hymns in his prayer book without destroying the words that were printed in each page. A fireproof corrugated box was developed by a group of Digital Equipment employees who were looking for a method to prevent their computers from being destroyed by fire during storage in various warehouses. American Airlines's frequent flier program, a novelty in that industry when first introduced, was the creation of the marketing manager. In 1956, another 3M employee spilled a new chemical on her tennis shoe. Some time later, she realized that that area was not becoming as dirty as the rest of her shoe. The result? A major new product for 3M called Scotchguard fabric protector.

These examples, and many more, are the result of *entrepreneurial employees*, not entrepreneurs.

---

5. Innovators are born. It's a trait of personality, and we just don't have any of these people around.

One of the worst impediments to new product creation is the thought that innovation is a trait of personality—in other words, that a few select people are born with that trait while the rest of the masses are not.

As Thomas Edison once observed: "Invention is 10 percent inspiration and 90 percent perspiration" (*Edison: Inventing the Century* by Neil Baldwin, Hyperion, 1995). The main reason that many people attribute the skill to personality is that most people who are good at new product creation cannot describe the process, or method, they use. Again, anything that cannot be codified cannot be explained.

Our contention is that the ability of people to innovate is a function of the *management system* in place in an organization rather than a trait of personality. How does one explain the hundreds, or even thousands, of product innovators that 3M has been able to attract to its company? Is it because 3M has an uncanny knack for finding all these people with this trait while its neighbors in St. Paul or its competitors do not? Even 3M isn't that superior in its personnel selection. Obviously, there is something else at work. 3M has, in our opinion, *institutionalized* a process to generate, capture, evaluate, and introduce new products more quickly and more successfully than its competitors.

Another example to prove our hypothesis that innovative behavior is a function of the process and not a trait of personality: China and Hong Kong. Why is it that for over 40 years, the Chinese in Hong Kong were so innovative while their brethren on mainland China were not? After all, they share the same genes. What, then, is different? The answer: the system. The economic system in Hong Kong caused innovation to flourish, while the Communist system in China suppressed innovation. There is even further and more recent proof. Since China has reformed its economic system in the last few years, innovation is starting to be seen on the mainland as well.

It is the *organizational process* used by management that will create an environment conducive to new product innovation. Product creation can be fostered in virtually any organization. The important point to emphasize is that, although it is true that business owners or so-called entrepreneurs can create new products or markets, it is usually employees in all sizes of companies that provide most new product concepts.

What the innovative organization requires is a method that allows concepts for new products or markets to be gathered and harvested in a systematic manner.

---

6. New product creation is too risky.

Although it is true that new product innovation can be risky, taking extreme risk is not a characteristic of entrepreneurs nor of innovative companies. Donald Trump, one of the premier entrepreneurs of the 1980s, said in his book, *The Art of the Deal* (Warner Books, 1989): "I've never gambled in my life. To me, a gambler is someone who plays the slot machines. I prefer to own the slot machines. Less risk."

David Singleton, another entrepreneur who built a very successful newspaper chain, has also reaffirmed this notion by saying: "To outsiders, our behavior may seem to be risky, but every risk was very carefully calculated."

The same is true of entrepreneurial organizations. As the former chairman of 3M once said to this author: "I prefer placing 50 small bets than one big bet."

Innovative organizations do take risks, but they are *prudent* risks. They know exactly what risks are there, and they have in place actions to contain such risk, as we will see when we study the process of new product creation and successful introduction in Chapter 12.

---

7. We don't have the resources necessary to innovate.

The perception that new product or new market creation requires a lot of resources is another major impediment to innovation. Such is not the case.

As Jeffry Timmons, author of *New Business Opportunities and Planning* (Brick House Publishing, 1990), stated:

> Entrepreneurship is a human, creative act that builds something of value from practically nothing. It is the pursuit of opportunity regardless of the resources, or lack of resources, at hand. It requires a vision and the passion and commitment to lead others in the pursuit of that vision. It also requires a willingness to take calculated risks.

The Need for Strategic Fit

After exploring the impediments to new product creation, we then looked for the elements that contribute to an organization's ability to create new products on an ongoing basis. The primary requirement was the ability to answer the following question: How well does this new product fit the strategy of the business? This is a key question that is often not asked but should be. Experience has shown that organizations that try to innovate outside the strategic framework of the business usually do not succeed.

By strategic fit, we mean the degree to which an opportunity fits a company's direction. The opportunity need not fit exactly at first, provided that it promises to fit well in the near future. So the issue concerns not just today's strategy but also the direction that the company is pursuing to ensure its future.

When an opportunity is pursued irrespective of strategic thrust, the results are usually disappointing or even damaging. Several years ago, Exxon decided to enter the office automation business and began an operation known as QXT. Despite the infusion of massive amounts of money and the work of some highly talented people, QXT was a disaster and Exxon eventually dissolved it. The office products market simply was not part of Exxon's direction and strategy as a company. That is, it could not be made a part of the nature and direction—the fabric—of Exxon's business. Consequently, it was doomed to failure from the start. A senior executive of Exxon recently told us that Exxon executives did not understand the office equipment business as well as they did the "trivia of the oil business," and thus they could not manage or even judge the opportunities of the former. There was *no* strategic *fit*.

Similarly, People's Express seemed to be making good headway toward its own goals when it was forced out of the sky by its acquisition of Frontier Airlines, a traditional carrier that did not fit very well with the vision and direction established by Donald Burr for People's Express.

New product or new market creation is not a question of unbridled enthusiasm spinning off into every direction of the compass at once. It is a question of organized, purposeful, and *focused* attempts to improve the organization's products, customers, and markets. The end result of innovation has to be an enhanced ability to meet and exceed the organization's *business goals*. Consequently, innovation must be undertaken within the purview of corporate strategy and its *future strategic profile*.

Create Products for the Future, Not the Present

During our research over the years for this book, we attempted to understand why many companies seem to concentrate their entire product creation effort on incremental or marginal improvements to existing products. This type of product innovation is a necessary part of business, but it leads only to *marginal* increases in revenue. The cause of such marginal results, in our humble view, is too much focus on the customer. In view of the great number of consultants who earn their living promoting the concept that firms today must get closer to their customers—be customer-driven as they call it—the fact remains that very few new product concepts come from customers. If the focus of a *new* product creation program is restricted to the analysis of customer needs, the company will more than likely end up with product extensions and not new-to-the-market product concepts.

The reason is simple. Customers are usually good at identifying performance gaps in products they are currently using, but they are not very skillful at identifying future trends and converting these into future needs. Most truly new-to-the-market products were conceived in the mind of the maker of the product, not the consumer of that product. The list of examples is limitless. No customer ever asked Thomas Edison to develop a light bulb. No customer ever asked Spencer Fry to develop a Post-it note. No customer ever asked Akio Morita to develop a Walkman. No customer ever asked Steve Jobs and Steve Wozniak to develop a personal computer. No customer asked Lee Iacocca to develop the Mustang. No customer ever asked Craig McCaw to develop a cellular telephone network. No customer ever asked Ted Turner to develop an international, all-news television network. No customer ever asked Hal Sperlich to develop a minivan. No customer ever asked Ray Kroc to build a chain of stores to sell hamburgers. No customer ever asked Wayne Huezinga to build a chain of retail outlets to rent videos. No customer ever asked Bill Gates to develop Windows software. The list is limitless!

The reason that new-to-the-market concepts do not originate in the minds of customers is very simple. Customers can convert performance gaps in current products into explicit needs, but these gaps are rarely needs that give birth to new-to-the-market product concepts.

One company that has been on a new-to-the-market product roll lately is Chrysler. Bob Lutz, Chrysler vice chairman, explains that company's success by endorsing our view:

> Being customer-driven is certainly a good thing, but if you're so much customer-driven that you're merely following yesterday's trends, then, ultimately, customers won't be driving your supposedly customer-driven products!
>
> Let's face it, the customer is, at best, just a rear view mirror. He can tell you what he likes among the choices already out there. But when it comes to the future, why, I ask, should we expect the customer to be the expert in clairvoyance or in creativity? After all, isn't that really what he expects us to be?

New-to-the-market product concepts come from the identification of implicit needs that stem from the interpretation of future trends. Furthermore, implicit needs are the result of two elements: (1) anticipation of future trends that identify implicit, future needs; and (2) understanding of strategic capabilities that can be leveraged to create concepts for new-to-the-market products.

The advantages of this approach are threefold. Identification of implicit needs:

1. Enables the conceptor to introduce *differentiated* products.

2. Allows the conceptor to build in *barriers to entry*, such as patents.

3. Provides a period of *exclusivity* that brings *premium* prices.

Fagor Electrodomésticos

Strategy for the New European Language

Jésus Catania
Chief Executive Officer

FAGOR Electrodomésticos is Spain's, as well as one of Europe's, most important manufacturer and marketer of "white goods" or domestic appliances. It is located in Mondragón, in Spain's Basque region, and is part of the Mondragón Cooperative Corporation, a unique Basque concept that makes all employees shareholders in the organization.

The cooperative is the most important industrial sector in the Basque region, with annual revenues of 300,000 million pesetas ($2,235,000,000 US) while the Domestic Appliance Division is a 56,000 peseta business. The division employs 3200 people, spread over nine plants. Approximately 20 percent of its production is exported to other European countries.

Jésus Catania has been managing director of the division for the last 14 years while also being a vice president of the Mondragón Cooperative responsible for all "home" products.

Mr. Catania called on DPI and used its *strategic thinking* when Spain entered the European Common Market. He foresaw that the "rules of the game" were about to change and he needed a catalyst to make his management team understand the depth of change that joining the EEC would bring.

"When we decided to apply DPI's *strategic thinking process* to our domestic appliance business," Mr. Catania tells us, "we were in the midst of very important changes here in Spain as well as throughout Europe."

"On the one hand, the disappearance of the protected market in Spain would make us more vulnerable to a host of new European competitors. On the other hand, we had to penetrate new markets in Europe where we would meet a number of alliances between European as well as North American manufacturers. We had never faced a situation like this before, and we needed to reorient our business strategy in order to succeed in these new circumstances."

The process at FAGOR included the top 20 managers of the division.

"In the first session, our impressions were very positive," continues Catania. "First, it's a highly participatory process which, in the case of a cooperative like ours, is well received. Second, there was unanimity at the end that we had constructed a strategy which would allow us to grow. The concept of *driving force* was a new one for the group and it represented a significant difference compared to other methods we had used before.

"Once we agreed on which element of the business should drive our strategy forward, it was relatively easy for us to develop a future strategic profile for the business which clearly delineated the products, customers, and markets we should and should not pursue."

Having settled on a future strategy, the group then concentrated on determining which strategic positions needed to be defended or captured to ensure the success of the strategy. From this discussion, FAGOR management decided that in order to be successful in penetrating new markets in other European countries, they had to defend their current position in Spain. As a result, a number of actions were put into place to ensure continued dealer and end-user loyalty to FAGOR products. To this day, other competitors have not made any significant inroads into the Spanish market while FAGOR has increased its share of other markets outside Spain. In fact, FAGOR has even increased its market share in Spain.

"The most important part of the DPI process" says Catania "is that it draws out the best knowledge of everyone in the room about every aspect of the business. Yet, it does this in a disciplined and objective manner. The DPI facilitator, however, does not allow us to make any false assumptions about ourselves. He challenged and provoked our thinking in a constructive manner.

"Over and above the development of a coherent strategy, the process also helped us identify a number of *critical issues* that needed to be resolved in order for us to implement the strategy successfully. Each of these programs were assigned to specific individuals who were made responsible for their execution. These critical issues and action plans then became part of our budget and business plan for the next two years.

"We had agreed during our strategy sessions that we needed to defend and consolidate our position in our home market, and this was our number one issue. And this objective has been met. Not only have we not lost market share," says Catania, "we have, in fact, increased our share of our domestic market in the last two years.

"A second critical issue the company identified was the need to improve its customer satisfaction index, as much at the distributor level as well as the consumer level. This was particularly important in view of the entry into the Spanish market of a number of new competitors. The rules of the game had changed overnight.

"I'm glad to report that with our distributors we have gone from third place to first place as reported by them. In terms of consumers, we decided to track after-sale service as an indicator and, in this area, we have improved by 20 percent over last year."

Another critical issue was the advent of major new competitors, international in scope, into the Spanish market. FAGOR saw a need to form an alliance with other partners in order to achieve the same economies of scale that these global players had.

"We were the first to make use of the EEC's new regulations to form an alliance with Thompson in France, GDA in the U.K., and Ocean in Italy. This alliance, called EURODOM, has become the second largest group in Europe, thus giving us economic advantages we would not have been able to achieve on our own," explains Catania.

A fourth critical issue was the recognition that FAGOR's products did not meet the more demanding North European standards. So a plan was put into place to become ISO 9000 certified, and that has also been achieved. "This certification allowed us to increase our sales of certain appliances by as much as 50 percent in a two-year period," says Catania.

Three years later, FAGOR has accomplished significant gains. In the area of productivity, the company has been able to reduce inventories by 40 percent and manufacturing space by 30 percent while increasing productivity and reducing costs.

"Compared to other strategy methods, the DPI process also forces you to explore different scenarios for the future of the business. In other words, *strategic thinking* is not linear in that it doesn't extrapolate the current strategy forward, but causes you to explore different alternatives before choosing the one most appropriate to deal with the environment the business will face in the future rather than the one it faced in the past. If necessary, the new strategy could represent a rupture from the current one if that is what is needed for the company to succeed.

"Finally, I would like to say a word about the need for a third-party, objective facilitator with a structured process. This role is indispensable. Otherwise the group and the discussion would meander all over the place. A third-party facilitator who understands the process better than we do is a better judge of the quality of the answers and can ensure that we have not skipped any steps that might lead to wrong conclusions. Furthermore, we have an expression in Spain that says 'One is never a prophet in one's backyard.' My management is more than likely to be more attentive to an outside person than they would be to me if I attempted to do this myself," Catania says.

12
Market Fragmentation

The Future of Successful New Product Innovation

As mentioned in Chapter 11, the "raw material" of new product creation is change. There is a direct linear relationship between the number of changes present in the environment of a business or industry and the number of new products being created. The more changes, the more new products appear. The fewer changes, the fewer new products that are created.

In our work with the CEOs and management teams of over 300 corporations worldwide, we are constantly being told by these executives that change, particularly technological change, is happening faster and faster. As a result, they claim, no one can keep up—much less predict anything—with the avalanche of changes facing a business today.

The Myth of Rapid Technological Change

Although a part of the above observation is sometimes true, the idea that technological change happens too quickly to be anticipated is somewhat of a myth. Our own work would offer a different hypothesis. Our view is that most executives get caught by surprise because they have not been looking! And when you have not been looking, every change catches you by surprise!

The fact is that technological change takes 20 to 30 years to find a commercially viable application and then another 50 to 70 years before it has an impact on all the nooks and crannies that it eventually will affect. However, if you have not been looking, even a change that is only creeping along will seem to hit you very fast. Two examples come to mind. The first is the invention of electricity. Although invented in the 1860s, it only found a few successful applications in the 1870s and 1880s. Most of the applications of electricity which are now taken as a given were not developed for another two to three decades. The same is true of robotics, lasers, and fiber optics—all technologies invented in the 1950s but barely finding commercially viable applications today— some 50 years later. The microprocessor is yet another example. Although invented in the 1960s, and although it gave birth to the personal computer in the 1970s, the fact is that in spite of the billions of dollars invested in these products by corporations all over the world, the products have had no effect on the productivity of these companies so far. Only now are we starting to see the potential impact that these machines might have. And we have only seen a very small percentage of the potential applications of the microprocessor.

Although corporate executives would claim that they are constantly bombarded by changes that affect their business, in reality there are very few *macro* changes that have significant impact on corporations. Failure to recognize these macro trends can mean corporate death. However, the company that does detect a macro change early in its evolution and constructs a strategy to capitalize on it can reap a substantial reward.

The Impact of Unnoticed Macrochanges

There are some changes, macro in nature, that affect every product made by every company on the planet. Frequently, unfortunately, many executives completely fail to notice these until it is too late.

It is a fact, today, that 50 percent of the population of the United States, Japan, and most European countries will be 55 years and older by the year 2010. No one can change that. And that change will have an effect on every product made by every company in the world.

For example, Caterpillar had better be thinking today of designing its large machines in a manner to be operated by frail old men or women. Why? Simply because there will not be enough big, young men with big biceps to move all those levers. Another example came out of our work with Texaco. When a group of their executives used the process described in this book, they started questioning the concept of the self-service gas station. They started asking themselves if the notion of asking people to get out of their cars to serve themselves might still be viable when people are older and less mobile. Therefore, why not have a small robot next to each pump that takes a customer's credit card, processes it, puts the nozzle in the gas tank, and activities it, and then hands you back the card. All accomplished without the customer leaving the driver's seat.

Although this concept was developed by these Texaco executives during one of our work sessions in 1988, the company decided not to pursue this novel idea. However, someone else did. BMW and Mercedes are jointly developing this machine, shown in Figure 12-1.

Macrochanges

Two such macrotrends are currently at work today. One is the demographic change just discussed—the aging population of most Western countries—which will affect every company in the world for the next 25 years. The other has already occurred but has been missed by most corporate managements, particularly in the United States. The most significant change of the last 15 years is that the majority of the economies of the Western world have gone from "push" economies to "pull" economies. "What's the difference?" you may ask. "Very substantial," I would answer.

Push to Pull Economy

In a *push economy* there is more demand than supply, and the *producer* reigns. From 1945 to the mid-1970s such was the case in the West. Most companies, particularly those in the United States, were riding this wave. Everything they produced was immediately gobbled up by long lines of customers craving their products. One only needs to go back to the introduction of television in the mid-1950s to understand this phenomenon. If you were around back then, you will remember how the entire neighborhood would gather at the window of the local appliance store to watch the TV set through the store window. The next morning, there was always a long line of customers waiting to purchase their first TV. It didn't matter much to the customer that resolution was poor and that the picture kept rotating on the screen; the goal was to get a set before the store sold out—more demand that supply. This situation lasted until the mid-1970s.

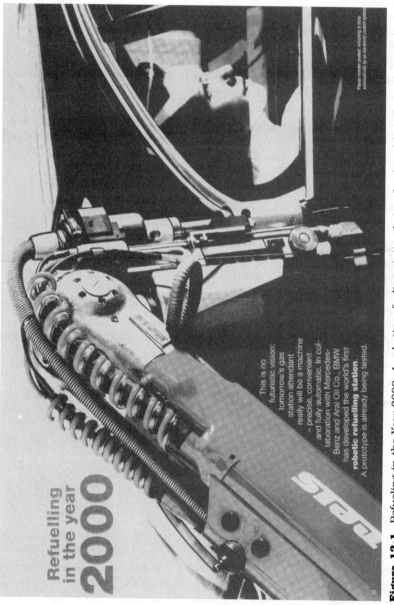

Figure 12-1. Refueling in the Year 2000. A robotic refueling station being developed by BMW in collaboration with Mercedes-Benz and Aral Oil Co.

202

Today, the opposite situation exists. With the advent of Japanese, Korean, Singaporean, Taiwanese, and European products, there is more supply than demand. As a result, the rules of the game have changed significantly. In a *pull economy*, the *customer* reigns. Unfortunately, few CEOs have noticed. Table 12-1 is a listing of the differences between the push and pull economies.

Table 12-1. Economy

Push	Pull
↑ Demand versus supply	↑ Supply versus demand
Producer is King	Customer is King
Market segmentation	Market fragmentation
Large number of customers with similar needs	Smaller number of customers with dissimilar needs
Generic product	Tailored product
Commodity prices	Premium prices
Long production runs	Shorter production runs
Efficient manufacturing (low-cost producer)	Flexible, effective, decentralized manufacturing
Long product cycles	Shorter product cycles
Strong brand loyalty	Little brand loyalty
Periodic product innovation	Continuous product and process innovation
Fixed rules	Changing rules
Sturdy and stable	Fast and nimble

Market Fragmentation versus Market Segmentation

How does one deal with a push versus a pull economy? In a push economy, the producer controls the market and the key to success is market segmentation. This is the concept of grouping large numbers of customers with *similar* needs together and providing them with a generic product. It's the Henry Ford approach to business. "You can have any color car you want as long a it's black." This has been the approach followed by all U.S. producers since the end of World War II. But unfortunately, it does not work in a pull economy, where a company must practice the opposite concept of *market fragmentation* to be successful.

The concept of market fragmentation means identifying smaller groups of customers with *dissimilar* needs and responding with *customized* products. The world's most successful companies today are practicing market fragmentation. Companies in trouble are still clinging to the outdated market segmentation. Again, a variety of examples exist.

In the automobile industry, which was probably the first to go from push to pull, one of the most successful companies is Toyota. The reason is simple. Toyota has so mastered its business and manufacturing processes that a customer can enter a dealer's office in Japan on Monday morning, configure the car he or she wants, and take delivery of it on Friday afternoon—custom-made to the buyer's specifications.

Even BMW, the German automaker, attributes its current success to market fragmentation. As *Business Week* reported in an article entitled "'Grill' to Grill' with Japan":

> In Europe, where BMW gets 75% of its sales, most cars are made to order. That's why BMW offers a big à la carte menu of models, engines, colors, and options. "Each customer can have a unique car," says Eberhard von Kuenheim (CEO). Japanese competitors offer far fewer choices. He complains: "They are building 100, 200, even 400 exactly identical cars a day."

I hate to think what he would say about the U.S. manufacturers.

Sony markets a different version of its Walkman in Norway than it does in Sweden, two if its smallest worldwide markets. Why? Sony discovered that these two areas had unique needs that required a slightly different product.

Twenty months after 3M introduced its unique Post-it notes, the company had developed more than 100 versions of the original product to cater to a variety of slightly different needs in the marketplace. No other competitor was able to keep up with such a pace of product proliferation.

Castrol, the oil lubricant specialist, has no oil reserves nor does it own any refineries or service stations. What Castrol does have, however, is over 3000 different formulas of lubricants, each tailored to a specific application. While the major oil companies try to satisfy the market with one or two generic lubricants, Castrol can provide a specific formula especially conceived to fulfill the requirements of each customer's specific application.

FLEXcon, a client based in Spencer, Massachusetts, has a similar approach. Whereas the giant chemical companies provide multipurpose, generic adhesives to printers who produce printed packaging material, FLEXcon develops a special formula for *each* printer. FLEXcon's ability to tailor a solution to meet each printer's specific need represents that companies competitive advantage.

In the retailing business, Sears is suffering from a double whammy. On one hand, a number of specialty retailers are fragmenting the market away from Sears. Sears' strategy of being all things to all people—as reflected by the broad array of merchandise, from furniture to financial services—is being decimated by a new brand of boutique retailers such as The Limited and The Gap, each catering to a much narrower range of needs. On the other hand, a couple of players such as Wal-Mart and Home Depot are changing the rules of play.

Even McDonald's is feeling the pinch of market fragmentation. A host of smaller, more nimble competitors are forcing McDonald's to rethink its entire strategy. Companies such as Chili's, Taco Bell, Olive Garden, and others are dividing and conquering what was once a large, homogeneous market for hamburgers.

In the mundane world of pens, pencils, and markers, the Sanford Company of Illinois produces a return on equity of 24 percent and sales increases of 14 percent per year. How? By fragmenting the market to pieces. Sanford keeps broadening the market by niching it to death. Sanford has markets for all types of applications, from markers for clothes in laundromats to nonsmearing markers for use on fax paper. In between, it has watercolor markers for toddlers of every age and talent. Again, the myth of the mature market has been proved to be false. As observed in an August 5, 1991, article about this company in *Forbes:* "As the fountain pen was dying 40 years ago, few would have thought Sanford would survive into the 1990s. Fewer still would have predicted that the market would price it like a growth stock."

In the beer industry most brewers are having a difficult time growing their businesses and maintaining their margins. The reason? A group of entrepreneurs, evolving as microbrewmeisters, are fragmenting the large brewers' markets to smithereens with a host of regional brands that many times sell only in their respective cities. It is reported that over 500 such regional brands have sprung up in the last five years. The national brewers, caught off guard by this phenomenon, should have anticipated it, since the same has occurred in Germany and Britain, where there is a brewery in every village, let alone every city.

Belgium may host the ultimate in terms of "market fragmentors." In one of the smallest countries in Europe (population 10 million), there are between 500 and 800 breweries. In Belgium, one finds market fragmentors that are fragmenting market fragments! One can find raspberry beer, wheat beer, red beer, golden beer, 12 percent alcohol beer, grape beer, beer made in abbeys, beer with spices, and even "dark" beer for Christmas. The concept of market fragmentation is strong and healthy in Belgium!

Even mighty American Express has discovered the concept of market fragmentation. After decades of offering only two versions of its cards, green and gold, the company has just announced that in the next 18 months it will scrap this approach and will introduce 13 new versions, each aimed at a fragment of these two initial segments.

The most successful manufacturer of home appliances in Europe, Electrolux, has also learned that market fragmentation works. Electrolux has recognized that Northern Europeans want large refrigerators since they shop only once a week, whereas the French want small ones since most shop each day. Northerners want their freezers on the bottom, while southerners like their freezers on top. And Electrolux has responded with a wide array of tailored products to satisfy all these needs. Whirlpool, on the other hand—relatively new to Europe—has taken the opposite track. It is trying to sell a standard product across Europe. Time will tell if this strategy will succeed.

Differentiated versus Commodity Products

One of the first impacts of market fragmentation is that it almost makes commodity products and their providers obsolete. Because the practitioners of market segmentation respond with generic products that attempt to satisfy large groups of users, these products are usually easily duplicated and, before long, become "commodity" items. Market fragmentation, however, results in a wide variety of custom-made products, each differentiated to satisfy a unique set of requirements. Because customer needs are always evolving, so too are the products. This make it more difficult for competitors to emulate.

In fact, the companies and industries that are struggling today are the ones that have not adjusted to market fragmentation and are losing ground to those that are practicing this concept. The strategy of the fragmentor is to identify large, commodity markets and to fragment them into smaller pieces to the fragmentor's advantage.

In the media industry, CBS, ABC, and NBC are going through this trauma. The industry is being fragmented by the cable providers who, in turn, are fragmenting programming to address the more specific needs of smaller segments of the audience. Thus, the remarkable growth and success of MTV, A&E, ESPN, and others. There is even a 24-hour-a-day Weather Channel!

Ted Turner is running ahead of the pack. Not only has he changed the rules of play with his worldwide news network CNN, but he is also practicing market fragmentation through cable television. In addition to his news network, Turner has introduced an all-movie channel for movie buffs, an all-sports network for sports buffs, and—an all-cartoon network for cartoon buffs.

Bill Ziff of Ziff Communications and Dale Lang of Lang Communications did the same thing to the barons of the print media. For several decades the goal of magazine publishers was to publish a magazine that could find an audience of seven to ten million readers. Several did at one time and became known as the *seven sisters*. These included *McCall's*, *Redbook*, and *Good Housekeeping*. Lang and Ziff have done exactly the opposite. Lang is the publisher of a number of women's magazines, each tailored to a unique set of feminine needs. One, for example, is called *Working Woman* and another is called *Working Mother*. Each has a subscriber base of only a million readers, but the magazines are highly successful. In fact, *Working Woman* has been the most successful of any magazine launched in the last decade.

Ziff, on the other hand, can be considered the founder of "special interest" magazines. He started such titles as *Car and Driver, Yachting, PC Magazine, MacUser,* and *Computer Shopper.* Ziff clearly detected the shift from market segmentation, as being practiced by the seven sisters, to market fragmentation. "When I started in this business, mass magazines were dominant. Today we live in an age of stratified, separated, targeted markets that are information-hungry. The future of all advertising-supported media is *narrow casting*, not broadcasting."

Hallmark once dominated the market for greeting cards. Today, 70 percent of the market has been fragmented by a dozen or so smaller companies that offer a card for just about any occasion, including no occasion.

In the 1970s, Adolph Coors, the brewing company, was in dire straits. Its growth had stopped and so had its profits. In the 1980s Coors discovered market fragmentation. When the "light" beer craze arrived, Miller and Anheuser-Busch each introduced one brand and tried to capture the largest share of the market. Coors, on the other hand, introduced three different brands, each tailored to a different set of customers. One in particular, called the Silver Bullet, was geared especially to women. As a result, Coors doubled its sales in the 1980s and has edged its way up to third place next to Busch and Miller. Coors' objective is to displace Miller in second place by the end of this decade by more fragmentation.

Premium Price versus Low Price

One of the disadvantages of the market segmentation approach is that it leads to generic products, as already mentioned, and to generic prices. Because all products are very similar, so are the prices. And most transactions have a tendency to drift to the level of "low price wins," because customers see no difference in one product compared to another.

The advantage of market fragmentation is often the opposite. Products have been tailored to very specific needs, so the "solution" is usually different from the generic product, and added value can be perceived by each customer. This allows for *premium* pricing, and each transaction is concluded on the basis of value instead of price. Higher margins are therefore possible.

Both Lang and Ziff get premium prices for their publications compared to the publishers of the seven sisters. The reason is simple. Their magazines deliver to a narrower but more targeted audience with differentiated needs. The same is true at FLEXcon.

Another example of market fragmentation that brought premium prices is a small but growing company called Message! Check Corporation. Located in Seattle and started by Priscilla Beard, this company makes personalized checks for groups or organizations who wish to personalize the graphics and the message on the blank check. It prints checks which carry messages from Greenpeace, Mothers Against Drunk Drivers, Vietnam Veterans of America, and a host of others. All these sell for twice what the traditional check printers charge, and Beard can't keep up with the demand.

In yet another industry where fragmentation is fast taking over, premium prices are being realized. This is the cable industry, where different channels are being programmed more and more by specialty broadcasters catering to smaller and smaller audiences but bringing higher and higher prices. There is, for example, a channel called the Military Channel, which reaches three million subscribers on military bases in the United States. Whereas CNN obtains $4.50 per thousand viewers for a 30-second spot, the Military Channel gets $7.50, an 80 percent premium.

A company called Quidel Corporation has devised the ultimate use of market fragmentation to justify premium prices. Quidel markets pregnancy test kits. One brand called Conceive is found in one part of a drugstore and retails for $9.99. Another brand called RapidVue is found in another part of the drugstore and retails for $6.99. The product inside each box is exactly the same. What's different? The packaging. The Conceive product has pink packaging with a smiling infant. The RapidVue one is in a plain wrapping with no picture. Why the difference? "The market definitely divides between the women who want babies and those who don't," says CEO Steven Frankel. He explains the difference in price: "People buy hope. In our case, they pay more for hope than for possible relief."

In the sunglass industry, two companies, Ray-Ban and Nikon, are trying to "outfragment" each other—and both at premium prices. Ray-Ban has taken the track of offering over 80 different frame styles. Nikon, on other hand, offers a wide variety of lens, each tailored to a slightly different use. There is the Nikon CE lens for skiers that allows a low percentage (6 percent) of light through. For divers, there's the Nikon LE lens which allows up to 22 percent of the light through. Then there are lenses for hiking, flying, shooting, and waterskiing—all at prices several notches higher than those for ordinary sunglasses. Nikon and Ray-Ban have both recognized that people's perception of a product can be changed and higher prices can be had.

In the telecommunications service industry a company called Mtel sells paging services, which are generally seen by all of its competitors as a commodity-type product, where lowest price wins. John Palmer, Mtel's CEO, doesn't agree, however, and he is proving the commodity view wrong. Under the Skytel name, the company offers basic nation-wide paging services. In 1996, the company introduced a new two-way wireless communication network aimed at travelers who not only need to be contacted but may also have to respond. This new service, called Destineer, is priced at a premium. The company sees all kinds of other customer fragments with special needs that could also be served through differentiated services at premium prices.

Fragmentation is also occurring in the tire industry. Another one of our clients, Steelcord (a division of Bekaert in Belgium), recently received a request to provide the steelcord to make tires for a new Honda sports car which will have four different tires—one for each wheel! Goodyear will probably be the manufacturer. In fact, the tire industry is an excellent example of one that is experiencing all phases of the switch from market segmentation to market fragmentation. The sequence went something like this: (1) a tire for all cars, (2) a tire for each size of car, (3) a tire for each model of car, and finally (4) a tire for each wheel.

Short Runs versus Long Runs

A great advantage of market segmentation is that it provides the producer with long manufacturing runs that enable it to attain maximum production efficiencies and, thus, profits. Unfortunately, the opposite is again the case in market fragmentation. Manufacturing versatility, not efficiency, is the key skill in this new mode. Again, U.S. companies have been slow to notice this change. As Michael Dertouzos, director of MIT's Laboratory for Computer Science, pointed out:

> U.S. industry clings to outmoded strategies, like inflexible mass production of a large number of standard goods that does not reflect the growing demand for individualized custom quality products. This system, pioneered by Henry Ford, can be likened to

a gigantic wheel of production, where workers, suppliers, and other participants are highly specialized cogs. The objective is to keep the wheel turning, no matter what. Anyone who misbehaves is replaced. By contrast, the new systems of production, both in the best-practice U.S. companies and abroad, entail a nimbler approach where broadly trained workers produce shorter runs of tailored goods. They are winning over the older system of mass production.

An industry currently undergoing the trials and tribulations of the transition from a push to pull mode is that of textiles. In the United States, textile manufacturers have concentrated on materials that can be produced in large quantities such as denim and sheeting. The problem they face, however, is that the retailers that are winning today are those that are fragmenting the market with a host of styles and fashions that require a much wider variety of materials and finishes but in smaller quantities. These are retailers such as The Limited and The Gap. Both these companies are going offshore to satisfy their requirements, not because these manufacturers are less costly but because they are more flexible. As Leslie Wexler, CEO of The Limited, said: "The problem with U.S. textile mills is that they don't make what we want to buy." In a pull economy, the customer is king!

Production Efficiency versus Production Versatility

Under a system that stresses long production runs and commodity products that can easily be duplicated by competitors, the key to winning is to become the low-cost producer. The concept of market fragmentation, however, focuses on production versatility. In other words, versatility is the ability to change from one product to another on the same line without losing efficiency.

In Germany, Heinz Grieffenberger took over an ailing company in 1983 called ABM Baumiller, a maker of motors and gearboxes for cranes. What he found was a company making a few standard products for a large number of customers. He quickly replaced the entire production process in order to tailor his products to individual customers' needs. "I can switch production to a different product within seconds," he boasted:

To be successful in the future, companies will have to learn to make their production processes as versatile as Toyota's without losing efficiency. FLEXcon, for example, prides itself on its ability to "tweak" its highly complex, volume-intensive coating process to supply custom-tailored orders of 200 yards when all other competitors demand 10 times the quantity for a minimum order. And FLEXcon has mastered this versatility without losing efficiency.

Dell Computers is another example of a company that has changed the rules of marketing PCs not so much through the use of direct marketing methods but by practicing market fragmentation. It has achieved the ability to customize every PC ordered to each customer's individual needs by transforming its assembly process into one of the most flexible in the industry. Dell has simplified its product and component configurations into a made-to-order manufacturing operation by pushing customization to the end of production and transmitting order information to the shop floor every 24 hours. This has resulted in three- to four-day production and delivery cycles.

If Shaquille O'Neal (7-foot-1-inch, 310 pounds) wanted a bicycle, he couldn't walk into any store and buy one. Because of his size and weight he would require one made to measure. Until Cannondale Corporation of Georgetown, Connecticut, came along, that would have been an almost impossible task. However, for Cannondale, it is one day's work. Cannondale's manufacturing process is so versatile that it can handle such requests as reinforced tubes, larger wheels, larger and stronger seats, and extended backs in a normal workday without disturbing the remainder of its production for that day—and at premium prices. In yet another study of the future of manufacturing, conducted by *Management Review,* the conclusions were pretty much the same as ours. Here's their view of the future:

> A woman peers at the image of a microwave oven on the personal computer in her home office. With the mouse on her PC, she selects from an array of options: size, color, digital display, rotating carousel. As she changes the specifications, the illustration represented on the screen changes. When she's satisfied with the results of her design, she "modems" an order for the microwave to the manufacturer, bypassing the company's order department completely. Presto! Her "personalized" microwave is manufactured that night and shipped the next morning.

The key to achieving such manufacturing prowess will be to *decentralize* and *delocalize* the manufacturing process. Several companies have already done this. One is Eyelab, which has taken the manufacturing of lenses for glasses from a large, centralized factory to a multitude of small, decentralized labs located in the back of the store where you buy your lens. Photofinishers, such as Moto-Foto, have done the same for the processing of film into finished photos. As a result, these companies have shortened the turnaround time from a week to one hour.

Product versus Process Innovation

Under a push economy, when there is always a long line of waiting customers for your product, the type of innovation needed is usually that of product innovation. This is so because there are few competitors, and the occasional introduction of new product versions is enough to succeed.

In a pull economy, however, with multiple competitors, product innovation alone is not sufficient to succeed. Process innovation is now a required skill. Historically, the United States has not been very capable at process innovation compared to the Japanese and the Germans. And the reason can be found by looking at where each country's R&D money has been invested over the last 30 years, as shown in the accompanying table.

	Product R&D (%)	Process R&D (%)
United States	70	30
Japan	30	70
Germany	50	50

Germany's balanced expenditure between product and process innovation probably explains why it has been even more successful than the Japanese since the end of World War II.

High versus Low Brand Loyalty

Another major effect of the pull economy and a contributor to the success of companies practicing market fragmentation is the change in the loyalty of consumers to traditional brands. In a push economy, there is strong brand loyalty because there is restriction of choice for the consumer and limited supply. As a result, the producer talks itself into believing that its products have strong brand following. In a pull economy, brand loyalty suffers and, faced with more choices of ever-increasing quality, the consumer's loyalty is to himself or herself and not the producer.

A result of this shift is the current cry among advertising agencies for higher advertising budgets to regain brand loyalty. The trend will continue to be in the opposite direction. A major winner in this shift from diminishing brand loyalty will be the providers of private label brands whose sales have been on the upswing for several years at the expense of the traditional brand. One of our clients, Torbitt & Castleman, has built itself into a very successful private brand company by pursuing this very strategy.

Changing Rules versus Fixed Rules

Under a push economy, the rules of play are set by the producer and forced onto customers. As long as a push economy exists, the producer enforces those rules and thrives from them. Under a pull economy, not only are the rules set by the customer but they are constantly changing, As a result, market fragmentators are very nimble people constantly monitoring and adapting to the evolution of customer needs in order to find new opportunities to identify slightly different needs that will lead to slightly different products, which will allow them to fragment the market even further and make it still more difficult for their competitors.

Once, as I was walking through one of Caterpillar's plants, I noticed a red tractor in one corner and a blue tractor in another. "Are those competitor tractors that you plan to strip down?" I asked. "No. They're ours," replied the vice president. "Some customers don't always want yellow."

Ten years ago this would have been heresy at Caterpillar. This company could do no wrong for most of this century. But then, in the 1980s even mighty Caterpillar was hit by the pull economy. Fortunately, Caterpillar has recognized the change and is responding. Today, Caterpillar is customizing 70 percent of its machines to the needs of each individual customer. "Personal products" is the new mantra.

As the CEO of Matsushita said, "In the future the mass markets will be the individual." A company that already practices this concept is the Karsten Company in Phoenix. It has taken a substantial share of the golf club equipment market by applying the same principle of fragmentation. Whereas most companies create generic clubs to fit all sizes of players, Karsten customizes each set to each player's physical dimensions. As its advertisements state:

> We, at Karsten, have always designed and built PING golf clubs to each customer's individual specifications. Just send us your golf glove size, height, and fingertip-to-floor measurements. These measurements help us make certain that the lie of each club rests properly on the ground. The lie of each iron must also be in proper rela-

tion to the length of the shaft. This is why a golfer's height is taken into consideration.

When was the last time you were asked these questions when you bought a set of golf clubs?

Companies that do not learn to practice market fragmentation, even to the level of single customers, will be the dinosaurs of the next century.

Cologne Life Reinsurance Company

The Cologne Life Re
COLOGNE LIFE REINSURANCE COMPANY

The Strategist as Weatherman

Michael Magsig
Chief Executive Officer

On September 22, 1938, a ferocious hurricane slammed into the East Coast of the United States, flattening everything in its path. The summer weather had been warm and sunny, and people went about their business unaware of the oncoming storm. Without today's sophisticated early warning systems, there was no time to react when the storm finally hit. A few hours' notice would have saved hundreds of lives.

In 1993, Mike Magsig, CEO of Cologne Life Reinsurance, faced a similar situation. Though his company was doing well, he saw storm clouds beginning to appear on the horizon. He needed a way to define those distant threats and focus his management's attention on them.

Magsig heads up Cologne Life Reinsurance, based in Stamford, Connecticut, which is owned by Cologne Reinsurance in Germany, the world's third largest reinsurer. With revenues of about $500,000,000, the company had just completed several record-breaking years and on the surface, the future looked bright.

"We had undergone a major organizational transformation back in 1990," he recalls. "It resulted in a significant downsizing of the organization and a strategic reorientation. We came out of that transformation with three consecutive years of record-breaking profit and revenue. We were able to reduce our expenses. We got out of some businesses that didn't have the prospects of being very profitable, and we streamlined the organization in such a way that we brought people who were involved in strategic development closer to the customers and the marketplace. So, '91, '92, and '93 were very strong years for us, but during '93, I began to have some concerns about our strategy. I sensed a vulnerability in our strategy that if we went down the 'if it ain't broke don't fix it' path, we could seriously impair our future ability to grow the business and outperform the competition.

"Some of the actions we had undertaken to develop this performance and transformation were actions that I believe certain of our competitors could easily duplicate if they so desired."

So the CEO's challenge was to focus management's attention on these potential problems, and develop a proactive analysis and strategy to avert them. He decided that DPI's *strategic thinking process* would be the best way to do it. "My biggest challenge at that point," he says, "was convincing management that we had a problem after three great years. And that is really the vital role that the DPI process played. It was met initially with a fair amount of skepticism. The process though, forced all of us into a broad-based strategic examination of our business, our environment, our company, its future. And through that process it gave us, I believe, more of a common basis of understanding. We had been working so hard in implementing these transformational changes and pursuing the benefits in the marketplace, that it was difficult for many to step back and reflect on what might be coming at us."

Employing the *strategic thinking process* enabled the management team to reason out its future strategic possibilities together. As they went through the process, the team was able to come to consensus on its future strategy with a full understanding of the internal and external challenges that lay ahead.

"And I think that one of the beauties of what DPI brings to the table is that they don't bring solutions," Magsig says. "They bring a process that becomes ours and something we can embody in the normal course of building our organization.

"It brings a greater discipline in establishing initiatives and improving our prioritization. It helps limit the number of initiatives we would be undertaking by helping us really weigh how central they are to the strategy.

"The process has elevated the organization's confidence in being able to continue to produce exceptional results. We have a means of examining the environment, the company, and opportunities in a way that I think can permit us to identify those opportunities much more quickly and cast off pseudo opportunities more quickly and systematically than we could have in the past.

"When we first set out on the transformation path," he recalls, "we had used the concept of a *driving force,* and as we went through this second examination with the help of DPI's facilitators, Mike Robert and Stephanie Angel, we were basically familiar with that concept. Our people were quite comfortable with it, fairly knowledgeable in discussing it, and we basically ended up confirming our driving force. But what became the added dimension through the process were the *areas of excellence* associated with our driving force. It caused us to examine more closely what we did well and what our marketplace and customers regarded as our unique strengths within the organization. It also caused us to reflect upon our potential for developing an additional strength or two that would serve us well in addressing any vulnerabilities."

One of the concepts in the *strategic thinking process* that Magsig found most intriguing was the idea of controlling the rules of the "competitive sandbox." By focusing on the specific niches and special types of opportunities, Cologne management felt they could limit the competitive field and choose the companies it wished to compete against. By narrowing the field to a few competitors against which it has a distinct advantage, the company could then control, or at least influence, the rules of play in that sandbox and tip the advantage in its favor.

"In terms of our competitive sandbox, we needed to redefine what was going to constitute success for us, and in doing so it lead us to a grid-type comparative that we update every few months in terms of our key competitors and where we are with regard to percentage increases and revenue growth and return on equity. What that causes us to do then is to look for certain types of niches and special types of opportunities and certain buying habits of customers that will permit us to retain that positioning on this grid," the CEO states.

As part of the implementation phase of the *strategic thinking process,* Cologne's management identified six *critical issues,* initiatives which are essential to the success of the strategy. These are carefully managed to assure that the planned results are realized.

"It's not something that is achieved by putting the organization on automatic pilot," says Magsig. "It couldn't have been achieved if we had been maintaining a business-as-usual mode. We are giving much more attention, through several critical issue groups, to action plans that are further developing certain of our strengths and permitting us to deploy those better in these niches that we're identifying.

"We have one individual who is designated as the owner of each of these six issues. That owner and a member of senior staff are responsible for presenting a quarterly update on the status of that initiative.

"Those critical issues are a linkage to strategy, to areas of excellence, and our strategic guidelines. By pulling all that together under a kind of umbrella of our vision, what this has all done is to sharpen our vision. And it has given more of an implementation orientation to realizing the vision we've created for this company."

Cologne Life Reinsurance has just completed its seventh consecutive year of record profits and revenue. And by using its strategic "early warning system," the management is confident that no future storms threaten the trend.

13

Alliances and Acquisitions

The Pursuit of Phantom Synergies

The buzz phrase heard most frequently throughout the corporate world today is *strategic alliance*. All the management gurus are on the bandwagon, espousing the need for strategic alliances in order to survive and prosper in the future. The concept is simple enough—if you can't fight them, join them. In other words, it's easier to form an alliance with a competitor than to fight that competitor.

Many of these alliances will fail, we believe, because they are being formed for the wrong reasons. In the first place, I must admit that I do not favor alliances. Alliances generally reduce competition, and reduced competition is not good for the consumer or the companies involved. Alliances usually produce higher prices for the consumer and breed complacency in the joined companies.

There are numerous examples of failed alliances—IBM's alliance with Apple to develop software around its PowerPC chip, IBM's alliance with Microsoft to develop an operating system for PCs (OS/2), and British Airways with both United and USAir. Cable & Wireless, the U.K. giant, recently announced the termination of its alliances with VEBA and RWE, two German utilities. La Compagnie Générale des Eaux, in France, also announced the end of its venture with Canal Plus.

There are similar examples to be found around acquisitions. Most acquisitions never produce the "synergies" they were acquired for and never produce the promised increases in shareholder value.

Some examples: Novell's purchase of WordPerfect; Sears' purchase of Coldwell Banker and Dean Witter; AT&T's purchase of NCR; Anheuser-Busch's purchase of Eagle Snacks; Quaker Oats' purchase of Snapple; Sony's purchase of Columbia Pictures...and the list goes on. All of these acquisitions produced major losses for the acquiring companies.

The reason, in my view, is management's obsession with the pursuit of *phantom synergies.* Management convinces itself that there are unexploited synergies to be derived which do not exist. In fact, the opposite is often the case. The two businesses have incompatible *driving forces* and *areas of excellence* that produce conflict rather than synergy.

However, if you feel your company must enter into such a venture, here are some dos and don'ts drawn from years of experience from our strategy consulting work.

Don'ts

Don't form an alliance to correct a weakness.

Many companies form alliances to correct a weakness they possess. This is not a good start. The reason is simple. The party that brings a weakness to the alliance will be, from that day forward, at the mercy of the other partner and subservient to that other party. Even though the alliance may be 50-50, the weak partner will never be an equal partner because weaknesses don't bring leverage in the marketplace.

A good example is General Motors' current alliance with Toyota in a joint manufacturing plant in Freemont, California. GM went into the venture to correct a weakness—its inability to manufacture high-quality small cars. GM thought it could acquire that know-how from Toyota through an alliance. Fifteen years later, GM still doesn't know how to make a good quality, small car. In fact, the car that bears the Toyota nameplate from the plant outsells the GM version six to one.

Another example, also from the automobile industry, is the Honda-Rover alliance in the United Kingdom. Rover's objective in this alliance was to correct a weakness—a lack of innovative car designs. It thought that by coproducing a Honda model it would protect its European share and help it penetrate the U.S. market. Neither of these two goals materialized. Rover became so dependent on Honda that Rover had no benefit at all. Honda derived all the benefit. Not only did the alliance give Honda an entry into Europe (300,000 cars in 1995), but Rover's capacity dwindled to less than 30,000. Finally, Rover was acquired by BMW, which quickly dissolved the alliance.

> Don't form an alliance with a partner that is trying to correct a weakness of its own.

The rationale, again, is simple. Your company will inherit that weakness! You may end up worse than you were before if you become the dominant partner in the alliance. The worst of all worlds is an alliance of two partners, each of which is trying to correct a weakness of its own. This type of marriage is doomed to failure from the start.

A current example of two companies struggling as a result of a merger of weakness is the "merger" of Upjohn and Pharmacia. The rationale for this merger was to correct Upjohn's weakness—not enough new drugs in its R&D pipeline—and Pharmacia's lack of U.S. distribution. To date, the merger has been a disaster.

Not only has the new company not been able to formulate a unified R&D strategy, it still operates three independent research facilities in Michigan, Sweden, and Italy. Not only did the two companies discover that they had different strategic capabilities (areas of excellence), but they couldn't even agree on where to locate the head office. So they chose a place that was inconvenient to everyone—London, where no one lived. The saga will continue for several more years.

Air France and Alitalia, two of Europe's weakest airlines, have this year entered into an alliance to "exploit all possible synergies" between the two companies. So the announcement said. The only result from a marriage of weaknesses is the creation of even more weaknesses.

> Never, never license proprietary technology.

One only needs to look at what has happened to the United States over the last 25 years to understand this rule. Sony acquired its transistor technology from Bell Laboratories for $25,000. A few years later, there were no more manufacturers of radios in the United States. Sony also acquired its videotape know-how from Ampex. In the United States, Ampex is no longer in the business. Unless you have very tight control of its use, licensing proprietary technology will always come back to haunt you!

C.K. Prahalad of the University of Michigan, made a study of eight such alliances and concluded that Western companies had too easily given up control of key technologies to the Japanese. Prahalad suggests that Western companies should think of these deals not as "strategic alliances" but as "competitive collaboration." He explains, "This would alert the organization to what they should protect." He also suggests, "Don't let your partner *underwork your core technology and skills.*" If you do so, "Japanese companies will build an ever more complex *competency* base and Western companies will surrender ever more control over their own competitiveness."

We would certainly agree with Prahalad. While working with owner-managed companies, we have noticed that these companies *never* license their *key skills* or *expertise* to anyone. Much more than in publicly run companies, the CEO in these organizations has a very clear understanding as to what area of the business drives the organization's strategy and what areas of excellence make that strategy work. And control over this strategic weapon is never relinquished!

Many U.S. multinationals are currently losing sight of that notion. The latest fad is to embark on "strategic alliances" with Japanese companies in an attempt to improve U.S. competitiveness. Unfortunately, these U.S. companies are losing sight of their driving force and are entering into alliances in which they are giving up control of their strategic weapon.

Don't form alliances around products or markets.

Most alliances fail because companies form alliances in order to exploit the similarity of certain products or markets. This rarely works. As proof, one only needs to review the multitude of broken alliances between companies that have attempted this.

Too often, alliances or acquisitions are made to fill "gaps" in the product line. This is not sound rationale. A few years ago, one of my clients asked me to critique an upcoming acquisition.

"Why do you want to make this acquisition?" I asked.

"To fill the gap between our low-end and high-end products," he replied.

"What is so attractive about this particular company?" I asked.

"They have mid-range products that are protected by patents," he replied.

"Have you done a patent search?" I asked.

"No," he replied, "but now that you mention it, I think I will do that."

To make a long story short, the firm had 17 patents. Twelve of the patents contained the names of the same two individuals. Do you think that these two individuals were included in the acquisition? Of course not! The seller wasn't that stupid. The moral of the story: You may not be acquiring what you think you are.

Dos

> Rule 1: Form an alliance to exploit a unique strength.

When forming an alliance, bring to the table a strength that you possess that is *unique* to you. In other words, no other competitor has this unique characteristic. The rationale? Only unique strengths can be sustained and defended over time. Even relative strengths—those that you have to a greater extent than a competitor but share with that competitor—are not the best upon which to build a successful alliance. Relative strengths can be acquired or duplicated but cannot be sustained over time.

> Rule 2: Form an alliance with a partner that has a unique strength of its own.

A marriage of unique strengths is the ideal. Looking to build a relationship by combining the synergy of strengths that are unique to each partner represents a venture with the highest probability of success.

> Rule 3: Form an alliance when neither party has the ability nor the desire to acquire the other party's unique strength.

This is the key rule of successful alliances. If one of the parties has the intention of acquiring the other party's unique strength, there will be no trust in the relationship from the beginning!

A good example of a successful alliance is 3M's venture with Squibb. 3M brings some polymer chemistry technology that can be applied to the development of drugs that Squibb cannot duplicate, and Squibb brings a distribution system to doctors and drugstores that 3M has no intention of replicating.

Corning is a premier example of a company that has engineered a series of successful alliances over the last few decades. The formula it has followed is the one just described. To each alliance, Corning brings its unique strength—its technology—and then seeks a partner that has a unique strength of its own. The other party is not usually in a position to duplicate Corning's technology, and Corning does not intend to acquire or duplicate the other party's unique contribution to the venture. The result? A string of successful ventures.

At Corning, alliances are an integral part of its strategy and its culture and not something out of the mainstream of business, which is usually the case in most other companies.

Rule 4: Form alliances around capabilities.

Rather than seek a marriage around products and markets, it is much wiser to form alliances around unique skills, capabilities, know-how, or technologies. Let the alliance develop products and markets later. The probability of success will increase many times.

Profit Is No Replacement for Strategic Fit

One deal that was announced earlier this year was Morgan Stanley's purchase of Dean Witter. The "strategic fit" is already being questioned. In a *Newsweek* article, here is what business editor Allan Sloan has to say about its prospects:

> Forgive me for not joining in the general huzzahs, but having lived through the ill-fated "financial supermarket" and "get as big as you can" manias of the 1980s, I have a funny feeling that the new Morgan Stanley, Dean Witter, Discover & Co. isn't going to work out as planned. The name alone is enough to give you pause—imagine having to say all seven words in one breath when you answer the phone. The joke going around Wall Street is that the new firm, which combines snooty Morgan Stanley with Middle American Dean Witter, should really be called "White Shoes & White Socks." This is a play on Dean Witter's adventure of 15 years ago, when Sears, Roebuck bought it and set up Dean Witter offices in Sears stores. Wall Street wags called this idea "stocks and socks," and it was a resounding flopperoo.

The folks running these companies say, in effect, that was then and this is now. Their rationale for combining Morgan Stanley and Dean Witter sounds great—but then again, it always does. If it didn't sound great, they wouldn't be doing it. Morgan Stanley, an investment-banking company that does business all over the world, is supposed to be a natural fit with Dean Witter, whose business is almost entirely U.S.-based. Morgan's main businesses—trading securities, advising corporations, selling new issues of stocks and bonds—are supposed to complement Dean Witter, which owns the Discover credit card and the nation's third largest retail stock brokerage. Morgan Stanley will help Dean Witter and Discover go global. Combining the firms will give Morgan Stanley outlets for its underwriting products and give Dean Witter brokers sexy new securities to sell. In the one part that makes clear sense, the firms would combine their mutual-fund businesses, creating one big mediocre fund company from the two existing mediocre fund companies. You can run one big fund business with far fewer people than it takes to run two smaller ones. Downsizing city, here we come.

My prediction of trouble ahead isn't because of "clashing corporate cultures," which is a polite way of saying that Morgan Stanley's high-paid investment-banker types aren't likely to become bosom buddies with Dean Witter's lower-paid employees. The culture problem is merely a symptom of the underlying problem. To wit: why do these businesses need to be combined? Dean Witter's 9,300 stock brokers aren't going to blindly peddle securities that Morgan Stanley is underwriting, and Morgan Stanley isn't going to put deals together just to create securities for Dean Witter's brokers to sell. If a Morgan Stanley deal is good, firms other than Dean Witter will happily take the securities. If the deal's not good, no one will take it, not even Dean Witter brokers.

History is a problem, too. Except for Merrill Lynch, which has managed to create a formidable investment-banking business largely from scratch, no firm that I know of has ever successfully combined investment-banking and retail-brokerage businesses for the long term. Certainly, no investment bank or brokerage house has successfully bought its way into the other business. And even Merrill hasn't been tested in a market downturn.

In the media and entertainment industries, 1995 and 1996 were banner years for acquisitions—Viacom's purchase of Paramount and Blockbuster Video, Time Inc.'s purchase of Warner Studios, Westinghouse's purchase of CBS, and Time Warner's purchase of Turner Broadcasting. Many financial analysts are asking themselves when they can expect to see the so-called synergies kick in. To date, none have been seen. In an attempt to build media conglomerates, these companies have spread themselves into everything from children's school books to video stores to animated cartoons to news reporting to trade magazines to cable television to X-rated movies. No single company

can master all of the skills to be successful at all these *different* businesses. As a result, growth has stalled in many of these companies, and the
stock prices of these conglomerates have nose-dived.

Even mighty Disney, which has achieved spectacular results under
CEO Michael Eisner, is being questioned about its purchase of Capital
Cities, Inc. What do animated motion pictures for families have to do
with farm magazines for farmers? Good question. Stay tuned.

Even companies in the so-called same industry have had difficulty
making so-called strategic acquisitions work. Two recent examples are
Novell's purchase of WordPerfect and Quaker Oats' purchase of
Snapple.

Novell, the powerhouse in software for local area networks (LANs)
in the 1980s, decided to enter Microsoft's sandbox—the market for
office applications—and acquired WordPerfect, a leader in word processing software. Although the two companies were headquartered in
the same city—Provo, Utah—they had radically different cultures,
organization structures, processes and systems, skills, and competencies. After paying $1.4 billion for the firm, Novell sold it to Corel,
another software company, for $200 million.

In 1994, Quaker Oats acquired Snapple, one of the decade's most
successful entrants in the soft beverage market, for $1.7 billion. Three
years later it sold the company for $300 million. What happened?
Although Quaker Oats was itself a powerhouse in that market with
other brands such as Gatorade, it could never understand or control
Snapple's marketing methods and distribution channels, which were
very different from those of Quaker Oats. While Quaker Oats had
excelled in marketing to and distributing through national chains, it
knew nothing about Snapple's reason for its success, which was its
strength in mom-and-pop stores across the country. The sale price after
three years: $300 million—a $1.4 billion loss. Furthermore, to pay for
the Snapple acquisition, Quaker Oats sold its candy and pet food divisions, two businesses that were profitable and kicked out a steady
stream of cash. Not only did it pay healthy capital gain taxes on those
two, but it also increased its cost of capital substantially for a triple
whammy against the company.

Conclusion

A few years ago, at our annual *CEO Symposium,* we invited four of our
CEO clients to speak about the pros and cons of alliances and acquisitions. Between the four of them, they had been involved in over 200
such ventures. To a person, they concluded that if they had to do it
over again, they would not repeat making any of these acquisitions.

The trauma of trying to merge organization structures, processes and systems, skills and competencies, and, most significant of all, cultures, is not worth the effort. Each of them offered that, after their experiences, they should have built these businesses in-house.

In fact, one CEO offered a remarkable piece of advice: "Rather than buy the company, buy their key people and grow the business yourself. It's much cheaper and much easier!"

——————Waverly, Inc.——————

Strategy "Sans Taches"

Ted Hutton
President and Chief Executive Officer

As a publisher of medical information, Waverly is squarely in the middle of two of today's most drastically changing industries: health care and information technology.

Over the course of more than 100 years, the company has built a successful business producing technical information in the form of magazines, journals, and books for doctors, nurses, educators, and other health professionals. Its "sans tache" (without blemish) motto is known as the mark of excellence in this specialized field around the world. Today the company's sales are in the neighborhood of $125 million and growing.

But, as in any business, change is constant, and Waverly has had to respond to more than its share. When Ted Hutton became Waverly's CEO nine years ago, it was at a point when the company's markets and technologies were in the midst of vast and accelerating changes. The health care and pharmaceutical industries (its customers) were headed into recessions, and the manner in which its information would be delivered was evolving because of the revolution in communications technologies. At the same time its competition was consolidating into fewer, larger players.

Hutton's task was to reshape the company and its strategy to compete effectively and grow in this new atmosphere.

"The company was at a critical juncture when I was brought in, " Hutton recalls. "The family owners were asking themselves, 'Do we sell out to a larger player, or do we remain independent and seek avenues of more accelerated growth?' Obviously they chose the latter as evidenced by the fact that I was brought in.

"In the first few years we tried to concentrate on changing the culture slightly, retaining good parts of the old culture, and adding new dimensions primarily aimed at reaching the standards to achieve growth. So we had some people changes and made several acquisitions, and at that point we brought in DPI to help us take a look at our strategy.

"We had grown larger," says Hutton, "and had brought on a lot of new players—two publishing companies in Philadelphia and one in Germany were acquired. We started to grow overseas, which had been going on well before I got here. Technology was changing dramatically, particularly electronic technology. The way in which we produce and distribute information products, publishing products, was changing and was going to change even more dramatically, because of the computer, primarily. Accepting authors' material on disk as opposed to a hard copy, manipulating and producing information electronically as opposed to the traditional manual and/or mechanical way...such changes are dramatically affecting both the printing and publishing businesses...and here we were one of the few companies in the U.S. that was both a printer and a publisher, and not a large one at that. In addition, health care was changing. At the time it was very clear that, while Clinton hadn't been elected at the point that DPI came in, there were going to be changes in health care because of the rising costs.

"Internally we were changing. We had a different look, a different size and different requirements, and I'd say the key was that we had to get the team, the new team, focused on the essential priorities. We went through the DPI process to identify those major issues on which we should focus. I chose this process because I liked its practical approach. It was not geared to having somebody come in and tell you what to do. DPI took us through a process of arriving at mutually agreed upon priorities.

"The advantage of this process is that it forces you to access all dimensions of your environment, internal and external, and focuses your attention on your strategic capabilities," Hutton says.

"From that understanding you can identify the areas requiring high-level attention. As Mike says, 'You all know what you need to do—it's a matter of getting everybody on the same page.' This process leads to action as opposed to a lot of talk. Too often in a retreat you have a wonderful time debating the issues but then there's no action thereafter. This process created momentum and leads to an action agenda that is carried out."

At the conclusion of the initial three-day work session, a set of critical issues was established—actions that would have to be accomplished to support the strategy. Teams were set up to work on those issues and over the course of the next two years, significant progress was made in all of them.

"In 1993, we experienced a recession in the health care market," Hutton says. "The pharmaceutical industry had severe margin problems and responded by cutting advertising significantly, thereby reducing revenue to our magazines and books. At the same time foreign markets such as Japan and Europe had economic problems. All that forced us to make a number of significant changes last year, for example, selling our printing company, and restructuring the publishing side.

"When we went through the *strategic thinking process,* we did not foresee the severity of the health care changes, nor did we anticipate the rapidity with which they have happened. Nevertheless, from that process we knew what had to be done and had secured agreement; we realized we had to do it faster. In some cases we executed pretty much along the lines that we had planned. In other cases, such as the restructuring, I had planned to do them over a three- and four-year period and instead did them over a four-month period. Some of those changes might not have been possible had we not gone through the process the year before."

Ted Hutton now concludes that Waverly is a stronger company that is better prepared to grow. That growth is supported by a management team that has a clear direction and that is now able to anticipate a changing environment and act quickly when new initiatives are needed.

"I think the best thing has been the bringing together of the management team. We've all been through a lot together, and I think that going through that process and the many changes thereafter has bonded our group. It should produce much better results for our shareholders."

14

The Logistics of the Strategic Thinking Process

Strategic thinking is the process used by a leader to formulate, articulate, communicate, and implement a clear, concise, and explicit strategy and vision for his or her organization. Unfortunately, in many organizations the strategy of the company is not always clear. It usually resides in the head of the chief executive exclusively. Other people around the CEO have to guess at what the strategy is. Because they have not been involved in the process, or because the CEO cannot clearly articulate the strategy, they feel no commitment to, or ownership of, that vision. Our own experience shows that most managers are so engrossed in operational activity that they have not developed the skills to think strategically. A CEO, therefore, might wish to involve his or her subordinates in a deliberate strategic process for strictly educational value. The problem, however, is that most CEOs practice this process by osmosis and are not conscious of its various steps. It is usually impossible to transfer to anyone else a skill that one cannot describe.

The Mechanics of a Strategy Project

Before describing how we work with the *strategic thinking process* in a client organization, it is important to say a few words about DPI's role in such an assignment. Our role, as an outside consultant, is not to set the direction of the client's organization. We feel quite strongly that no outside consultant can or should attempt to dictate a client's strategy. No outside consultant can ever learn enough about his or her client's business or ever know as much about that business as the people who run it. Nor should a consultant attempt to set the strategy if the consultant is not going to have to live with the results of that strategy.

The role that a consultant can undertake, however, is to facilitate the process of *strategic thinking*. As facilitators, we can keep the forum on track and bring objectivity to the discussions. We do not use the word *facilitator* to mean having someone in the room to take notes. Our meaning is that a *trained* facilitator follows a predetermined process and uses *predesigned instruments* to ensure that all the necessary questions are raised and debated. A facilitator's role is to place the participants in the appropriate discussion groups in order to tap everyone's knowledge and expertise in an orderly way. It is with this understanding of our role that we can then assist clients in setting their own direction following a time-efficient formula, which we will now describe and which is shown graphically in Figure 14-1.

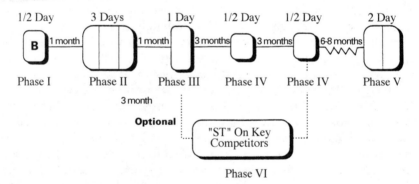

Figure 14-1. Strategic thinking project flow chart.

Phase I: Prework

Each member of the management team answers our two questionnaires, the *Current Profile Survey* and the *Strategic Input Analysis Survey*. This work requires three to five hours of effort by each person and is done without consulting one's colleagues. Our objective is to extract each person's best thinking on all the key elements of the business and its environment. The answers are sent to us for editing and collating.

Phase II: Three-Day Work Session

With the sum of views from the two questionnaires as our major inputs, we now come together to establish a strategy and a *future* strategic profile. During the work session, management discusses all of these inputs in subgroups using predesigned discussion instruments that raise all the necessary questions and activate the debate.

The three-day work session, which is divided as follows, is described in more detail later in this chapter.

Day 1

- We obtain agreement on the current profile and the current driving force.
- We review all the strategic inputs and agree on the two or three most important ones in each category.

Day 2

- We use the abridged strategic inputs from day 1 to choose two or three potential driving forces.
- We develop profiles for each potential driving force and compare them to the current profile.
- We choose a tentative strategic profile.

Day 3

- We develop competitive strategic profiles.
- We test the tentative strategic profile and bring to the surface critical issues. We shape and mold the final strategic profile.

Phase III: One-Day Strategic Objectives

After a three- to four-week break, we reassemble for another day that is dedicated to advancing the process by the development of:

- Strategic objectives for the organization
- Operational goals for each function/unit

Strategic versus Operational Objectives

Another element we encountered while working with client organizations worldwide is that many people have great difficulty distinguishing between strategic and operational objectives. Most organizations, in fact, seemed to be quite competent at generating operational objectives, but few knew how to formulate strategic objectives. Understanding the difference between these is an important nuance to master if one wants a strategy to be implemented.

Let me first define *operational objectives*. In most organizations, there is an annual ritual that occurs whereby each function, or department, assembles and makes projections for the following year's revenues and costs. It then establishes for itself goals and objectives to achieve which, hopefully, are somewhat higher than the goals of the current year. Activity goes on in these and other major functions: sales, marketing, manufacturing, accounting, human resources, research, and customer service.

Sometimes these objectives are congruent; sometimes they are not. They are all, however, extrapolations of history. People look back five years and, based on the history over that period, make adjustments for inflation and such, and then extrapolate forward.

Strategic objectives are very different in nature. Strategic objectives relate to four elements of the profile of the business, each of which is a key part of the future strategic profile or vision. These elements are:

1. Products
2. Customer groups
3. Market segments
4. Geographic markets

Strategic objective is a concept that comes from the military. A *strategic objective* is a strategic "position" that a strategy must protect or capture. The concept is simple. In a military sense, the commander must know that of the three hills that he or she possesses on the right-hand side of the battlefield, the one on the left, and the one on the right can be abandoned, but the one in the middle must be defended to the last person because from it is an unobstructed view over half the battlefield. On the other side of the battlefield, the hill on the right and in the middle are not important, but the one on the left must be captured because it will give an unobstructed view of the other half of the battlefield.

The same concept applies to business. The CEO and the management team must clearly understand which "hills" must be defended at all costs and which hills must be captured to win the war.

Some years ago I was a brand manager for a consumer packaged goods firm, and I was responsible for a core product—margarine. At the time, we had approximately 65 percent of the market. We, as a group, had made a conscious decision that we would never let our share drop under 60 percent. It was our view that a 60 percent share was the acceptable minimum for economies of scale on both the manufacturing and marketing sides of the business. And we had decided to defend that position against all comers. This was a strategic defensive position that was to be protected at all costs because the margarine business was considered to be the company's "crown jewel." As a result, a series of defensive tactics were automatically triggered whenever there was a one-point drop in share—everything from additional advertising at 64 percent to special in-store merchandising programs at 63 percent to price discounts at 61 percent. These would stay in place until the competitor gave up. We defended this position for as long as it took against all comers.

On the other side, offensive strategic objectives are also formulated. They represent "new hills" that need to be captured and that will serve as signals that our strategy is working. Naturally, offensive tactics are then developed to ensure that these will materialize.

The defensive and offensive strategic objectives then become the framework for the development of operational objectives in each of the company's functions or departments. The establishment of strategic objectives is the tool required to cascade the strategy down into the ranks of the organization and to ensure congruency of goals—in other words, to ensure that everyone in the boat is rowing in the same direction.

Phase IV: Critical Issues Meeting

There will be two half-day quarterly meetings with the CEO and his or her "inner circle" to review progress on the critical issues. At these meetings, the "owners" of the issues will be expected to report progress.

These meetings give the CEO an opportunity to:

- Assess the progress on each issue
- Determine whether the issue is "on-track or off-track"

- Judge whether progress on the issues are proceeding at the proper pace
- Remove any obstacles that the owners are running into
- Make any midcourse corrections

Phase V: Two-Day Review

Some 8 to 10 months after the first work session, we reconvene as a group to revisit our strategy. Because the conclusions of the first three-day session were reached on the basis of assumptions that were made about what might or might not occur in the environment, we now need to reassess those assumptions. This reassessment will also allow us to fine-tune our strategic position and bring to the surface any new critical issues.

During this process, the facilitator compiles, edits, collates, and produces all discussion papers and final reports.

General Observations

"Three days to set the direction of an organization is not enough time," some people will say. Our answer to that is, "That is true when you don't have a process." Without a process, executives can literally spend months and sometimes years trying to get agreement as to the future direction of the organization. This happens because the lack of methodology forces strategy formulation to be done on-the-run and in a haphazard way. With a good process, three days is more than ample time, as we've proved in a large number of client organizations.

Many of the systems that we have seen used in companies are overly complex and time-consuming. Too frequently they end up producing volumes of paper that are shelved together with the pictures and the awards.

Our process produces a strategic profile that a person can remember easily and practice daily. When transcribed to paper, it should not be more than two or three pages in length. The most successful organizations are those that keep things simple and do a few things extremely well. The same is true of strategic thinking.

The Process: Phase II

Our *strategic thinking process* in phase II (Figure 14-2) incorporates eight steps. These are:

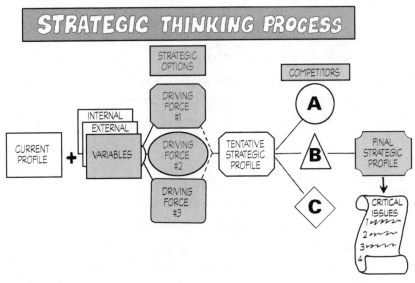

Figure 14-2.

1. Clarification of the current profile
2. Analysis of strategic variables
3. Exploration of different driving forces and possible strategic profiles (strategic options)
4. Development of a tentative future strategic profile
5. Development of competitive profiles
6. Anticipation of the implications of your strategy
7. Final strategic profile
8. Identification of critical issues

Clarification of the Current Profile

The first step in the process is taking stock of where the organization currently is. To do this one needs to take a "photograph" of the organization in its present state. One cannot have intelligent discussion as to "what we want to be" unless we clearly understand "what we look like today." Therefore, one needs to know:

- The scope of current products and services
- How these products or services are grouped

- The trends or cycles they experience
- The scope of the geographic areas they serve
- The user groups they have attracted
- The growth of these groups in the last few years
- Their market share and that of the competition
- The organizational structure in place to support the identified product/market division
- The return of each product/market division
- The organization's current driving force
- The organization's current business concept
- The organization's current areas of excellence

Collection of this information provides management with a "snapshot" or current profile of the organization (Figure 14-3). This is the composition of the organization as it is presently being propelled by a certain driving force.

Figure 14-3.

Analysis of Strategic Variables

Any sound strategy must allow the organization to successfully deal with its environment. Thus, the second step in strategic thinking is an analysis of the strategic variables that will be working for or against the business in the future (Figure 14-4). These variables, however, usually reside inside the heads of the management team and must be extracted and debated in a structured and objective forum with an outside person facilitating the process.

These variables are usually highly subjective in nature and are each person's view of what may or may not occur inside—but more importantly, outside—the organization. These differing views must be discussed in a rational manner in order for everyone involved to agree on the most important factors that the business will have to face.

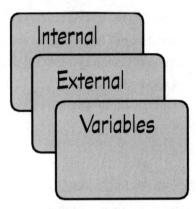

Figure 14-4.

The old saying "garbage in, garbage out" is very applicable in strategic thinking. The quality of the strategic inputs determines to a great extent the quality of the outcome of such an exercise. However, in order to obtain high-quality inputs, there is no need to undertake massive and costly studies about the future and its negative predictions. The best inputs are stored in the minds of the key people who run the company. Future direction is greatly influenced by the experience and perceptions of these people about the internal and external environment in which the organization exists. The trick is to tap this wealth of knowledge and bring it forward in an objective forum.

To do this, we have developed a strategic input survey that each member of management answers. The survey obtains everyone's view on 10 key areas of the internal and external environment: products, geographic markets, user segments, corporate beliefs, strengths, weaknesses, internal opportunities, competition, opportunities/threats, and strategic vulnerability areas.

Internal Environment

Products

- The common characteristics of products or services
- The exceptionally successful products
- The characteristics of their success
- The exceptionally unsuccessful products
- The characteristics of their failure

Geographic Markets
- The common characteristics of geographic markets
- The exceptionally successful geographic markets
- The characteristics of their success
- The exceptionally unsuccessful markets
- The characteristics of their failure

User Segments
- The common characteristics of user segments
- The exceptionally successful user segments
- The characteristics of their success
- The exceptionally unsuccessful user segments
- The characteristics of their failure

Corporate Beliefs
- The principles, beliefs, and values that guide corporate behavior

Strengths
- The unique strengths of the organization
- The strengths possessed to a greater extent by the organization than by the competition
- Traits that may become strengths later

Weaknesses
- The unique weaknesses of the organization
- The weaknesses possessed to a greater extent by the organization than by the competition
- Traits that may become weaknesses later

Internal Opportunities
- Short-term internal opportunities
- Medium-term internal opportunities
- Long-term internal opportunities

External Environment

Competition

- Direct competitors (present and future)
- Indirect competitors (present and future)
- Their strengths
- Their weaknesses
- New forms of competition
- Suppliers or customers that may become competitors

Opportunities/Threats

- Short-term external opportunities/threats
- Medium-term external opportunities/threats
- Long-term external opportunities/threats

Strategic Vulnerability Areas

- Raw materials
- Technology
- Labor
- Legislation
- Capital

Using the preceding categories, our strategic input survey consists of 42 key questions that are asked of each member of the management team. Their answers to these questions are all the data required as a basis for the development of a strategic profile for the organization. The consolidation of the information extracted from each person is the best environmental "scan" one can do. As mentioned before, this information is highly qualitative in nature, nevertheless, it is the foundation of sound strategic thinking.

Exploration of Different Driving Forces and Possible Strategic Profiles

Explore Different Strategic Scenarios. Once the management team has agreed to the variables that will work for or against the orga-

nization in the future, participants can explore which components of
the business can best be leveraged in the company's favor and around
which a successful strategy can be developed (Figure 14-5). There are

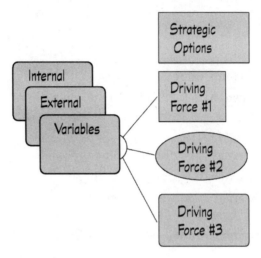

Figure 14-5.

usually two or three areas of the business around which a strategy can
be formulated. No company has access to all 10 driving forces, but
most have access to two or three. And most companies, over time,
have built up capabilities in two or three areas of the business that can
serve as the root of a future strategy.

It now becomes important for management to clearly understand
what the two or three areas are and then to draw "profiles" as to where
each one would lead the organization and what the organization
would "look like" if that avenue were pursued. Each area requires
emphasis or deemphasis on different products, customers, market segments, and geographic areas so that each picture will turn out to be
"different." At this juncture, management can make a choice as to
which pictures they like better and wish to embark upon.

Determine the Business's Future Strategic Heartbeat.   Once
management has agreed (and it's not an easy task) on what is currently
driving the business, they need to consider these questions: What
should drive the business in the future? Should we continue to be driven as we have been, or should we explore another driving force? If
so, which one should that be? What implications will that have on the

choices we make on the nature of products, customers, and markets we currently offer or do not offer? What will we end up looking like as an organization if we change the driving force of our company?

The management team can then identify which component of the business is *strategically* more important to the organization's survival and is the *key determinant* of the company's products, markets, and customers. In other words, which part of the business is at the root of the organization and can be leveraged by the company as its strategic weapon against its environment in the future?

Develop a Coherent Strategy and Business Concept. It is now imperative to develop a statement of strategy, which can be communicated to those who will be called upon to carry it out, around the element of the business that will drive the organization forward. The statement needs to be articulated in terms precise and concise enough so that people can carry it around in their heads. It should represent the *conceptual underpinning* of the organization and its *raison d'être*.

Translate the Strategy into a Strategic Profile and Vision. The next step is to translate the strategy into a vision of what the business will look like sometime "down the road." This vision should be a description of the products, customers, market segments, and geographic markets that the organization will emphasize and deemphasize in the future. This vision or profile then serves everyone as a test bed for the allocation of resources and the types of opportunities that are to be pursued in the future.

A strategic profile should be short enough that it can be carried around in one's head, and the boundaries should be clear and precise enough that managers can use it daily as a test bed for their decisions. Like picture painters, the master strategist must know what to include in the strategic profile. The following section describes the items that need to be clearly articulated.

Development of a Future Strategic Profile

Time Frame. A suitable time period for strategic thinking needs to be agreed upon. There is no rule, and it should be determined by the nature of the business.

Driving Force and Business Concept. The driving force that will propel the organization should be clearly established. This should be accompanied by a short description of the business concept that will be pursued in this mode. Because it is possible for two competitors within the same industry to have the same driving force but different business concepts, the particular description each one attaches to the driving force may influence greatly the direction it pursues. Volkswagen and Daimler-Benz, for example, are both product-driven companies. However, the definition that each gives to its product leads the two automobile companies down different paths in everything they do, including product design, pricing, advertising, distribution, and manufacturing. BMW and Porsche describe their respective products in yet a slightly different manner, which gives each company its own uniqueness and separates them from both Daimler-Benz and Volkswagen.

The description of the driving force is the description of the singular business concept or purpose of the organization. It is the conceptual underpinning of the business that sets the parameters for the scope of products, geographic markets, and user segments (Figure 14-6).

Figure 14-6.

Although corporations may get very large, the original idea that got them started is usually very simple and can be described in one or two sentences. It needs to be clear and crisp so that it can easily be retained by the dozens, hundreds, or thousands of people who are called upon to perpetuate it.

Akio Morita's concept of "using electronic technology in ingenious ways" is a good example of a technology-driven business concept that was at the root of Mr. Morita's vision and has been propelling Sony ever since.

CEOs who have difficulty articulating and disseminating their business concept will have great difficulty getting their key executives' commitment to any one direction. Furthermore, the inability to clearly define and articulate the business concept leads to the failure to establish an "edge" in the marketplace.

Areas of Excellence. The next elements to clearly establish are those two or three activities within the company that require excellence to a greater degree than any competitor has achieved, or to a greater degree than anything else the company does, if the business concept is to maintain its strength. Every organization excels in two or three areas, and it is this excellence that gives the business concept its strength. For a business concept to maintain its strength in the future, the areas of excellence that fuel this strength need to be identified and cultivated.

A product-driven company, for example, will need to excel at product development in order to improve current products and develop new ones. These skills are normally accompanied by excellent selling skills in order to convince more and more clients to buy the products. The areas of excellence vary from one driving force to another. Knowing which one is to be perfected will determine how resources are allocated.

Product Scope. Management must now turn its attention to listing the types of current and future products that are suited to this business concept and that will receive more emphasis in the future. They must also list those current and future products that are not suited to the business concept and will therefore receive less emphasis. This short list will serve as a filter for future product opportunities and test for a "fit." A product that falls on the less emphasis side should serve as a red flag to the company, telling it that the company is not organized to support this type of product opportunity and it should not be pursued.

Market/User Scope. The same is done for geographic markets and user groups. In each instance, management will draw a list identifying those markets and user groups that will be pursued and those that will not. Again, the objective is to construct a screen for future market or user opportunities.

Size/Growth Guidelines. The next part of the profile is to clarify the size and growth guidelines that the organization should achieve during the strategic time frame. The key word here is *guidelines*. These are usually ranges of numbers in categories such as sales, revenues, turnover, and growth.

Return/Profit Guidelines. The return/profit category specifies numbers that reflect guidelines for profit and return. The size/growth, return/profit guidelines should be representative of the financial performance required to provide the necessary cash flow to enable the organization to achieve its strategic profile.

Corporate Beliefs.   One executive described corporate beliefs as "moral guidelines, written or unwritten, that a company sets for itself in dealing with its environment." Although corporate beliefs are not part of the strategic profile of an organization, they are integral to the strategic thinking of the organization's leaders. The values, beliefs, and principles that these people own go a long way toward setting the tone of corporate behavior and molding the scope of its products and markets. They are to the strategic profile what the frame is to the painting.

Corporate beliefs exist in every company even though they are not always visible or known. However, once they have been drawn out of top management, our recommendation is that they always accompany any publication of the strategic profile, because they are the moral foundation upon which the company is based.

To illustrate their importance, two examples come to mind. We once worked with a tobacco manufacturer who, during one of our sessions, identified as an opportunity the possibility of obtaining distribution in one of the largest department store chains. Because this chain did not carry tobacco products, distribution alone would have meant a sizable initial order and a chance to significantly increase market share. The company set about devising an elaborate plan to approach the chain's buyer. By coincidence, we had also worked with the department store and knew that this possibility would never materialize. We informed the tobacco manufacturer of our opinion. "Why?" he asked. The reason was simple. The founder of the department store chain was a devout abstainer, and no tobacco or alcoholic products would ever be offered for sale in his stores. His personal belief, then and now, dictates corporate behavior.

The second example occurred when I was with Johnson & Johnson in the 1960s. Baby oil is one of its products, and the company started noticing that teenagers and adults used it every spring as a suntan lotion. It works well when used this way because baby oil has no sunscreening ingredient. We saw an opportunity, and every spring Johnson & Johnson started promoting its baby oil in the suntan market. It was so successful that within a few years J&J had the market's largest share. At the same time, however, there was emerging research indicating that overexposure to the sun might be a possible cause of skin cancer. J&J—at that time and to the present day—has a corporate belief that says it would "never offer for sale any product that may prove to be a hazard to a person's health." The suntan market experience was violating this belief. A decision was made in 1969 to withdraw all promotional funds and activities from the suntan market with a resultant loss of 15 percent in baby oil sales.

These corporate beliefs, known as the Credo, existed then and still dictate J&J's corporate behavior today. *Fortune* magazine once did a story on J&J, and a large segment of the article was naturally devoted to "The General's Credo."

The force that holds J&J together is an improbable one—the Credo, a 291-word code of corporate behavior that has a mystical but nonetheless palpable influence in the company. The Credo is a legacy of "the General," Robert Wood Johnson, the son of one of the founding Johnson brothers and the man who, during his long rule from 1938 to 1963, shaped the company. Rare is the conversation with a J&J executive in which the Credo does not come up. Several years ago, company officers debated for hours before changing a paragraph in the document. When one looks at the scope of J&J products and markets, one can look to the Credo as a key filter to the choices this company has made in the areas of its strategic profile.

Some outsiders might consider the Credo not so much corny, as wrong-headed: It commands that the company service customers first (especially mothers, nurses, doctors, and patients), employees second, the communities in which the company operates third, and the shareholders last. J&J has sometimes sacrificed earnings in what is perceived to be the best interest of the customers. Its behavior in the Chicago Tylenol case is a good example of adherence to this Credo.

Development of Competitive Profiles

As outsiders, it is still surprisingly easy to determine the driving force of an organization's key competitors (Figure 14-7). One only needs to look at their actions in the marketplace. By knowing their driving force, one can then anticipate what they will do in the future. We were working with a film manufacturer not too long ago, and it identified that one of its major competitors was production capacity–driven. In a soft market, such an organization usually resorts to price cutting in order to maintain volumes. Our client anticipated this type of behavior from that one competitor and, sure enough, a week later that is exactly what the competitor did. This time, however, our client was ready, and the competitor's action had little effect.

Next in the *strategic thinking process* is the construction of future profiles for the organization's three or four major competitors. By identifying each competitor's driving force, one can easily anticipate which products, markets, and user groups it will pursue and which ones it won't. These profiles will be valuable to have in order to proceed to the next step—the test step.

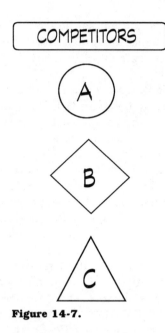

Figure 14-7.

Anticipation of the Implications
of Your Strategy

Often, when chief executives change the strategy and direction of their organization, they do not take time to think through the implications of that change. As a result, they end up reacting to these changes as they "bump" into them. Every change in strategy—even a minor one—will bring implications of one kind or another. If you want your strategy to succeed, you must devote some time and thought to identifying the issues that stand in the way of making your strategy work. What are all the changes that need to be addressed in order for the strategy to work? These changes become what we, at DPI, call *strategic critical issues*. These issues become management's agenda; each is assigned to a specific person who becomes the "owner" of the issue and who is held responsible and accountable to get the issue resolved. My friends at 3M call this "pin the rose" time. It is the successful management and resolution of these issues that will ensure the implementation of the strategy.

The test of the future strategic profile has three parts:

1. Versus the current profile

2. Versus the strategic inputs

3. Versus the competitive profiles

Versus the Current Profile. This test consists of comparing the future strategic profile to the current profile (Figure 14-8). The type of questions asked are:

- How large are the gaps between the two profiles?
- What changes need to be made to go from the current product scope to the new product scope?
- What changes need to be made to go from the current market scope to the new market scope?
- What changes need to be made to go from the current user groups to the new user groups?
- What new resources/skills will be required?
- Is it realistic to achieve this within this time frame?
- How should the strategy and profile be modified in view of the preceding?

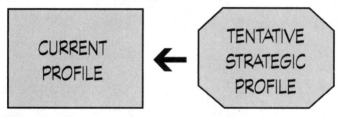

Figure 14-8.

Versus the Strategic Inputs. This test consists of comparing the future strategic profile to the original strategic inputs about the external and internal environment (Figure 14-9). The questions asked are:

- Are the organization's unique strengths being exploited?
- Are its unique weaknesses being minimized?

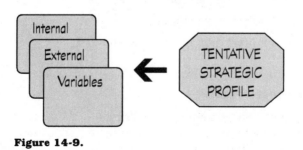

Figure 14-9.

- Are any corporate beliefs being violated?
- Are all major opportunities being exploited?
- Are all major threats being avoided?
- How should the profile be modified?

Versus the Competitive Profiles.   This test consists of comparing the future strategic profile to each of the major competitors that will be attracted to your strategy (Figure 14-10). The questions asked are:

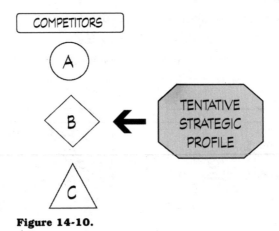

Figure 14-10.

- Is our strategy running up against their strengths?
- Are their weaknesses being exploited?
- How will they react to this strategy?
- How can their actions be counteracted?
- What is driving their strategy?
- How can we offset their areas of excellence?

Final Strategic Profile

The three-part test just completed brings to the surface a number of issues and provides an opportunity to try to "shoot holes" in management's thinking. It also affords management the chance to reshape the

organization's strategy and profile one more time before adopting it
(Figure 14-11).

Figure 14-11.

Identification of Critical Issues

Determining the final strategic profile will also bring to the surface a
number of key issues that management will need to resolve if the organization's future strategic profile is to become a reality (Figure 14-12).

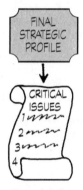

Figure 14-12.

These critical issues are the bridge between the current profile and the
final strategic profile. Setting the direction of the organization has been
achieved. Now managing that direction starts, and managing that
direction on an ongoing basis means the ongoing management of the
critical issues.

Notes and Sources

Chapter 1

Page

8   *As one executive of Chaparral Steel said:* Terrence P. Pare, "The Big Threat to Big Steel's Future," *Fortune,* 1991, p. 107.

9   *Even Gillette, the inventor of the razor blade:* "We Had to Change the Playing Field," *Forbes,* February 4, 1991, p. 82.

11   *The conventional approach:* Alicia Hills Moore, "Biotech Firms Tackle the Giants," *Fortune,* August 12, 1991, p. 78.

13   *In many industries:* Michael Porter, "Operational Effectiveness Is Not Strategy," *Harvard Business Review,* November/December 1996, p. 61.

Chapter 2

Page

29   *Not in a very:* Peter Drucker, "The Theory of Business," *Harvard Business Review,* September/October 1994, p. 94.

Chapter 3

Page

42   *My success in business:* Bill Gates, "Ability to Think Well Ahead Holds Key to Success in Business," *The Straits Times,* July 25, 1995.

45   *An article in:* Charles Hill, Michael Hitt, and Robert Hoskisson, "Declining U.S. Competitiveness: Reflections on a Crisis," *The Academy of Management Executives,* February 1988, pp. 53–55.

47   *Management should understand:* Milton Lauenstein, "The Failure of Business Planning," *Journal of Business Strategy,* March 1986.

Chapter 4

Page

64   *Behind each corporation:* William Waddell, "The Outline of Strategy," *Planning Forum,* Oxford, Ohio, 1986.

Chapter 6

Page

92   *A leader is:* Russell Mitchell and Judith H. Dobrzynski, "Jack Welsh: How Good a Manager," *Business Week,* December 14, 1987, p. 96.

93   *Followers want to know:* Wilton Woods, "The U.S. Must Do as GM Has Done," *Fortune,* February 13, 1989, p. 161.

95   *Every Enterprise:* Alfred Sloan, *My Years with General Motors,* Doubleday, New York 1972.

95   *Strategy is the:* Henry Mintzberg, "Planning on the Right Side, Managing on the Left," *Harvard Business Review,* February/March 1980.

96   *Every organization:* Peter Drucker, "The Theory of Business," *Harvard Business Review,* September/October 1994, p. 96.

Chapter 7

Page

109   *Bill Marriott of:* Walter Kiechel III, "Corporate Strategy for the 1990s," *Fortune,* February 29, 1988, p. 38.

112   *The thing that:* Bill Saporito, "ALLEGHENY Ludlum Has Steel Figured Out," *Fortune,* June 25, 1984, p. 40.

112   *The thing that scares me:* Robert P. Bauman, "Creating a Global Health Care Company," *Journal of Business Strategy,* March/April 1992.

113   *When he declared to:* Joseph Weber, "Mr. Nice Guy with a Mission," *Business Week,* November 25, 1996, p. 132.

114   *We've got new:* Suzanne L. Oliver, "Sticking with It," *Forbes,* May 13, 1991, p. 88.

115   *As David Glass, CEO of Wal-Mart:* "Will Wal-Mart Take over the World?" *Fortune*, January 30, 1989, p. 52.

115   *Fred Smith, CEO:* Interview in *The Journal of Business Strategy*, July/August 1988, p. 19.

115   *In this area, Shell has:* Toni Mack, "It's Time to Take Risks," *Forbes*, October 6, 1986, p. 125.

116   *Even its competitors:* Gary McWilliams, "The Undersea World of Shell Oil," *Business Week*, May 15, 1995, p. 78.

117   *We aren't likely to deviate:* "J.P. Morgan, Banking's Class Act," *Dun's Business Month*, December 1986, p. 36.

Chapter 8

Page

124   *We've been accumulating:* Neil Gross, "Sharp's Long-Range Gamble on Its Innovation Machine," *Business Week*, April 29, 1991, p. 52.

129   *Even the union executive:* James E. Ellis, "United Swallows Hard—and Goes for Growth," *Business Week*, May 15, 1989, p. 34.

Chapter 9

Page

154   *MCI is starting:* Christine Gorman, "Smooth Operator," *Time*, September 18, 1989, p. 60.

Chapter 10

Page

164   *The problem:* "The Failure of Business Planning," *Journal of Business Strategy*, March 1986.

Chapter 11

Page

186   *Its CEO, Neil Shaw:* Rita Koselka, "Back to What We do Best," *Forbes*, June 24, 1991, p. 48.

186   *In a market:* Jennifer Reese, "His Cup Runneth Over," *Fortune*, November 4, 1991, p. 173.

188   *There are always:* Joyce E. Davies/Ricardo Sookdee, "Pepsi Opens a
      Second Floor," *Fortune,* August 8, 1994, p. 64.

194   *Being customer-driven:* Jerry Flint, "Chrysler: Company of the Year,"
      Forbes, January 13, 1997, p. 83.

Chapter 12

Page

207   *When I started:* Christopher Palmeri, "The Idea That Print Is Dead Is
      Preposterous," *Forbes,* June 10, 1991, p. 43.

209   *U.S. industry:* "How Serious Is America's Industrial Position?" *Chief
      Executive,* November/December 1990.

210   *As Leslie Wexler, CEO of The Limited:* Robert Budesi/Mark Maremont,
      "Why Leslie Wexler Shops Overseas," *Business Week,* February 3,
      1992, p. 80.

211   *A woman peers:* Jenny C. McCune, "Tomorrow's Factory," *Management
      Review,* January 1993, p. 19.

213   *In the future:* "Matsushita-san, the Teacher," *EuroBusiness,* June 1989,
      p. 13.

Chapter 13

Page

222   *C. K. Prahalad of the University of Michigan:* Marc Beauchamp, "Use a
      Long Spoon," *Forbes,* December 15, 1986, p. 122.

Chapter 14

Page

247   *These corporate beliefs:* Lee Smith, "J&J Comes a Long Way from Baby,"
      Fortune, June 1, 1981, p. 59.

Bibliography

Publications

Business Week
"Jack Welch: How Good A Manager?" (December 1987).
"Why Leslie Wexner Shops Overseas" (February 1992).
"The Consumer Drives R.J. Reynolds Again" (June 1984).
"Alcan Goes Toe to Toe with Alcoa" (August 1984).
"The Perils in Financial Services" (August 1984).
"The New Breed of Strategic Planner" (September 1984).
"Do Mergers Really Work?" (June 1985).
"Continental: In for the Short Haul" (December 1993).
"The Steering Column: Competition Heats Up in Auto Insurance" (August 1994).
"Why Continental's CEO Fell to Earth" (November 1994).
"The Schwab Revolution" (December 1994).
"Kodak's New Focus" (January 1995).
"The Undersea World of Shell Oil" (May 1995).
"A British Publisher's Dreams of Empire" (November 1996).
"Read All About It—In *Marlboro Monthly*" (November 1996).
"Wells Fargo Bets Big on Minibanks" (November 1996).
"Mr. Nice Guy with a Mission" (November 1996).
"What Price the Snapple Debacle?" (April 1997).

The Economist
"Triple Whammy?" (March 1997).

Excellence
"Avon Calling...What's New in Management" (October 1985).

Forbes
"Import Quotas: The Honda Dealer's Best Friend" (December 1983).
"Good-bye Animal House" (November 1984).
"Like the Kid at F.A.O. Schwarz" (May 1985).
"The Antique Shop in Athol" (November 1985).

"Best Car Wins (January 1986).
"It's Time to Take Risks" (October 1986).
"Store for Our Times" (November 1986).
"Use a Long Spoon" (December 1986).
"What Makes a Survivor" (January 1987).
"We Had to Change the Playing Field" (February 1991).
"It's My Favorite Statistic" (September 1994).
"Forbes Informer: When the Going Gets Tough..." (January 1995).
"The Magazine Factory" (May 1995).
"Acquisition Is Fine, But Organic Growth Is Better" (December 1996).
"Flaming Success" (November 1996).
"The Odd Couple" (November 1996).
"Would You Rather Do Business with a Computer?" (December 1996).
"The Makeover" (December 1996).
"The Price Is Right" (December 1996).
"How an Outsider's Vision Saved Kodak" (January 1997)

Fortune
"The Big Threat to Big Steel's Future " (July 1991).
"J&J Comes a Long Way from Baby" (June 1981).
"Corporate Strategists Under Fire" (December 1982).
"Allegheny Ludlum Has Steel Figured Out" (June 1984).
"Breaking Out of a Niche Can Hurt" (July 1984).
"Exxon Rededicates Itself to Oil and Gas" (July 1984).
"Merrill Lynch's Not-So-Thundering Recovery Plan" (August 1984).
"Fare Wars: Have the Big Airlines Learned to Win?" (October 1984).
"America's New No. 4 Automaker—Honda" (October 1985).
"Pioneer Hi-Bred's Crop of Profits" (October 1985).
"How to Make Money in Mature Markets" (November 1985).
"Merck Has Made Biotech Work" (January 1987).
"Gillette Knows Shaving—And How to Turn Out Hot New Products" (October 1996).
"The Rent-a-Car Jocks Who Made Enterprise #1" (October 1996).
"Is AT&T Getting Something Right?" (March 1997).
"Could the Very Best PC Maker Be Dell Computer?" (April 1997).
"Biotech Firms Tackle the Giants" (August 1991).
"The U.S. must do as GM has Done" (February 1989).
"He's Saving Big Blue" (April 1997).

Harvard Business Review
"Planning on the Right Side, Managing on the Left" (February 1980).
"The Theory of the Business" (September–October 1994).
"Operational Effectiveness Is Not Strategy" (November/December 1996).

Inc.
"Excellence in Medium-Sized Companies" (December 1983).
"That Daring Young Man and His Flying Machines" (January 1984).
"Murphy's Law" (July 1984).

Insight
"Auto Industry's Power That Was" (November 1986).

International Business
"Interview with Masaru Ikuba" (January 1982).

International Management
"Voices & Views" (October 1984).

Journal of Business Strategy
"The Failure of Business Planning" (March 1986).

Newsweek
"Rowing Nowhere Fast" (February 1997).

Planning Review
"Fortune 500 Dropouts" (May 1986).

Time
"D-Day for the Home Computer" (November 1983).
"Slimmed Way Down and Styled Up" (November 1986).

U.S. News & World Report
"Effective Leadership: The Exception, Not the Rule" (April 1983).
"When a New Breed of Bosses Takes Over" (February 1984).
"A New Picture at Kodak" (September 1994).
"Loser Layoffs" (November 1996).

Venture
"How Entrepreneurs Maintain Their Imprint" (May 1982).
"Lessons Learned When Blue Chips Fail" (May 1982).
"Publishers Shift to Small Presses" (June 1983).

World Business
"British Companies Plan by Hunch" (May 1983).

Newspapers

The Straits Times
"Ability to Think Well Ahead Holds Key to Success in Business (July 25, 1995).

Wall Street Journal
"Cross-Border Merger Results in Headaches for a Drug Company" (February 1997).

Books

Ansoff, H. Igor. *The New Corporate Strategy.* New York: John Wiley & Sons, 1988.

Brant, Steven C. *Strategic Planning in Emerging Companies*. Menlo Park, Calif: Addison-Wesley, 1981.

Clifford, Donald K., Jr., and Richard E. Cavanagh. *The Winning Performance: How America's High-Growth Midsize Companies Survive*. New York: Bantam Books, 1985.

Drucker, Peter F. *Innovation and Entrepreneurship: Practice and Principles*. New York: Harper and Row, 1985.

Georgantzas, Nicholas C., and William Acar. *Scenario-Driven Planning*. Westport, Conn.: Quorum Books, 1995.

Graham, John W., and Wendy C. Havlick. *Mission Statements*. New York: Garland Publishing, 1994.

Guth, William D. *Handbook of Business Strategy*, 3 vols. Boston: Warren, Gorham & Lamont, 1985, 1986, 1987.

Hamermesh, Richard. *Making Strategy Work: How Senior Managers Produce Results*. New York: John Wiley & Sons, 1986.

Harvard Business Review. *Strategic Management*. New York: John Wiley & Sons, 1983.

Henderson, Carter. *Winners: The Successful Strategies Entrepreneurs Use to Build New Businesses*. New York: Holt, Rinehart and Winston, 1985.

Hickman, Craig R. *The Strategy Game*. New York: McGraw-Hill, 1993.

Kotler, Philip, William Fahey, and S. Jatusripitak. *The New Competition*. Englewood Cliffs: N.J.: Prentice-Hall, 1985.

Krause, Donald G. *The Art of War for Executives*. New York: Perigee Books, 1995.

Mintzberg, Henry, and James Brian Quinn. *The Strategy Process*. Englewood Cliffs, N.J.: Prentice-Hall.

Moris, David J., Jr. *Market Power and Business Strategy*. Westport, Conn.: Quorum Books, 1996.

Morita, Akio et al. *Made in Japan: Akio Morita and the Sony Corporation*. Edited by Jennifer Josephy. New York: E.P. Dutton, 1986.

Pattison, Joseph E. *Breaking Boundaries*. Princeton, N.J.: Patersons/Pacesetter Books, 1996.

Porter, Michael. *Competitive Advantage: Creating and Sustaining Superior Performance*. New York: Free Press, 1985.

—*Competitive Strategy: Techniques for Analyzing Industries and Competitors*. New York: Free Press, 1980.

Quigley, Joseph V. *Vision: How Leaders Develop It, Share It, and Sustain It*. New York: McGraw-Hill, 1993.

Rich, Stanley R., and David Gumpert. *Business Plans That Win Dollars: Lessons from the MIT Enterprise Forum*. New York: Harper and Row, 1985.

Ries, Al, and Jack Trout. *Marketing Warfare*. New York: NAL, Plume Books, 1986.

Rothschild, William E. *Putting It All Together: A Guide to Strategic Thinking*. New York: AMACOM, 1986.

Sawyer, Ralph D. *Sun Tzu: Art of War*. Boulder, Colo.: Westview Press, 1994.

Shanklin, William L., and John K. Ryans, Jr. *Thinking Strategically*. New York: Random House, 1985.

Shenkman, Michael H. *The Strategic Heart*. Westport, Conn.: Quorum Books, 1996.

Sirower, Mark L. *The Synergy Trap*. New York: Free Press, 1997.

Sloan, Alfred P., Jr. *My Years with General Motors.* Edited by John McDonald and Catherine Stevens. New York: Doubleday, 1972.

Von Senger, Harro. *The Book of Stratagems.* New York: Viking Press, 1991.

Waddell, William C. *The Outline of Strategy.* Oxford, Ohio: Planning Forum, 1986.

Yip, George S. *Total Global Strategy.* Englewood Cliffs, N.J.: Prentice-Hall, 1992.

Index

About the Author

Michel Robert is founder and president of Decision Processes International, Inc., a consulting firm headquartered in Westport, Connecticut which has 60 partners in 15 countries. His clients include such major companies as Caterpillar, 3M, and GATX. A noted lecturer and the author of six books including *Product Innovation* and *Strategy Pure & Simple: How Winning Companies Outpace Their Competitors*, his writings have appeared in many business magazines and journals. He lives in Litchfield, Connecticut.

FOR A FREE SUBSCRIPTION TO OUR QUARTERLY MAGAZINE

THE STRATEGIEST

Please Mail This Page to the Address Below

Name _____

Title _____

Company _____

Address _____

City _____ State_____ Zip _____

Telephone _____ Fax_____

Decision Processes International
10 Bay Street
Westport, CT 06880
Fax: (203) 226-5802